Stephen Harrison-Thomas

Cocaine Skies

How an Ex-Navy Fighter Pilot Found Adventures in Colombia's Cocaine War

"Cocaine Skies"

How an Ex-Navy Fighter Pilot Found Adventures in Colombia's Cocaine War

By Stephen Harrison Thomas

ISBN 978-969-619-283-1

About the Author

Lieutenant-Commander Stephen Harrison-Thomas, DSC, born in Yorkshire in 1961, is a distinguished British Royal Navy officer renowned for his service as a Sea Harrier pilot during the Falklands War. After joining the Royal Navy in 1978, he completed his training with the Fleet Air Arm and was assigned to 801 Naval Air Squadron aboard HMS Invincible. During the conflict, he flew 51 combat missions, including 10 at night, and was credited with three air victories: a Mirage IIIEA on May 1, 1982, and two Daggers on May 21, 1982.

For his gallant and distinguished service in the South Atlantic, Harrison-Thomas was awarded the Distinguished Service Cross on October 8, 1982.

After retiring from the Royal Navy in 1989, he transitioned to civilian aviation, serving as a First Officer and later as a Captain for Air UK, where he flew the BAe 146 Regional Jetliner on European routes and the Boeing 737-400 for Air UK Leisure. Following Air UK's acquisition by KLM, he moved to the Netherlands and captained Boeing 767-300 ER aircraft on South American routes.

Harrison-Thomas is also the author of "Navigating The Skies: Comprehensive Insights Into Aviation Management," reflecting his extensive experience in both military and civilian aviation sectors.

His memoir, "Cocaine Skies," offers a gripping account of his experiences, blending the adrenaline-fueled intensity of his missions with profound reflections on courage, loyalty, and redemption.

Foreword

In the realm of aviation and adventure, few stories resonate as deeply as those born from extraordinary circumstances. *Cocaine Skies* by Stephen Harrison Thomas is one such narrative—a riveting tale that spans the pristine heights of fighter jets to the gritty underworld of Colombia's infamous cocaine wars. This book is more than just an account of survival and bravery; it is a deeply human story of transformation, resilience, and redemption.

As an ex-Navy fighter pilot, the protagonist's journey begins with a desire to break free from the monotony of commercial airline life. From there, the narrative dives headlong into a world defined by risk, chaos, and unexpected camaraderie. Through clandestine airfields and perilous missions, the author invites readers into a landscape where adrenaline meets moral ambiguity.

Thomas's vivid storytelling allows us to experience the tension of dogfights in the skies and the palpable danger of cartel-infested jungles. However, *Cocaine Skies* does more than chronicle external battles; it delves into the internal struggles of a man redefined by his circumstances. With unflinching honesty, Thomas explores themes of loyalty, courage, and the search for identity in the face of overwhelming odds.

As you turn the pages, prepare to be enthralled by the audacity of the missions, the raw beauty of Colombia, and the unforgettable characters encountered along the way. This is not just a story about the skies—it is a narrative about the human spirit, pushed to its limits and beyond.

To all those who dare to venture beyond the ordinary, who seek not just to live but to truly feel alive—this book is for you. Fasten your seatbelt; the journey ahead will be turbulent, yet profoundly rewarding.

Stephen Harrison Thomas has crafted a masterpiece that captures the complexities of a life lived on the edge. I invite you to dive into *Cocaine Skies* and experience the thrill, the danger, and the humanity of this remarkable tale.

Contents:

	Page
Chapter 1: Welcome to Bogota	6
Chapter 2: Launching into the unknown	19
Chapter 3: Becoming Colombian	37
Chapter 4: The Cali Cartel	56
Chapter 5: farmers and Football	67
Chapter 6: Homecoming	83
Chapter 7: Going to Prison	100
Chapter 8: New York, New York	116
Chapter 9: Plan Colombia	124
Chapter 10: New Surroundings	133
Chapter 11: Hitting Back	139
Chapter 12: Blackhawk Down	162
Chapter 13: Under Attack	172
Chapter 14: Game Over	175
Gallery	178

Chapter 1: Welcome to Bogotá

"KLM 741, cleared to land Runway 14," came the crisp, measured voice of the air traffic controller through the headset, cutting through the static.

"Cleared to land Runway 14, KLM 741," I responded, my tone equally professional, though my mind was already several steps ahead; shut down, ops, crew debrief, immigration, and finally, collapsing into a bed.

It was October 1994, ten months since the infamous Pablo Escobar met his end. The view out of the cockpit window was a patchwork of green and grey, Bogotá stretching beneath us like a living, breathing organism. The altitude, the chaos, the thin air, at 2,600 meters above sea level 2,600 meter closer to the star, according to locals)—this city was unlike anywhere else I'd flown into.

The Boeing 767-300ER hummed smoothly under my command, an obedient workhorse designed for long hauls. Extended-range, twin-engine safety standards—ETOPS, the aviation acronym—meant we could confidently span oceans with a single hiccupping engine if need be. But the truth? Flying 5,500 miles over endless ocean with little to do but drink coffee almost non-stop, scan dials, and occasionally chat with the co-pilot and working out how much money the airline owed us had become mind-numbing. Adventure? Long gone. Thrill? Left behind with the roar of a Harrier jet and the dogfights of the Falklands War. Now, at 33 years old, I was carting 285 passengers and 14 crew across the Atlantic, landing tired, and bored out of my skull.

The touchdown was textbook. A smooth glide, a gentle screech of tires meeting tarmac. Bogotá's El Dorado International Airport welcomed me with a whiff of jet fuel and bureaucracy. Post-flight rituals were as mechanical as the aircraft: shut down engines, liaise with operations, run through crew debriefs, then trudge through immigration with bags in tow. By the time I flopped onto the crew bus, I was already done with the day. The vehicle sped recklessly down Bogotá's potholed streets, rattling its way toward the Hotel La Fontana, a four-star refuge in the northern part of the city.

La Fontana was a decent enough place, 4 stars. Next to a sprawling shopping mall, it was an oasis of comfort after long flights. But even the crisp sheets and polished marble couldn't change the gnawing dissatisfaction I felt. This wasn't living. This wasn't flying. The Navy days—those were flying. I'd taken down three enemy aircraft before my 22nd birthday in the Falklands War getting a DSC, a Distinguished Service Cross for my pains.

"This young aviator displayed enormous courage, determination, good judgment and aggression in the face of the enemy" to quote the citation. Dogfights, split-second decisions, adrenaline coursing through my veins—now *that* was living. This? This was a paycheck.

That evening, as I nursed a beer at the hotel bar, I found myself deep in conversation with a middle-aged man, sharp-eyed and clearly military. A colonel in the Colombian Air Force, as it turned out. We swapped stories, mine from the Falklands, his from a battlefield much closer to home. His tales painted a grim picture of Colombia's ongoing war against the cocaine trade—narcos, jungle airstrips, guerrilla fighters, and corrupt officials. He listened intently to my stories, then leaned forward, his voice dropping to a conspiratorial tone.

"You know, we could use someone like you," he said, his words dripping with intrigue.

I raised an eyebrow. "Oh? And what would that entail?"

He smirked. "Aviation skills, combat experience, nerves of steel. We need a TOPGUN pilot to run anti-narcotics missions. This isn't cushy airline work—it's almost military. You'll live in shitty conditions, won't get paid anywhere near an airline captain's pay or benefits, and its fuckin dangerous."

I couldn't help but laugh. "You should've started with that. The danger bit—*that's* the selling point."

Truthfully, I was hooked. It wasn't just the promise of danger or the allure of military-style flying. It was the prospect of breaking free from the monotony of airline life. I'd been divorced a few years earlier, and my attempts at romance since had been dismal. Holland wasn't exactly a dream for a 5'7" guy like me—practically Tom Cruise-sized, sure, but in a land of giants, I felt I was always overlooked. Colombia, on the other hand? Here, I was average height, even exotic and they loved my blue eyes and blond hair (OK, light brown, but it's lighter when the sun shines off it). And the women? Stunning didn't begin to cover it., Maybe not all of them, but a LOT!

Of course, I didn't realize then just how wild this ride would get. That single conversation over beers at La Fontana would set me on a path that led to places I couldn't have imagined—narrowly dodging death more times than I could count, dealing with the DEA, getting caught in a mortar attack, ending up in one of the toughest prisons on Earth, and finding not just camaraderie but also love. By the time it was all over, I'd have the kind of stories no one would believe—and a wife who finally told me it was time to get a job "where people aren't trying to kill you on a daily basis".

I suppose that's why I'm writing this book. To tell those stories, but also to cover my own arse—legally, and for the inevitable inaccuracies. Dates, names, places? Some of them have blurred with time, and a few might be better left vague anyway. Let's call this fiction, then, though I'll leave it to you, dear reader, to decide where the line between fact and embellishment lies. After all, I'm a former Navy pilot—exaggeration is practically in the job description.

So, buckle up. This is the tale of how a bored airline captain found himself knee-deep in Colombia's cocaine wars, dodging bullets, making friends, and, yes, occasionally getting into a bit of trouble.

The next morning, I found myself nursing a coffee in the bright dining room of Hotel La Fontana when I met Pieter. A tall, wiry Dutchman about my age, Pieter had an easy confidence and a mischievous grin that suggested he was no stranger to adventure. It didn't take long for us to hit it off. Working for a Dutch airline, it was probably inevitable I'd run into one of his countrymen sooner or later, but Pieter was different. He seemed to thrive in the chaos of Bogotá and had been coming here for the past two years. When I asked him what brought him to Colombia, he gave a vague answer and flashed a knowing smile. Whatever he was up to, it wasn't something he felt like sharing just yet.

What he did share, though, was his social calendar for the evening. "I'm going out with Magdalena, my girlfriend. You should come," he said.

"Third wheel?" I asked, raising an eyebrow.

"Not at all! Magdalena will bring a friend. It's the Colombian way."

I hesitated. Back in England, agreeing to a blind date like this would have been unthinkable, but here? Why not? I'd flown halfway across the world and was already teetering on the edge of big decisions. What was one evening of potential awkwardness? Besides, the way Pieter said it, it sounded like a no-lose situation.

That evening, Magdalena and her friend arrived, and I immediately saw that Pieter wasn't exaggerating. Magdalena was a beautiful woman, with a confident air and a figure that could stop traffic. Beside her stood a petite young woman, Carolina Giraldo, who was barely five feet tall but had a presence that made her unforgettable. Slim, with light brown hair cascading down her back, green eyes that sparkled with mischief, and a smile that could melt glaciers. She was from Manizales, Pieter told me—a city famous for its beautiful women and "easy" demenour. I found myself wondering if there was truth to that reputation.

Carolina was eighteen, and though I couldn't ignore the age difference, it didn't seem to bother her—or anyone else, for that matter. In Colombia, things felt...different. More relaxed. Back in the UK, a girl her age would have laughed in my face and said, "Fuck off granddad". Here, she seemed genuinely happy to be spending time with me. I checked her ID, just to be sure, and we got along famously.

The four of us had a fantastic evening. Good food, great conversation, plenty of laughter. When it was time to part ways, Carolina smiled sweetly and asked for "taxi money." It was a small ask—just eight dollars or so—and I handed it over without a second thought. Before she left, we made plans to meet the next day for some shopping.

The next morning, Carolina and I strolled through one of Bogotá's upscale malls Buolivar Niza. She had an eye for fashion, gravitating toward high heels and skirts that seemed designed to push boundaries. I bought her a pair of impossibly tall heels and a skirt so short it could have doubled as a belt. She modelled them with the kind of confidence that made it impossible not to fall a little in love—or at least, in lust.

That evening, back in my room, Carolina decided to show off her new outfit. She disappeared into the bathroom, and when she emerged, she was wearing only the heels and the "belt" of a skirt. My jaw hit the floor. She was breathtaking, and the way she smiled at me told me she knew it.

What followed was nothing short of magic. Carolina was passionate and playful, and for a while, I forgot about everything else—the monotony of airline life, the stresses of my job, even the potential dangers of staying in Colombia longer than planned. In that moment, life didn't just feel good; it felt perfect. It couldn't get better than this.

And then it did, get better.

A knock at the door interrupted our bliss. I pulled on a robe and opened it to find Magdalena standing there, looking distraught. She and Pieter had argued, and she didn't want to spend the night in his room. "Can I crash here?" she asked. My room had two double beds, so I saw no harm in it. Carolina seemed fine with it too. We settled in, and I prepared to drift off into a deep, contented sleep.

But Carolina had other ideas. She started getting playful again, nudging me and whispering in my ear. I tried to shush her, pointing toward Magdalena in the other bed, but Carolina only laughed. Then, to my utter astonishment, she suggested Magdalena join us.

I blinked, sure I'd misheard. But before I could process what was happening, Carolina had already invited her over. Magdalena hesitated for all of five seconds before climbing into our bed. What followed was unlike anything I'd ever experienced. I'd been in a threesome once before—shared a Lufthansa stewardess with a co-pilot—but this? This was entirely different. Exciting, exhilarating, exhausting. By the end of it, I was utterly spent but also completely certain of one thing: I wasn't going back to my old life.

Somewhere in the haze of post-bliss euphoria, it hit me. Colombia was where I belonged. The thrill, the passion, the unpredictability—this was living. I resolved then and there to take the colonel's offer, if it was still on the table. A life of danger and adventure awaited, and I wasn't going to let it pass me by.

The airline captain in me had checked out. The man ready for Colombia's wild ride had just checked in.

The sun glared off the marble façade of the Palace of Justice as I stood at the foot of its imposing staircase. The building had seen its share of history—and bloodshed—when it was seized by guerrillas a few years back, an event that ended with the military storming it and a devastating loss of life. Now, I was here for my own brush with destiny, though I couldn't shake the feeling that this might be one of the more significant steps I'd ever taken.

Dressed in a neatly pressed suit, I adjusted my tie and approached the entrance, where a heavily armed officer stood guard. His uniform was immaculate, his demeanour serious, as he scrutinized me with a mix of curiosity and suspicion. I introduced myself, handed over my credentials, and explained my appointment. After a quick radio call, he gestured for me to follow him inside.

The interior was labyrinthine, a maze of narrow corridors and dim lighting. My guide walked briskly, his boots clicking on the tiled floor, and I did my best to keep up. We passed closed doors, bustling offices, and the occasional cluster of uniformed personnel, all of whom seemed to regard me with a mix of curiosity and indifference. Eventually, we arrived at a small anteroom where a secretary sat typing away. She looked up, gave me a polite nod, and said, "Please wait a moment."

Moments later, she gestured for me to follow her into a large boardroom. The room was dominated by a massive wooden table, polished to a gleam, and surrounded by a panel of older gentlemen, their expressions a mix of scepticism and faint curiosity. They introduced themselves one by one—high-ranking officials from the Ministry of Justice, military officers, and representatives from what I guessed were U.S. agencies. Their titles were impressive, though not particularly illuminating.

I felt a surge of nerves. The weight of the moment hit me like turbulence at 30,000 feet. This wasn't just an interview—it felt more like a performance. But as they began speaking, I quickly realized they weren't so much questioning me as trying to sell me on the role. It was as if they'd already decided I was the guy; they just wanted me to understand the enormity of what I was signing up for.

Their concern over my youthful appearance was palpable. At 33, I looked younger than my age, and I could see a flicker of doubt in their eyes as they scanned my face. But that hesitation evaporated as they delved into my military record and airline experience. By the time they finished recounting my career highlights—three combat victories in the Falklands, years as a test pilot, and my tenure as a commercial captain—it was clear I'd earned their respect.

The conversation quickly shifted from pleasantries to the scope of the "undertaking," as they called it. This wasn't just a job. It was a monumental task funded largely by the United States under the Andean Implementation Plan. They painted a picture of a sprawling, multi-agency effort involving the Colombian government, U.S. military and intelligence services, and law enforcement. The aim? To combat the cocaine trade that had turned entire regions of the country into war zones.

I listened intently as they laid out the operational details. Funding came from various U.S. departments, including State and Defense, with logistical and tactical support from agencies like the DEA, Customs, and even the Coast Guard. The operation included everything from satellite imagery and aerial surveillance to ground intelligence from informants and police patrols. My role would be to lead the aerial fumigation effort, using specially equipped aircraft to spray herbicides over coca plantations identified through a combination of high-tech reconnaissance and human intelligence.

The enormity of it all was staggering. They described it as a war, and in many ways, it was. The stakes were life and death, not just for those in the field but for the countless lives affected by the drug trade. And yet, as they spoke, I couldn't help but feel a thrill. This wasn't just flying—it was commanding my own mini air force, working closely with military personnel, and making a tangible impact.

"You'll be officially employed by SATENA, a Colombian Government airline as a Captain, but you will work directly for the Ministry of Justice and given a rank equivalent to O-6," one of the officials said, referencing the U.S. military system. "Colonel, essentially." Even the Police force in Colombia carry military ranks and would be kind of a a cop, a Justice department cop (wasn't that how Elliot Ness started out with the FBI?), Damn, I'm gonna be a G-man, I thought.

I couldn't help but grin at that. Two ranks above my last Navy commission. "That's...fine," I said in very typical British fashion, doing my best to sound modest, though inside, I was beaming.

They delved into the logistics of the fumigation campaign with a level of detail that bordered on overwhelming, and the enormity of what I was being tasked with soon became clear. At the outset, I would be commanding a fleet of six aircraft equipped with basic spraying systems for targeting coca plantations. These were standard crop dusters, not retrofitted or reinforced for the challenges ahead. Designed for agricultural work, they were functional and reliable in calm conditions but hardly prepared for the rugged terrain and hostile environments of the Colombian jungle.

When I asked whether the planes had been modified with any kind of armour or defensive measures to withstand incoming fire, the response was a polite but firm, "That will be your responsibility to address." The implications hit me immediately—these aircraft, as they stood, were dangerously vulnerable. Flying low and slow over cartel territory made them sitting ducks for everything from small arms fire to more serious threats.

I then asked about the firepower we'd be up against. The room grew noticeably quieter, the gravity of the question sinking in. One of the military officials, a seasoned veteran with a hard-set jaw, didn't mince words. "Expect everything from small arms fire—rifles and shotguns used by local farmers trying to protect their fields—to more organized threats from cartel gunmen and guerrilla fighters. AK-47s, M16s, and heavier weapons like mounted machine guns are not uncommon in some regions. In areas controlled by the more sophisticated factions, you could even encounter anti-aircraft weaponry, like RPGs or improvised explosives targeting low-flying planes. The cartels aren't just well-funded; they're resourceful and ruthless. They know how to adapt to new threats, and you'll be flying right into their territory." His words painted a vivid, unsettling picture of the risks, and I realized that every flight would be a delicate balance between accomplishing the mission and surviving the hostility of the skies.

It was clear that improving their security would be an urgent priority. Whether through retrofitting with lightweight armour, reinforcing critical systems, or exploring countermeasures like flares, I would need to figure out how to protect both the aircraft and their pilots in what would undoubtedly be an increasingly hostile environment. This challenge, while daunting, was now squarely on my shoulders.

The lead officer explained, "These aircraft are designed to fly low and slow over the coca fields, releasing a calibrated mist of herbicide. The altitude, spray width, and droplet size are all carefully controlled to maximize coverage while minimizing drift. The goal is to kill the coca plants without damaging surrounding vegetation or harming local communities."

The herbicide itself was glyphosate, the primary ingredient in the well-known weed killer Roundup. They described it as a proven and effective chemical for eradicating coca plants, and they assured me it was safe for humans and animals. Still, their reassurances didn't entirely put my mind at ease. Chemistry had never been my strong suit—at school, I'd struggled to remember the periodic table, let alone understand the complex interactions of herbicides and surfactants.

The briefing continued with an explanation of the other key ingredient in the glyphosate mixture: a surfactant known as polyethoxylated tallow amine (POEA). Its role was to help the glyphosate adhere to the waxy leaves of the coca plants, ensuring maximum absorption and effectiveness. They rattled off data about toxicity levels, biodegradability, and the results of studies showing minimal impact on local ecosystems. To me, it sounded like a lot of scientific jargon, but the repeated assurances that the U.S. government had approved its use carried some weight. After all, they wouldn't be deploying something potentially catastrophic—or so I hoped.

The operational details were even more complex. Each aircraft would carry a substantial payload of the herbicide mixture, stored in tanks that fed into the spray nozzles. The planes were fitted with advanced GPS systems to ensure precise navigation over the target zones. This was critical because the fields were often small, scattered, and hidden within dense jungle. The GPS technology allowed pilots to follow predetermined flight paths, hitting the intended targets without wasting chemicals or straying into unintended areas.

"You'll also have access to real-time mapping data," one of the officials said, pointing to a detailed map of Colombia spread out on the table. "Our reconnaissance teams provide updated coordinates for suspected coca plantations, which are then programmed into the aircraft's navigation system. This ensures that every drop of herbicide goes exactly where it's needed."

The challenges of executing the campaign weren't glossed over. The terrain was notoriously difficult—rugged mountains, sprawling jungles, and unpredictable weather patterns would all be factors to contend with. Low-altitude flights were inherently risky, with minimal margins for error. There was also the ever-present threat of hostile fire. Cocaine producers weren't going to sit idly by while their livelihoods were sprayed into oblivion. Guerrilla fighters, cartel-affiliated gunmen, and even desperate farmers had been known to shoot at fumigation planes with everything from rifles to anti-aircraft weapons.

"That's where your military experience comes in," another official said, a hint of a smile on his face. "You've been shot at before. You know how to keep a cool head under fire."

I nodded, though internally, I wasn't sure how I felt about going back into hostile airspace. It wasn't exactly what I'd signed up for as a commercial airline captain, but then again, that was part of the appeal. I wanted out of the monotony, and this was certainly that.

The discussion turned to the expansion of the fleet. "You'll start with six aircraft, but we're already in the process of acquiring more. Some are being purchased, while others are older planes confiscated from drug traffickers and repurposed for our operations. You'll also have access to helicopters for reconnaissance and support, and additional fixed-wing aircraft for logistics."

When the discussion turned to funding, the panel spoke with an air of confidence about the financial backing of the Andean Initiative. Tens of millions of dollars, they assured me, had been allocated for the campaign, courtesy of U.S. support and the broader war on drugs. On paper, it sounded incredible—a treasure chest of resources—but I wasn't entirely convinced I'd see much of it in action. The bureaucracy involved, not to mention the competing interests across agencies, made me sceptical. Still, the sheer mention of such funding set my mind racing. I began to imagine what I could do with it—how I could transform this rudimentary operation into a well-oiled, elite unit. *My squadron,* as I was now thinking of it, could be more than just crop dusters. I pictured adding supply aircraft to keep us operational in the remote jungle regions, transport planes to move personnel and equipment efficiently, and, most excitingly, reconnaissance helicopters. With a couple of thousand hours logged in helicopters, I had a deep love for flying them and knew firsthand their versatility and value. A fleet of helos equipped with advanced surveillance systems could give us the eyes we needed in the skies and the ability to scout ahead of fumigation missions. With the right resources, I could turn this ragtag operation into something extraordinary—a squadron that could adapt, survive, and succeed in the toughest conditions. The thought of building it all from the ground up filled me with an almost boyish excitement.

Hearing this, I couldn't help but picture myself as the commander of a small, highly specialized air force. It was both daunting and exhilarating. They emphasized the importance of maintaining the fleet, pointing out that every plane was a critical asset in the fight against the cartels. "You'll need a reliable team of mechanics and ground crew," they said. "Spare parts can be hard to come by, especially for the older aircraft, so creativity and resourcefulness will be essential."

The operational tempo would be intense. Each mission would require meticulous planning—determining the target zones, coordinating with reconnaissance teams, ensuring the aircraft were fully prepped, and managing the logistics of refuelling and resupplying in remote locations. Missions could last hours, with multiple sorties per day, depending on the size of the targeted area.

Finally, they touched on the broader implications of the campaign. "This isn't just about spraying coca plants," one of the officials said, his tone serious. "It's about disrupting the entire supply chain. Every field you destroy represents thousands of kilos of cocaine that won't make it to the streets. It's a blow to the cartels and a step toward reclaiming these regions from their control."

I sat back in my chair, absorbing it all trying to convey an air of confidence. The sheer scale of the operation was staggering, and the responsibility they were placing on my shoulders was immense. But as daunting as it was, I couldn't deny the allure. This wasn't just a job; it was a mission—a chance to make a real difference, to bring my skills to bear in a way that mattered. Sure, the herbicide's safety claims might have been over my head, and the risks were undeniable, but for the first time in years, I felt a spark of excitement. This was the kind of challenge I'd been waiting for.

"How do you know where the plantations are?" I asked, my voice tinged with genuine curiosity. "Colombia's massive, and a lot of it is dense jungle. Surely you can't just fly around hoping to spot a patch of coca leaves."

The men on the panel exchanged knowing smiles, clearly expecting the question. One of them, a grizzled officer with sharp eyes and a commanding presence, leaned forward and began to explain.

"You're right—Colombia is vast, and its geography can be unforgiving. That's why we rely on a multi-pronged approach that combines the best of modern technology and tried-and-true intelligence gathering. First and foremost, we utilize satellite imagery. The U.S. government, particularly agencies like the CIA and the National Geospatial-Intelligence Agency, provide us with high-resolution satellite data. These satellites are equipped with advanced imaging technology that can distinguish the unique spectral signature of coca plants from other vegetation. It's a bit like finding a needle in a haystack, but with the right tools, the needle practically glows."

Another official chimed in. "But satellites are just the start. We also conduct aerial surveillance using specialized reconnaissance aircraft provided by the U.S. These planes—Lockheed P-3 Orions and others—are outfitted with state-of-the-art sensors that can operate even in the challenging conditions of Colombia. For example, infrared sensors detect heat signatures, making it possible to spot coca fields even under dense jungle canopies. Multispectral imaging systems analyze vegetation at different wavelengths, further enhancing our ability to identify coca plants."

He paused for effect, letting the weight of the technology sink in, before continuing. "Then there's Synthetic Aperture Radar—SAR for short. This system allows us to penetrate cloud cover and thick foliage. In Colombia, where it's often cloudy or the jungle is impenetrable from a visual perspective, SAR is invaluable. With these tools, we can identify potential coca plantations with remarkable accuracy."

Another panelist, a civilian advisor with a practical air about him, picked up the thread. "Of course, all the high-tech gadgets in the world can only do so much. That's where on-the-ground intelligence comes in. We have networks of local informants—farmers, community members, even defectors from the cartels themselves—who provide valuable information about where plantations are being cultivated. These people are often the first to know when a new coca field has been planted, and their tips guide our efforts."

"Then there's the military and police," added the first speaker. "They regularly patrol regions known for coca cultivation and update our intelligence. These patrols are dangerous—they encounter guerrilla fighters, narco-militias, and booby traps—but they provide us with critical, firsthand data."

"And let's not forget captured cartel intel," the civilian advisor interjected. "Raids, interrogations, and seized documents often lead to new discoveries. A single map or logbook can reveal the locations of hidden fields, supply routes, and even processing labs. Every piece of intel adds to the bigger picture."

I nodded, impressed. "So, you're cross-referencing all this data?"

"Exactly," he said with a grin. "It's like assembling a puzzle. We feed all this information—satellite imagery, aerial surveillance data, and ground intelligence—into Geographic Information Systems. GIS software lets us create detailed maps of suspected coca cultivation areas. We also use predictive modeling to identify likely new hotspots based on factors like proximity to trafficking routes, historical trends, and even soil and climate conditions."

"Speaking of history," the officer said, "we rely heavily on records of known cultivation areas. Certain regions—Nariño and Putumayo in the south, Guaviare and Meta in the central jungles, and Catatumbo near the Venezuelan border—have long been coca hotspots. These are starting points for our operations, but the cartels are always adapting. They move fields deeper into the jungle, disguise them among other crops, or use new techniques to evade detection."

The complexity of it all was staggering. This wasn't a haphazard operation; it was a meticulous, multi-layered effort combining cutting-edge technology with old-fashioned human intelligence. Every tool, every tactic, and every piece of data served a single purpose: to locate the coca fields that fueled the global cocaine trade. It was a war fought on multiple fronts, with an enemy that was as resourceful as it was ruthless.

I leaned back in my chair, my mind racing. It was one thing to imagine the scale of the drug problem, but hearing about the lengths to which they went to fight it was another thing entirely. The sophistication of the operation was unlike anything I'd encountered before. I had been a fighter pilot, a test pilot, and a commercial captain, but this was a whole new level of complexity and precision. And now, they were asking me to lead a critical piece of it.

"Your job," ("should you decide to take it, Mr Phelps" -is what I heard, straight out of Mission Impossible TV series) one of the officials said, leaning forward with an air of authority, "will be to take all this data and turn it into actionable results. Identify the plantations, organize the fumigation flights, coordinate with multiple agencies, and ensure the mission's success. Ultimately, you'll be responsible for seeing that these coca fields are eradicated and that our resources are used efficiently."

His words hung in the air, heavy with expectation. There was no room for misinterpretation—I would be the one making the decisions, pulling together threads of intelligence from satellites, reconnaissance planes, ground teams, and informants. It wasn't just about flying planes or organizing sorties; it was about strategy, execution, and accountability on an unprecedented scale. "Holy shit!" was said silently in my mid, I just hope my face didn't give away my amazement or incredulity.

For nearly three hours, the conversation unfolded like a tactical briefing. They covered every angle, every nuance, and every possible scenario. My mind spun as I tried to absorb it all, jotting down notes and asking question after question. I asked about logistics, chain of command, operational protocols, contingency plans, and even the political ramifications of our actions. They answered with a mix of candour and confidence, their responses sharp and precise, revealing an intricate web of interagency cooperation and strategic planning.

At one point, I leaned forward and asked, "What happens when we encounter resistance? These cartels won't just stand by while we spray their fields into oblivion."

One of the military officers, a man with a hard-set jaw and an air of seasoned authority, replied, "You will encounter resistance. Make no mistake—this is a war, and the cartels will fight back. Your aircraft will be fired upon. You'll deal with everything from small arms fire to anti-aircraft guns, depending on how deeply entrenched the cartels are in the region. That's why your pilots must be prepared for evasive manoeuvres and quick decisions under fire."

I nodded, swallowing hard. It wasn't that I hadn't anticipated the danger, but hearing it spelled out so plainly made it all the more real. Still, there was a part of me that felt a thrill at the challenge. This was what I'd been missing—the adrenaline, the stakes, the sense of purpose.

As the meeting wore on, I found myself alternating between fascination and apprehension. The scope of the operation was mind-boggling. It wasn't just about dropping herbicide over fields; it was about coordinating a high-stakes campaign involving dozens of moving parts, each one as critical as the next. The politics alone were enough to make my head spin—U.S. funding, Colombian sovereignty, interagency rivalries, and the constant scrutiny of the international community. One misstep could have far-reaching consequences, both on the ground and diplomatically.

Yet, as daunting as it all seemed, there was a fire inside me that refused to be extinguished. This was the kind of mission I'd dreamed of back in my Navy days, the kind of challenge that made you feel alive. And when doubt began to creep in, I pushed it aside with the same fighter pilot arrogance that had carried me through dogfights over the South Atlantic. This was just another mission, I told myself. Another test of skill and nerve. If I could face enemy planes at 22,000 feet, I could certainly handle this.

As the meeting drew to a close, the mood in the room shifted. There was a sense of approval from the panel, a subtle nod of respect for the way I had handled myself. Smiles replaced the initial guarded expressions, and handshakes were offered all around. When I stood to leave, one of the officials clasped my hand firmly, looked me squarely in the eye, and said, "This is a unique opportunity. We hope you'll use it to make a real difference—not just for us, but for the people of Colombia."

The words carried a weight that lingered as I stepped out of the boardroom and into the darkened corridors of the Palace of Justice.

I stepped out of the Palace of Justice into the blazing Bogotá sunlight, momentarily blinded by the glare. The cacophony of the city enveloped me—honking horns, the distant clatter of helicopters (police ones, no doubt), the chatter of pedestrians. For a moment, I stood still, letting it all sink in. I had just committed to one of the most ambitious and dangerous undertakings of my life, and the weight of it pressed down on me like the humid air around me.

But as I started walking, that weight began to lift, replaced by a mix of excitement and determination. This was more than I had ever bargained for, true, but it was also exactly what I had been searching for—a mission with purpose, a chance to make a difference, and an opportunity to push myself to the limit. Plus, the chance to meet lots of hot women.

I didn't just feel alive. I felt unstoppable.

Chapter 2: Launching into the unknown

In December 1994, I boarded a KLM flight to Bogotá, my resignation from the airline finalized, my apartment in Amsterdam left in the capable hands of a friend who would cover my mortgage. I was carrying everything I owned for this new life in just one suitcase and a carry-on. The flight itself felt strange. For the first time in years, I was traveling as a passenger rather than the one in the cockpit, and this time, the destination marked the beginning of an entirely new chapter.

Before I left Amsterdam, my friends and colleagues didn't hold back in telling me I was completely mad. "You're going to *Colombia*?" they'd say, wide-eyed, their voices dripping with disbelief. The country's reputation preceded it—bombings, shootings, kidnappings. To them, I was walking into a war zone. "Why would you throw away a career like yours?" they asked. "You're on track to become a 747 captain, flying prestigious international routes. Instead, you're going to fly tiny planes in a country that might get you killed? It's career suicide, if not ACTUAL suicide." They weren't wrong, at least not from a traditional perspective. Taking this job wouldn't earn me any points with the airlines, and it certainly wouldn't help me climb the corporate aviation ladder. But the truth was, I didn't care. The thought of spending the next 20 years bored out of my mind at 30,000 feet in the plush but predictable seat of a jumbo jet sounded like a slow death. The most common comment from them was: *"You're stark raving mad to go to Colombia! You'll get yourself killed!"* I tossed this off as being widely excessive and unrealistic. I craved something more. I wanted excitement, danger, purpose, plus let's not forget those beautiful hot women. This was a chance to live—to relive the intensity and camaraderie I'd experienced during my military days. Those had been the best years of my life, and if this mission gave me even a fraction of that thrill, it would be worth the risk.

Landing in Bogotá, the city greeted me with an overcast, drab sky. The air was cooler than I'd expected for a city near the equator, but at 8,600 feet above sea level, Bogotá had its own unique climate. This time I had to take a taxi to the familiar Hotel La Fontana, I no longer had access to the KLM crewbus. I looked out at the sprawling city and couldn't shake the mixture of excitement and trepidation bubbling within me. This was it—the leap into the unknown I'd been craving.

As I sat in my Bogotá hotel room, it struck me how exposed I felt without the safety net of a corporate giant like KLM surrounding me. For years, I'd been cushioned by its vast infrastructure—the steady paycheck, the polished reputation, the resources to handle anything from mechanical failures to emergencies halfway around the globe. KLM was more than a job; it was a shield, a structure that kept everything in order. Leaving it felt eerily similar to the day I left the Royal Navy. Back then, walking away from the tight-knit camaraderie and the sense of purpose that came with serving felt like abandoning a family. Now, I felt that same sense of vulnerability, like I'd willingly removed the armour that had protected me. Yet, as unnerving as it was, it was also thrilling. This wasn't the predictable world of major airlines or the regimented hierarchy of the military—this was me, stepping into the unknown, entirely responsible for what came next. Scary, yes, but it was a kind of freedom I hadn't felt in years.

The first week passed in a blur of bureaucracy. I spent my days shuttling between various government offices, being introduced, vouched for, and stamped into the system. The paperwork seemed endless, but some of it carried an undeniable thrill—like getting permission to carry a firearm. Guns were generally forbidden for foreigners in Colombia, but my position with the Ministry of Justice came with special allowances. I think they knew the danger I would be in and I needed this.

They handed me a permit, and while the actual Glock 19—a compact 9mm pistol with a 15-round capacity—would be sent to my eventual posting in Tumaco, I couldn't resist getting a leather hip holster for it. Back at the hotel, I practiced my quick draw in front of the mirror like a cowboy preparing for a showdown. It felt a bit absurd, but also oddly satisfying. Later, a local acquaintance told me it was smarter to wear the gun at the back of my waist, where it looked like I was reaching for my wallet if I were ever held up. The comment was unnerving—this wasn't something I'd dealt with before in the Netherlands or the UK—but it was a crash course in the realities of my new environment.

Oddly, the most challenging part of the week wasn't the gun permit, but securing a Colombian driver's license. The bureaucratic maze for this simple task was mind-boggling. I was told I needed a certificate from the Colombian consulate in the UK to verify my British license, then have that document translated and notarized back in the UK before presenting it to the Ministry of Transport in Bogotá. The thought of traveling 11,000 kilometers just for a license made me want to pull my hair out. Thankfully, I "met a guy."

Hovering near the transport office, this *tramitador*—a sort of unofficial fixer for government paperwork—offered his services. For 90,000 pesos (about $45 at the time), he promised to sort everything for me. True to his word, three hours later, I was holding my new Colombian driver's license. To my amusement, it also allowed me to drive an articulated truck—something I had never been qualified for before. It seemed the Colombian approach to licensing was as fast and flexible as it was, well, creative.

Next on my to-do list was reporting to the SATENA offices at the airport. SATENA was the Colombian state airline that technically employed me as a captain, even though my real mission was entirely separate. It was a peculiar setup. I was issued an employee ID and was told I might have to get type-rated on their Fokker F28 jets. These 65-seat regional planes felt tiny compared to the Boeing 767s I'd flown for KLM. Still, I took the news in stride, though I couldn't resist snickering at the endless stream of childish Fokker jokes that came to mind.

As I wandered through the Colombian airline's installations, taking in the mix of Fokker F28s and AVRO HS-748 turboprops, I felt a strange mix of curiosity and detachment. These planes were far smaller than what I was used to, but they had a certain rugged charm, clearly suited for Colombia's challenging landscapes. Their utilitarian design and compact size were a stark contrast to the Boeing 767s I had flown for KLM, but there was something endearing about their no-nonsense practicality.

As I moved past the main hangars, I entered an area that looked, at first glance, like a boneyard—or perhaps even an aviation museum. A line of old aircraft sat baking in the sun, their paint faded, some with visible patches of rust. One immediately caught my eye: a Douglas DC-3 with *Lineas Aéreas Petroleras* painted on the fuselage in peeling letters. It looked like something straight out of a World War II film, its vintage curves and distinctive design making it an icon of a bygone era. A few steps away sat a Convair jetliner, a relic of the early 1950s, its age showing in the worn edges of its airframe and the streaks of grime trailing from its rivets.

But the most striking of the lot was an Antonov An-32, its massive turboprop blades unmistakable even at a distance. The Soviet-designed workhorse had clearly seen better days, its once-proud exterior now a patchwork of mismatched paint and scrapes. It looked well-used—functional, yes, but far from the polished machines I was accustomed to.

Standing among these aging giants, I couldn't help but feel a pang of unease. This was a far cry from the sleek, cutting-edge Navy fighters I had flown during my military days, or the modern, glass-cockpit Boeing 767s that represented the pinnacle of commercial aviation. These planes, with their rugged appearances and clear signs of wear and tear, seemed more like survivors of a long and arduous battle than tools of a thriving operation. My mind began racing as I wondered what aircraft I'd be assigned. Surely, I wouldn't be flying any of these antiques—or at least I hoped not.

Still lost in thought, I rounded a corner near one of the hangars and spotted two male mechanics working on an engine. They were deep in conversation but stopped as soon as they noticed me. To my surprise, they began pouting their lips and blowing what appeared to be kisses in my direction. I froze, utterly confused. Were they joking? Flirting? My mind raced as I tried to process what was happening.

Coming from Amsterdam, I was no stranger to the LGBTQ+ community—it was a celebrated and visible part of life there, and I had plenty of friends who were openly gay. But I hadn't expected such apparent openness here in Latin America, where I had assumed the culture to be more conservative about such things. I forced an awkward smile and quickly walked away, trying to appear unfazed even as my thoughts spiraled. Had I misunderstood their intentions? Was I reading too much into it?

Later, over coffee in the operations office, I recounted the incident to a local colleague. He laughed and shook his head. "No, no, they weren't flirting! That's just how Colombians point." He explained that instead of using a finger to indicate something, Colombians often pout their lips in the direction they want to highlight. It was both a revelation and a relief, though I couldn't help but feel a bit sheepish for misunderstanding. It also hit me how much I had to learn—not just the Spanish language, but the subtle, unspoken nuances of Colombian culture. Every gesture, every interaction seemed to carry layers of meaning that I had yet to decipher. Clearly, my immersion into this new world was going to be more complex than I'd anticipated.

By the end of the week, my checklist was complete: my *cédula extranjero* (foreign resident ID), a shiny new Justice Department employee badge, my SATENA ID, my gun permit, my leather holster, and even my Colombian driver's license. I had a fresh uniform hanging neatly in my closet and the attention of Carolina, my stunning Colombian girlfriend. I'd gone from an British Airline pilot (in a dutch airline, I know) to something resembling a Colombian action hero in just a matter of days.

The feeling was intoxicating. For the first time in years, I felt like I stood out in the best way possible. Back in Amsterdam or the UK, I was just another guy—another face in the crowd. But here in Bogotá, I felt important, noticed, like I was someone. Even the speed at which things got done amazed me. While Europe was bogged down in endless red tape and required permissions for every minor detail, Colombia had its own "unofficial" system of getting things done. For a few thousand pesos here or there—a negligible amount to my European sensibilities—you could bypass hours or even weeks of bureaucracy. It was pragmatic, fast, and strangely liberating.

But Bogotá wasn't all sleek efficiency and charm. The city had its rough edges, from the sprawling, chaotic streets of its poorer districts to the palpable tension that seemed to hang in the air in certain areas. Still, there were neighborhoods that could rival any European city in beauty and amenities. Shopping malls, parks, and streets lined with restaurants offered a cosmopolitan flair, and the prices were astonishingly cheap. Add to that the abundance of gorgeous women, and I was starting to see why Pieter had been so enamored with the place.

Reality hit, however, when I looked up Tumaco on a map. Located on Colombia's Pacific coast, it was a world away from Bogotá in every sense. Tumaco was a remote, humid, and notoriously rough area—a key battleground in the drug trade. The realization that this would be my posting left me both intrigued and apprehensive. I knew it wouldn't have the malls and fine dining of Bogotá, but I also knew it was where the real adventure would begin.

As I packed my things for the next leg of my journey, I couldn't help but feel a strange mix of excitement and foreboding. The city I had come to appreciate would soon be in my rearview mirror, and I'd be heading into the unknown. But that was what I'd signed up for, wasn't it? And in a way, it was exactly what I'd been searching for—a place to feel alive.

Touching down at Tumaco's La Florida Airport in a SATENA Airlines Fokker F28, I felt a mix of pride and nerves. I was wearing my freshly pressed captain's uniform, complete with medal ribbons for my South Atlantic Medal and the Distinguished Service Cross (DSC). These small tokens of my military past were more than just decorations—they were my armour, a way to command respect. Being a short, young-looking guy had often made me feel like I had to prove myself, whether in the Royal Navy or the corporate halls of KLM. Once, as a lieutenant, I'd even been accused of wearing my dad's uniform. Today, I wasn't taking any chances.

The airport was quaint, to put it mildly. The terminal was smaller than my old three-bedroom house in Manchester, and the single asphalt runway stretched just 1,600 meters. Despite its modest size, it could still handle the likes of Boeing 737s and Douglas DC-9s, a testament to its importance in this remote region.

The first thing that struck me as I stepped off the plane wasn't the heat, though it was sweltering, but the air of rugged utility that hung over the place. The SATENA building, where I'd officially reported in, was functional but sparse. Just to the side of it was the military installation—a collection of low, single-story brick and wooden buildings, interspersed with tents. The perimeter was ringed by a chain-link fence, and beyond that was a dirt road lined with shanty-style houses that looked like they had been pieced together by their owners. Scattered around the installation were several sandbagged gun positions, crude but effective. Seeing those sent a chill down my spine. This wasn't a training exercise or a simulation; this was the real deal. I was in a war zone.

I was directed to the base commander's office, where I met the man in charge. He was older—mid-fifties, I guessed—with a neat, short-sleeved uniform and an impressive collection of medal ribbons that instantly made me glad I'd pinned mine on. He greeted me warmly, his demeanour professional but friendly, and seemed genuinely pleased to see me. Perhaps I was a relief for him, someone who could shoulder a bit of the burden. Our conversation was brief, and after a firm handshake, he handed me over to a junior officer to get settled in.

The officer led me to the base's officers' mess, where I was assigned a room. It was far from luxurious—basic, to say the least. A single bed with a thin mattress, an old wooden cupboard, a wardrobe, a desk, and a metal chair made up the furnishings. The walls were bare, and the air was heavy with humidity. I was assured that better quarters would be available later, though I wasn't holding my breath. Still, it was functional, and I set about unpacking the few clothes and belongings I had brought with me.

That afternoon, a captain gave me a tour of the base and introduced me to the crew and staff. Most of the personnel were U.S. civilian contractors working under a contract with DynCorp Aerospace Technologies through the U.S. State Department. They were mostly my age, with a couple of older hands in the mix. None of them, however, had combat experience. A few had served in the U.S. National Guard, but that was as close as it got. When they found out about my military background, particularly my time flying Sea Harriers in the Falklands, they were full of questions. They'd heard about the Harrier's legendary vertical take-off and dogfighting capabilities and seemed genuinely impressed by my stories. That respect made it easier for me to assume command. I could tell they were sizing me up, but the mix of my military history and my airline experience seemed to cement my credibility.

As I continued the tour, I was shown the six AT-802 Air Tractor aircraft that would form the backbone of our fumigation campaign. These planes were massive for agricultural aircraft, capable of carrying 800 gallons of herbicide in a single load. Their wings stretched nearly 60 feet, and they cruised at over 200 mph—impressive for what were essentially flying crop sprayers. But their size and payload capacity weren't the only things that stood out. These planes were unarmoured, leaving them dangerously vulnerable to the small arms and heavier firepower we would inevitably encounter.

The pilots had already tried to address this with makeshift solutions. They'd fashioned "protected seats" using bulletproof vests. Beneath the seat, on the sides, and even behind the headrests, they had layered Level III body armour vests, the ones with steel plates in them—designed to stop 7.62mm NATO rounds and AK-47 fire which is the main weapon of the guerilla fighters who would be protecting the cocaine plantations. They had put 2 vests under the seat to protect the "family jewels" against through-the-floor shots. The armour was held together with duct tape—"Cinta americana," as they called it here. It wasn't exactly standard-issue, but it was ingenious and, more importantly, effective. I couldn't help but admire their resourcefulness, though it was a stark reminder of what we were up against.

As I continued to inspect the aircraft, I noticed the registration numbers painted boldly on the sides of each plane, like "PNC 1046." Curious about their significance, I inquired and was told that PNC stood for *Policía Nacional de Colombia*. These weren't just fumigation planes; they were officially designated police aircraft. The realization struck me—I would be flying a plane marked as part of the Colombian National Police, a symbol of authority in the fight against illicit activities. I thought it was pretty cool to be associated with such an emblem, even indirectly. However, I was also informed that we could only operate PNC-registered aircraft, not those marked with Army or Air Force insignia. This distinction, I learned, was crucial to maintaining clear jurisdictional boundaries and ensuring operational compliance within the intricate framework of Colombian law enforcement and military protocol.

I was also briefed on the operational logistics. The Narcotics Affairs Section of the U.S. Embassy provided the herbicide, fuel, and technical advice, while our missions were coordinated with Colombian National Police crews. Spray aircraft were always accompanied by escort helicopters—another thrilling aspect of the job for me. With over 2,000 hours logged flying helicopters, I had a deep appreciation for their utility. Seeing the sleek UH 60 black hawks and a couple of older Vietnam War era UH-1 Iroquois "Hueys" and other models on the tarmac made me itch to get behind the controls. Reconnaissance and escort missions were an essential part of the operation, and I hoped to play an active role in both. I wondered what my ride would be.

The base's facilities were as modest as I'd expected, but the atmosphere was welcoming. Most of the crew wore military-style overalls, which immediately made me feel overdressed in my captain's uniform. I'd brought along my old Navy overalls, minus the badges that could easily be Velcroed on, and made a mental note to switch into something more practical. As much as I appreciated the authority the uniform lent me, I didn't want to stand out too much among the team. I would be wearing my 4 bar captain's epaulettes to maintain my identity as the boss though.

The sense of camaraderie among the crew was palpable, even in those first few hours. They were a diverse group—Americans, Colombians, and a guy from Guatemala—all brought together for a mission that was as dangerous as it was important. There was a shared understanding of the risks, but also a determination to get the job done. As I settled into my role, I felt a growing sense of responsibility—not just for the mission, but for the people I would be leading.

By the end of the day, as I sat in my spartan room, I reflected on the stark contrasts I'd experienced so far. From Bogotá's cosmopolitan charm to Tumaco's makeshift installations, this wasn't just a change of scenery—it was a transformation of my entire life. The base's crude defences, the improvised armour on the planes, and the palpable tension in the air were constant reminders that this was no ordinary job. Yet, I felt alive in a way I hadn't in years. This was exactly the challenge I had been searching for, and I was ready to meet it head-on.

The morning after I arrived in Tumaco, I was ushered into a briefing room by one of the senior officers at the base. A large map of Colombia hung on the wall, marked with bold red and blue lines that I would soon come to recognize as representing guerrilla-held territories and areas of paramilitary influence. A long, low table was scattered with folders, charts, and coffee mugs, the scene exuding a sense of urgency and order.

I had expected an orientation of sorts, perhaps an overview of the fumigation program or a rundown of logistics. What I received instead was a masterclass on the tangled web of Colombia's history, a story of war, politics, and drugs that left me reeling.

The officer, a man whose demeanour spoke of years in the field, began with the origins of Colombia's conflict. "The armed conflict officially began in 1964," he said, pointing to the map, "when two guerrilla groups, the FARC and the ELN, were formed. But the violence—well, that started long before."

He described how Colombia had been plagued by civil wars throughout the 19th century, battles fought between political elites vying for control. The violence escalated dramatically in 1948, following the assassination of Jorge Gaitán, a charismatic Liberal Party leader who had captured the hopes of the working class and peasant farmers. His murder sparked a decade-long period known as *La Violencia*.

"Over 200,000 people were killed during that time," the officer explained, his tone sombre. "Entire villages were wiped out. Families destroyed. Much of it happened in rural areas, among the peasants. The government couldn't control the chaos, and the seeds of the guerrilla groups were planted."

By the 1960s, these seeds had grown into organized insurgencies. The FARC (*Fuerzas Armadas Revolucionarias de Colombia*) consolidated control over vast swathes of rural Colombia, eventually controlling nearly 40% of the country's territory. They used these regions, many of which were ideal for coca cultivation, as strongholds to fund their activities. At its peak during the late 1990s, the FARC was the largest guerrilla group in Colombia.

The group's manpower was estimated to be between 16,000 and 20,000 combatants and its influence spanned a wide geographical area, including rural and jungle regions.

The FARC also had thousands of supporters and militia members who were not full-time fighters but contributed logistical support, intelligence, and financial backing through extortion and the drug trade.

The ELN (*Ejército de Liberación Nacional*) emerged with a similar ideology, though often clashing with the FARC over territory and tactics. By the 1980s, these guerrilla groups had become entrenched, waging war against the state while operating as shadow governments in the territories they controlled. The ELN was smaller in comparison to the FARC, with an estimated size of 3,000 to 5,000 fighters during the 1990s.

While it shared some ideological similarities with the FARC (Marxist-Leninist roots), the ELN focused more on ideological rhetoric and less on the drug trade (though it did engage in extortion and kidnapping for revenue).

The ELN operated primarily in different regions, including the Andean highlands and areas near key oil infrastructure, which they frequently targeted.

By the time the officer began explaining the rise of the drug cartels, I was already struggling to wrap my head around the sheer scale of the conflict. But nothing could have prepared me for the story of the cocaine trade and its role in transforming Colombia's war into a nightmare of global proportions.

"Pablo Escobar," the officer said, his voice tightening as he spoke the name. "The King of Cocaine. His Medellín Cartel was a global empire in the 1980s and early '90s. At its peak, they controlled nearly 80% of the cocaine entering the United States."

I had, of course, heard of Escobar. His death in December 1993 was international news, a supposed victory in the war on drugs. But what I hadn't realized was how deeply embedded the cocaine trade had become in Colombia's economy and its conflict. Escobar's Medellín Cartel wasn't just a criminal organization—it was a shadow state, complete with its own militias, networks of influence, and a stranglehold on the government.

When Escobar fell, I naïvely assumed that had marked the end of the cocaine trade in Colombia. But I couldn't have been more wrong. As the officer explained, the vacuum left by Medellín was quickly filled by the Cali Cartel, an equally powerful and far more sophisticated organization.

"The Cali Cartel didn't operate like Medellín," he said. "Where Escobar ruled through terror and brutality, Cali worked behind the scenes. Bribery, infiltration, calculated violence. At their height, they controlled over 80% of the world's cocaine supply. Billions of dollars, untold influence. They weren't just a Colombian problem—they were a global threat."

Complicating matters further was the rise of paramilitary groups in the 1980s. Initially formed by large landowners, business leaders, and even the Colombian Army as a response to the guerrilla threat, these groups quickly morphed into something far more dangerous. Funded heavily by drug cartels, they targeted leftist organizations and any perceived threats to their economic interests.

"These paramilitaries," the officer said, "didn't just fight guerrillas. They massacred civilians, assassinated political activists, and operated with near-total impunity. They had deep support within the state, which only made things worse."

By the 1990s, the conflict had devolved into a chaotic free-for-all. The FARC, ELN, and paramilitaries all relied heavily on the drug trade to finance their operations, leading to a tangled web of alliances and betrayals. Meanwhile, the civilian population bore the brunt of the violence. Kidnappings, extortion, massacres—it seemed no one was safe.

As if the situation wasn't complex enough, the officer explained how the United States became deeply involved in Colombia's conflict, particularly after the rise of the cocaine trade. What began as an effort to eradicate marijuana crops in the 1980s quickly expanded into a full-scale counternarcotics campaign.

The U.S. provided billions of dollars in aid, military equipment, and technical support, largely under the banner of the Andean Initiative. DynCorp, the private military contractor overseeing much of our operation, was a key player in this effort.

"DynCorp will take care of most of the heavy lifting," the officer said, and I could feel a weight lifting off my shoulders. "They handle recruiting, training, maintenance, and a lot of operational support. Your focus will be on finding and destroying the coca plantations. They'll give you the tools; you'll make it happen."

Learning about DynCorp's extensive role in the operation gave me some relief. I had worried about being bogged down in logistics, but with the contractor managing so much of the backend work, I could focus on the mission itself. Still, the sheer scale of the problem was daunting.

As part of my induction into the operations in Tumaco, I was given an overview of the aircraft fleet operated by the Policía Nacional de Colombia. These machines were critical to their counter-narcotics and law enforcement efforts, providing the mobility, surveillance, and logistical support necessary in a country with such challenging terrain. From rugged mountains to dense jungles and sprawling urban areas, the fleet had to be versatile and robust, capable of adapting to both the extremes of geography and the dangers of the mission.

Helicopters were the lifeblood of operations, their versatility unmatched in Colombia's diverse and often unforgiving landscapes. They were used for everything from transporting personnel to conducting surveillance and even engaging in direct-action missions.

The crown jewel of the fleet, at least in my eyes, was the Bell 212 Twin Huey. A twin-engine upgrade of the legendary Huey, it offered greater payload capacity and reliability, making it perfect for troop deployments and cargo missions. When I learned about its role in the fleet, my imagination immediately took flight. I could see myself piloting one of these sleek, powerful machines, ferrying crews and supplies deep into cartel territory or swooping into action for a daring extraction.

Unfortunately, that dream was cut short almost as soon as it started. When I asked if I would be assigned a Twin Huey, the response was swift and unequivocal. "No, you'll be flying a Bell 206 JetRanger," I was told. For a moment, I felt a pang of disappointment. The JetRanger, a single-engine utility helicopter, was certainly a fine machine—agile, reliable, and well-suited for reconnaissance and patrol missions—but it lacked the raw power and capacity of the Bell 212. Still, the idea of having my own helicopter, even if it wasn't the Twin Huey, was enough to keep my spirits high.

The JetRanger wasn't a bad consolation prize. With its sleek lines and dependable performance, it was the go-to helicopter for law enforcement and corporate fleets around the world. In many ways, it was the Swiss Army knife of helicopters: light, manoeuvrable, and perfect for solo or small-team missions. It also meant that I would have a personal helo for missions tailored to the fumigation effort or anything else that might require quick mobility. I kept the questions about its role and specifics to myself for now, preferring to wait until I actually had the thing in front of me before diving into operational details.

The Policía Nacional also operated a range of fixed-wing aircraft, essential for long-range transport and surveillance. Among them were the Cessna 208 Caravan and the Beechcraft Super King Air, both dependable and versatile machines capable of ferrying personnel and conducting aerial reconnaissance.

Then there was the Douglas DC-3, an aircraft that has filled many a museum. A relic of World War II, the DC-3 had a reputation for being sturdy and reliable, but it was ancient—far older than any plane I had flown. I respected its legacy, but the thought of trusting my life to one of those old birds made my stomach turn. As far as I was concerned, someone else could take that risk. I'd stick to modern machines, thank you very much.

The fleet wasn't just a collection of aircraft; it was a vital tool in Colombia's fight against the cartels and insurgent groups. Helicopters were used for rapid troop deployments, surveillance, medical evacuations, and supply drops in areas too remote or dangerous for ground access. Fixed-wing aircraft handled long-range logistics, intelligence gathering, and fumigation missions to eradicate coca fields.

The missions were high-risk and often conducted under fire. Guerrilla fighters and cartel gunmen knew the value of these aircraft to government operations and targeted them relentlessly. Pilots had to be skilled, resourceful, and unflinching in the face of danger. I couldn't help but feel a surge of pride and excitement at the thought of joining their ranks. This was what I had signed up for—adrenaline, purpose, and the chance to make a real difference.

I couldn't help but linger on the thought of flying the Bell 212 Twin Huey. Its twin engines, larger payload capacity, and enhanced performance were tailor-made for the kind of missions we'd be running. The idea of sitting in its cockpit, with the hum of dual turbines in my ears and the thrill of a mission ahead, was intoxicating. But the reality was clear: I wasn't getting the Bell 212.

Still, the JetRanger was no slouch, and I was chuffed to have a helicopter assigned to me at all. I'd flown many types of aircraft in my career, but there was something special about helicopters. The precision required to maneuver in tight spaces, the ability to hover and land almost anywhere, the connection you felt to the machine—it was a completely different experience from flying fixed-wing planes. I couldn't wait to take the JetRanger for its first mission, to see how it performed in the challenging conditions of Colombia.

As the briefing wrapped up and I mulled over the details, I found myself tempering my excitement with a dose of realism. The stakes here were higher than anything I'd encountered before. The aircraft might be tools of the trade, but they were also targets, and every flight came with risks. The guerrillas and cartels were well-armed, and the thought of being shot down was a sobering reminder of the dangers we faced.

For now, I decided to take things one step at a time. I would get to know the JetRanger, understand its capabilities, and learn how to use it effectively in the field. I had a lot of questions—about its armament (if any), its defensive capabilities, and how it would be deployed—but I held them back. Better to get hands-on experience first than to pester the seasoned crew with premature concerns.

One question I couldn't hold back, however, was about the *rules of engagement*. After all, this wasn't just crop dusting or passenger transport—this was a shooting war. I needed to understand exactly how we were supposed to defend ourselves. Sitting with one of the more experienced contractors over coffee, I raised the subject, trying to sound as nonchalant as possible.

"So, what's the deal with defending ourselves out there?" I asked, leaning back in my chair. "Are we allowed to shoot back, or is it one of those situations where we have to wait to get shot at first?"

He gave me a wry smile. "You've got it," he said. "Rules of engagement are strict. We can only return fire if we've been fired upon first. And even then, only if there's no other way to extract ourselves from the situation. We're here to spray crops, not pick fights. The Colombian government and the U.S. Embassy are very clear on that."

I nodded, though the answer didn't do much to put my mind at ease. I couldn't shake the thought of my meagre Glock 19—a compact 9mm pistol—being my only personal line of defence. Sure, it could hold 15 rounds, and I was reasonably confident I could handle it in a pinch, but against a guerrilla or narco wielding an AK-47, it felt more like a token of reassurance than a meaningful deterrent. The image of myself awkwardly leaning out of the helicopter's window, trying to return fire with my pistol, was more comedic than comforting.

He seemed to pick up on my concern. "You won't be out there alone," he added. "You'll have an escort."

That got my attention. "An escort?"

"Yeah. Blackhawk helicopters," he said casually, as though he were describing a taxi service. "They'll have miniguns mounted. Those things can fire up to 6,000 rounds per minute. Trust me, the sound alone is enough to make most people think twice about shooting at you."

I blinked, letting that sink in. The M134 Minigun, a legendary piece of hardware, was essentially a rotating, multi-barrel Gatling gun that could spit out a torrent of bullets faster than anything I'd ever encountered. It wasn't just a weapon; it was a statement. The thought of a Blackhawk flying overhead, its minigun ready to deter any threats, was reassuring in a way my Glock never could be.

"Have you seen it in action?" I asked, my curiosity piqued.

"Once or twice," he replied, a glint of something between respect and fear in his eyes. "Let's just say it gets the job done. It's not about engaging in firefights—it's about making sure they think twice before starting one."

It made sense, but it also underscored the risks. We were entering hostile territory, flying low and slow, making ourselves vulnerable targets. The Blackhawk's minigun might be an intimidating presence, but it was also a reminder of how precarious the situation really was. If we needed that level of firepower to keep us safe, it wasn't because we were casually flying over friendly skies.

As I sat there digesting the information, I couldn't help but feel a mix of admiration and trepidation. The operation was meticulously planned, and the resources we had—escorts, advanced aircraft, and experienced crews—were impressive. But I was also acutely aware that this wasn't just a technical challenge or an adventure. This was real, and the stakes were as high as they could get. My mind drifted back to my friends in Amsterdam and the UK, who had called me crazy for coming here. Maybe they weren't so far off the mark.

Still, I couldn't deny the thrill of it all. The thought of flying into the jungle, protected by a Blackhawk bristling with weaponry, wasn't just daunting—it was exhilarating. This was the kind of mission I'd been searching for, the kind that made you feel alive. I just hoped I wouldn't have to test the limits of those rules of engagement anytime soon.

By the time the briefing ended, my mind was spinning. I had thought I understood the task ahead—fly planes, spray crops, disrupt the drug trade. But the reality was so much more complex. This wasn't just a fumigation campaign; it was a war within a war, a conflict fueled by layers of corruption, greed, ideology, and despair.

The scale of the issue was staggering. Millions of hectares of coca fields stretched across Colombia, hidden in remote jungles and guarded fiercely by those who relied on them.

Entire communities were tied to the drug trade, either through coercion or necessity. The money involved was beyond comprehension—billions of dollars annually, enough to corrupt politicians, fund militias, and destabilize entire regions.

And then there were the dangers. The guerrillas and cartels weren't just going to let us spray their livelihoods into oblivion. They had the firepower and the resources to fight back, and every flight would be a gamble.

As I stepped out of the briefing room into the humid Tumaco air, my thoughts unexpectedly drifted to my friends back in Amsterdam and the UK. Their voices, full of disbelief and concern, echoed in my mind: *"You're stark raving mad to go to Colombia! You'll get yourself killed!"* At the time, I had laughed it off, chalking up their warnings to exaggeration and a misunderstanding of the situation. But now, after hearing the unvarnished history of violence, the staggering scale of the drug trade, and the brutal realities of the guerrilla and paramilitary war, I felt a chill run down my spine. For the first time, I realized they might have been right. This wasn't just a tough assignment—it was a war zone where every decision could mean the difference between life and death. Their words, once dismissed, now felt like a sober reminder of the precarious line I was walking. I felt a mix of emotions.

As I absorbed the full scale of the briefing, one thought stood out above the rest: I was now working against the largest, most powerful criminal organization in the world. The Cali Cartel alone controlled billions of dollars and held sway over entire regions of Colombia, while the guerrilla groups were armed to the teeth and entrenched in their jungle strongholds. The enormity of it left me both awed and daunted. I had always sought adventure, but this wasn't just a test of skill or courage—this was stepping into the crosshairs of an empire. And yet, amidst these lofty, almost cinematic realizations, a far more childish thought popped into my head: *When does my gun arrive?* The absurdity of it made me smile to myself, but it also underscored how real and personal the danger had suddenly become.

There was fear, of course—fear of the danger, fear of failure. But there was also determination. I hadn't come all this way to turn back now. This was the adventure I'd been craving, a chance to test myself in a way I hadn't since my Navy days.

As I walked back to my quarters, I couldn't help but smile. I had my own helicopter, a real role in the fight against the cartels, and a new adventure unfolding before me. The disappointment of not getting the Bell 212 faded as the excitement of what lay ahead took over. This was why I had come to Colombia—to fly, to fight, and to be part of something that mattered.

This was more than a job. It was a mission, and it was time to get to work.

I spent the next few days getting to know my new surroundings, acclimating to the base, the routine, and the people who would be my colleagues in this dangerous yet fascinating endeavour. It quickly became apparent that to lead this operation effectively, I had to understand not only the mission but also the tools we were using. That meant getting to know the Air Tractor 802, the aircraft at the heart of the fumigation campaign.

It had been ages since I'd flown anything so small. My aviation career had taken me from the cockpit of a sleek executive jet—a Hawker, during my early civilian training days—into progressively larger aircraft: the AVRO RJ100, the Boeing 737, and finally the mighty 767, a machine that weighed in at 187 tonnes when fully loaded. The Air Tractor, by comparison, was a featherweight at just over 7 tonnes fully fueled and under 3 tonnes empty. It felt like piloting a toy in comparison, but I knew that underestimating it would be a mistake. This was a purpose-built workhorse, designed for utility and toughness in ways my jetliner background couldn't quite prepare me for.

When I climbed into the cockpit, the first thing I noticed was how basic it was. This wasn't a sleek, glass cockpit with computerized displays; it was simple, functional, and no-nonsense. The controls were robust and mechanical, with gauges and switches that wouldn't have looked out of place in a tractor, which, to be fair, made sense given its name. But what struck me most was the visibility—the cockpit's bubble canopy offered a nearly uninterrupted view of the ground and sky, critical for low-altitude flying and precision fumigation.

Despite its simplicity, the Air Tractor felt reliable. Its rugged design gave it a reassuring solidity, and when I started up the Pratt & Whitney PT6 turboprop engine, the deep, throaty hum sent a wave of confidence through me. This was a machine that wasn't built for finesse but for getting the job done, no matter the conditions.

The opportunity to fly the Air Tractor came sooner than I had anticipated. I was told about a coca plantation that had been sprayed a few days earlier in the Sanquianga National Park, about 100 kilometers northeast of Tumaco. The purpose of the flight was to familiarize myself with the aircraft while also seeing firsthand the aftermath of a successful fumigation mission.

Taking off from Tumaco, I climbed into the sky, heading out over the Pacific Ocean before turning inland across a vast expanse of dense jungle. The Air Tractor handled beautifully, its stability at low altitude making it feel more like an extension of my own body than a machine. It was surprisingly nimble for its size, responding to every input with a reassuring steadiness.

As I crossed the Patía River and followed its winding path, the enormity of the country became strikingly clear. To the west, the rivers spread like veins into the ocean, while in every other direction, the jungle stretched endlessly to the horizon. It was humbling to realize just how vast and remote these areas were, and how challenging it would be to make even a small dent in the coca production that thrived in this environment. As I followed the Patía River's winding path, marveling at the vast expanse of jungle stretching endlessly to the horizon, a sobering thought crept into my mind: my single-engine status. The Air Tractor 802, as dependable as it was, had only one engine, and if that failed out here, there would be no soft landings. Below me was a relentless sea of trees, their dense canopy a deceptive cover for what was surely a brutal web of branches and trunks that would destroy any aircraft on impact. At this low altitude, there wasn't enough glide range to get anywhere safe. The absence of roads, clearings, or even the faintest hope of a flat patch of ground to attempt an emergency landing was unsettling, to say the least.

My mind wandered to my new ride—the single-engine JetRanger. I had done plenty of autorotations during training, practicing engine-off landings where the helicopter's rotor blades freewheeled to provide enough lift to descend in a controlled glide. In the Bell 206B JetRanger III, the best glide ratio is about 4 to 1, meaning for every foot of altitude lost, you could travel forward about 4 feet. At 5,000 feet, under perfect conditions, that would give you a mere 6 kilometers of distance before gravity forced you into the trees. Out here, flying over 100 kilometers from any realistic landing site, those odds were sobering. The numbers danced in my head like a cruel joke: glide ratios, distances, and the unavoidable reality of this terrain. It was a calculated risk every time you went up.

I pushed the thought aside for now, focusing on the mission and the immediate task of getting the job done. But the awareness lingered, a quiet reminder of the stakes we were playing for every time we climbed into the cockpit.

When I reached the target area, it was easy to spot the coca fields. The edges of the plantation were still a vivid green, but the bulk of the crop had turned a dull grayish-brown, evidence of the herbicide's effectiveness. The stark contrast made the plantation look almost like a scar on the jungle's otherwise unbroken green canopy. The sight was both satisfying and sobering—satisfying to see the success of the operation, but sobering to realize the sheer scale of the task ahead. For every field like this, there were hundreds, perhaps thousands, more.

The plantation appeared abandoned, so I had no concerns about ground fire. This gave me the freedom to push the aircraft a bit, testing its handling in the same conditions my pilots would face. I made several tight turns at the end of short runs, simulating the flight paths required during fumigation. The Air Tractor proved its worth—it was agile, predictable, and surprisingly forgiving, even when I pushed it harder than I probably should have.

The thrill of swooping low over the jungle and climbing sharply to escape imaginary threats was exhilarating. It reminded me of my Navy days, the dogfights over the South

Atlantic, and the raw joy of flying a machine that responded so perfectly to my commands. This wasn't a fighter jet, but it brought back some of that same adrenaline-fueled satisfaction.

On the way back to Tumaco, I took a meandering route, enjoying the rare opportunity to soak in the scenery. The rivers below shimmered in the afternoon light, and the jungle seemed to roll on forever, its mysteries hidden beneath the dense canopy. I thought about the people who lived here, the farmers, guerrillas, and traffickers who all played roles in the tangled web of Colombia's conflict. I wondered how many of them had been affected by the spraying I had just witnessed, and how many more fields like this one would need to be targeted before the drug trade felt even a fraction of the impact we were hoping for.

Returning to base, I felt a renewed sense of purpose. The Air Tractor might not be a fighter jet or a sleek airliner, but it was a vital tool in this fight—a machine designed to tackle the impossible conditions of Colombia's jungles and make a real difference. Flying it gave me a deeper respect for the pilots under my command and a clearer understanding of what I was asking them to do. It was dangerous, yes, but it was also necessary.

As I shut down the engine and climbed out of the cockpit, I couldn't help but grin. This was exactly the kind of adventure I had been looking for—a mission that combined flying with purpose, danger with satisfaction, and challenges with opportunities to prove myself. For the first time in a long while, I felt like I was exactly where I was meant to be.

As the days passed, I found myself exploring Tumaco in my downtime, though I mostly stuck to the area near the airport on Morro Island. The island had a quieter, small-town feel compared to the bustling chaos of Tumaco Island, the adjacent island where the main city sprawled. Tumaco Island was a tangle of narrow streets crammed with one- and two-story buildings packed tightly together right up to the water's edge. It was as if the concept of urban planning had never reached this corner of the world. Coming from Amsterdam—a city that had mastered the art of organizing every inch of its waterfront—I was struck by the haphazard nature of Tumaco. I think I only saw two buildings taller than two stories, which stood out like giants amidst the sea of low rooftops.

While Tumaco Island buzzed with activity, it also came with a reputation for being dangerous, which was enough to keep me rooted near Morro Island. There, life felt a little less chaotic, the streets a little more navigable. Still, Tumaco as a whole had the unmistakable look and feel of a third-world town. It wasn't glamorous, but it had its own rough charm, and I quickly found a spot that became my go-to refuge: a small bar-restaurant-juice bar run by a man who was the spitting image of Lou Diamond Phillips.

The resemblance was uncanny. He was tall, dark, and swarthy, with that ambiguous mix of features that suggested Latin and Native American heritage. His English was impeccable—pure American, in fact. I learned he was Colombian but had spent years in the U.S. before somehow finding his way back to this remote corner of the Pacific coast. He was a warm, welcoming guy, and we hit it off immediately. He became more than just the owner of my favorite hangout; he became my unofficial cultural and language teacher.

He saved me more than once from embarrassing situations, especially after a few of the guys at the base decided to play some harmless tricks on the new guy. One day, they convinced me that "huevón" meant friend—a word I quickly learned was more akin to "dumbass" or "idiot" depending on the tone. Another time, they told me "hijueputa" (a contraction of *hijo de puta*, or "son of a bitch") was an affectionate term. My new friend intervened after I nearly started a fight by cheerfully calling a local that. "Yeah, don't use that unless you're ready to throw some punches," he advised with a laugh. I was grateful to have someone to steer me through the minefield of Colombian slang.

December rolled on, and the atmosphere on the base shifted. Everyone began talking about their plans for the holidays, which were rapidly approaching. I learned that we would all be heading home for a break. For most of the contractors, that meant a flight back to the U.S., while the local staff prepared to spend time with their families here in Colombia. I had no intention of going back to Amsterdam—I wasn't even sure it still felt like home anymore. Instead, I made arrangements to head back to Bogotá, where I booked myself into the familiar comfort of the Hotel La Fontana.

As I packed my things and prepared to leave Tumaco for the holidays, I reflected on everything I had experienced so far. This strange little town on the Pacific coast had been my introduction to a new life, one full of challenges, dangers, and unexpected friendships. I felt a growing sense of belonging—not just to the mission, but to the people I was working alongside. It wasn't always easy, but for the first time in years, I felt alive. Tumaco had marked the beginning of something bigger, and as I boarded the plane to Bogotá, I couldn't help but wonder what lay ahead in the new year.

Chapter 3: Becoming Colombian

The hotel wasn't expensive by European standards, but it was clear to me that staying there long-term wasn't practical. I had decided to plant roots here, at least for the foreseeable future, and the recent signing of a two-year contract—extendable to five—cemented that plan. If the fumigation campaign continued as expected, I would be in Colombia for a good while, and having my own space felt like the next logical step.

With that in mind, I started the search for an apartment. Bogotá's northern neighborhoods, known for their relative safety and amenities, seemed like the best option. After some digging, I found a lovely two-bedroom place in a quiet, well-maintained building not far from the shopping mall next to my hotel. The apartment was bright and tastefully furnished, with a cozy sitting-dining area that felt like it could quickly become home. It wasn't lavish, but it was exactly what I needed—comfortable, convenient, and secure.

Getting the lease, however, was an entirely different matter. The landlady asked for documentation, which I had thanks to my affiliation with the Ministry of Justice, but they also wanted a reference. This posed a bit of a problem. I had only been in Colombia a short time, and no one here knew me well enough to vouch for me. I explained this to the landlady, but she wouldn't budge.

Frustrated, I mentioned the situation to a colleague at the "office," who nodded knowingly. "Don't worry," he said with a grin. "I know a guy." That phrase, I would soon learn, was a cornerstone of Colombian life. Sure enough, for 100,000 pesos—about $56—this mysterious "guy" produced a glowing letter of recommendation two days later. It was typed neatly on Ministry of Defense letterhead, complete with an official stamp and the signature of a senior general. The letter described me as a "highly recommended" individual of impeccable character. It was both flattering and absurd, considering the general in question had never met me.

Still, the document worked like a charm. The landlady's demeanour shifted immediately, and within hours, I had signed the lease. I couldn't help but marvel at the way things got done here. In Europe, the process would have involved weeks of back-and-forth, endless checks, and a mountain of bureaucracy. Here, all it took was a little cash, the right connections, and a willingness to accept that the system operated in shades of grey. It wasn't ideal, but it was effective, and I couldn't argue with the results.

With the keys in hand, I felt an odd sense of pride as I stepped into my new apartment for the first time. I was no longer just passing through—I was a resident of Colombia now. I unpacked my few belongings and arranged the space to my liking, enjoying the feeling of having a home base again. The north of Bogotá had a distinctly cosmopolitan vibe, and the streets around my building were lined with cafes, shops, and small parks. It felt worlds apart from Tumaco's chaotic sprawl, and I quickly realized how much I appreciated the contrast.

The convenience of my location was another perk. The shopping mall near my hotel was within walking distance, and I found myself drawn there regularly, whether for groceries, a quick meal, or just to people-watch. The mall was bustling with activity, a vibrant mix of locals and expats going about their days. It was a stark reminder of the stark economic divide in the country—here, life seemed polished and modern, far removed from the struggles of rural Colombia where I had just been working.

As I settled into Bogotá, I continued to learn the quirks of Colombian culture. The pace of life was slower than I was used to, and people seemed to operate with a certain flexibility that could be both charming and maddening. Appointments were suggestions rather than firm commitments, and bureaucracy often required creative problem-solving. But the warmth of the people more than made up for these frustrations. My neighbours were friendly, and I quickly became a regular at a small café down the street, where the staff greeted me like an old friend after just a few visits.

Language was still a barrier, though I was improving. I had picked up some Spanish during my time in Tumaco and was determined to get better. I enrolled in a local language school and started practicing every chance I got, though my accent and occasional missteps provided endless entertainment for the locals

By the time Christmas rolled around, I was beginning to feel at home. Bogotá during the holidays was a sight to behold. The city lit up with colourful displays, and the streets were filled with the sounds of people getting "Merry", vendors selling festive treats, and families enjoying the season. I wasn't close enough to the city center to see the grandest displays, but even in my neighbourhood, the holiday spirit was palpable.

I spent the holidays quietly, Carolina had gone home to her family in Manizales, so I was on my own. I took the time to reflect on the whirlwind of changes that had brought me here. The year had been transformative—leaving KLM, moving to Colombia, and stepping into a role that combined danger and purpose in equal measure. As I sat in my new apartment, watching the lights of the city flicker in the distance, I couldn't help but feel a sense of gratitude. This wasn't the life I had planned, but it was exactly the adventure I had needed.

The new year was just around the corner, and with it, a renewed sense of determination. The mission hadn't even begun, and I knew the challenges ahead would test me in ways I couldn't yet imagine.

The new year began quietly enough, but it didn't take long for the reality of my new life in Colombia to sink in further. The apartment I had settled into was comfortable and located in a relatively safe part of Bogotá, close to an army base. At first, this proximity gave me a sense of security. Soldiers regularly patrolled the local streets, their presence a reassuring reminder that the state was actively trying to maintain order. However, it wasn't long before I learned that living near a military installation wasn't necessarily a comfort—it also made the area a potential target for guerrilla attacks. What had initially felt like a layer of protection now felt like a double-edged sword.

I began to pay more attention to the local news, tuning into channels like RCN and Caracol, even though my Spanish was barely more than a few words and phrases, but the stories and images were clear enough: reports of shootings, kidnappings, and massacres were a daily occurrence. It was violence on a scale I couldn't have imagined growing up in the UK. The numbers were staggering, and the sheer brutality of the incidents reported left me reeling.

One report that stood out was about a massacre in a village in the north of Colombia, well away from where I was working, a couple of months earlier, around 20 armed men, some hooded and others dressed in military clothing, stormed the village. They rounded up the residents, fired shots into the air, and looted their belongings and killed 3 people. The killers were believed to be members of a paramilitary group.

What shocked me most wasn't just the savagery of the attack but the apparent complicity of the military. A checkpoint and a Mobile Brigade post were reportedly located near the village, and an army tank passed through shortly after the massacre—but no effort was made to intervene or capture the perpetrators. This wasn't an isolated case. It was one of many stories that painted a grim picture of a country where violence was deeply entrenched and often ignored by those in power.

Another recent story from a couple of weeks earlier described how, in the early hours of the morning, a group of armed men believed to be paramilitaries descended on a small village They intimidated the residents, read out a list of names, and then murdered three members of a family, including a 72-year-old man. The reports were relentless—stories of farmers, union leaders, teachers, and even journalists being targeted, tortured, and killed. It seemed no one was safe.

The news often referenced paramilitary groups, and as I dug deeper, I began to understand their role in Colombia's ongoing conflict. These groups had roots stretching back decades, initially formed in the 1980s as "self-defence" organizations by large landowners, business leaders, and even the Colombian army. Their original purpose was to combat guerrilla forces like the FARC and ELN, but they quickly devolved into something far more sinister.

Funded heavily by drug cartels, these paramilitary groups became known for their brutal tactics, targeting not just guerrillas but civilians, opposition leaders, and anyone else they saw as a threat. Despite government attempts to outlaw these groups they continued to operate with impunity. In many cases, the state itself seemed complicit, with military commanders denying the existence of paramilitaries or dismissing them as "farmers defending themselves."

Even the new government under President Ernesto Samper, which had taken office in August 1994, struggled to address the issue. Samper had made promises to dismantle paramilitary groups and improve human rights during his campaign, but progress was slow. While he launched a human rights program in September 1994, stories of massacres and atrocities continued to dominate the headlines.

As I watched these stories unfold, I couldn't help but feel a growing unease. My apartment in Bogotá felt like a haven, but the reality outside its walls was far different. This wasn't just a country struggling with crime—it was a nation at war with itself. The lines between guerrillas, paramilitaries, and the state were blurred, and civilians were often caught in the crossfire.

There were moments when I thought back to my friends in Amsterdam and the UK, the ones who had called me mad for coming here. Watching these news reports, I began to wonder if they had been right. The risks I had taken to be part of this mission felt more real with every passing day. Living near an army base, seeing soldiers patrolling my street, and hearing about massacres in far-off villages were constant reminders that I was no longer in the relative safety of Europe.

But despite the fear, there was also resolve. I had come here for a purpose, and every report of coca fields being destroyed, every step toward curbing the drug trade, felt like a small but meaningful victory. The scale of the violence and the entrenched nature of the conflict often made the mission feel overwhelming, but I clung to the belief that even small actions could make a difference.

As I turned off the news and stared out at the Bogotá skyline, I reminded myself that this was why I had come—to challenge myself, to face danger, and to be part of something larger than myself. Colombia was chaotic, violent, and unpredictable, but it was also a place of resilience, hope, and potential.

While strolling through the bustling streets of Bogotá, I stumbled upon a small bakery tucked into a quiet corner of the city. It was the kind of place you could easily miss if you weren't paying attention. A one-man operation with an attached shop, its modest exterior and faded signage didn't promise much, but something about it caught my eye. Through the window, I could see outdated machinery—mixers, ovens, and proofing cabinets that looked like relics of a bygone era. To anyone else, it might have seemed unimpressive, but to me, it was like stepping back into my childhood.

My father had been a baker and confectioner, and as a boy, I had spent countless hours in bakeries, helping out in whatever way I could. He crafted all kinds of bread, pastries, and elaborate cakes for weddings and birthdays, and I had grown up surrounded by the smell of flour and yeast, the clatter of machinery, and the heat of ovens. The equipment in this little Bogotá bakery was identical to what I remembered from the 1960s and 70s, and the nostalgia hit me like a wave. I couldn't resist stepping inside.

The baker, a slim wiry man in his mid 30s with a warm smile, greeted me from behind the counter. To my surprise, he spoke quite good English, and after a few minutes of conversation, I learned his name was Pedro. I told him about my dad's background, and he seemed delighted, inviting me into the bakery to show me around. As we talked, I let slip what I was doing in Colombia—perhaps a little too freely—and Pedro revealed that he was a former soldier who had served with the Colombian Army in Sinai as part of a UN peacekeeping mission. It was an unexpected connection, and we hit it off immediately. Before I left, I even offered to help out in the bakery when I had free time. Pedro chuckled at the idea but seemed genuinely pleased by the offer.

A couple of days later, Pedro suggested we go out for a drink. He knew a place, he said—a great bar in an upscale part of town that was popular with foreigners. It sounded like a good way to meet people and get a feel for the expat community in Bogotá, so I agreed. That evening, we set off for The Scottish Bar.

The bar was in a safer, upmarket area of the city, and its exterior had a polished, welcoming look. An armed security guard stood at the door—a sight I was still getting used to. When he saw Pedro and me, he gave a nod and opened the door with a friendly smile. Inside, the place felt like a typical British pub, with dark wood furniture, warm lighting, and an assortment of flags draped across the ceiling. I spotted the Union Jack, the Stars and Stripes, and a few others, including the Colombian flag, proudly hanging amidst the collection.

The clientele, as Pedro had promised, were mostly foreigners. The crowd wasn't large, but the atmosphere was lively enough, with clusters of people chatting over drinks. I guessed most of them were Americans, though I quickly learned that a few of them were Brits working for oil companies. The bar had the comforting feel of familiarity, and for a moment, it felt like I was back in Europe.

Feeling confident, I walked up to the bar, scanning the selection of beers for something recognizable. Seeing nothing familiar, I asked the bartender—a burly man with a sharp wit—if they had Heineken. I wasn't expecting the response I got.

"Sorry, we don't sell *American* beers," he said with a deadpan expression.

For a moment, I was so stunned I didn't know what to say. Heineken, *American*? I nearly laughed out loud at the absurdity of it. Either he was the worst barman I'd ever encountered, or this was some bizarre inside joke I wasn't in on. Deciding not to argue, I ordered a Club Colombia on Pedro's recommendation. It turned out to be a decent beer, though the encounter left me shaking my head.

As the evening went on, I began to mingle with the other patrons, hoping to strike up some conversations and maybe make a few connections. But to my surprise, the expats were surprisingly closed off. The Brits, Americans, and a smattering of other nationalities stuck to their own tight-knit groups, giving off an air of polite but firm disinterest in engaging with newcomers. Even my fellow Brits seemed uninterested in striking up a conversation, which was disappointing.

The few exchanges I did manage to have were brief and frustrating. When I asked about life in Colombia, most of them shrugged and said they didn't watch local news or follow what was happening. Some admitted they didn't even speak Spanish, despite having lived here for years. It was baffling. Here they were, living in one of the most dynamic and troubled countries in the world, and they seemed completely insulated from its reality.

The stark contrast between their ignorance and my own growing awareness of Colombia's complexities left me feeling disconnected. I had expected camaraderie and shared experiences, but instead, I found cliques and apathy. It became abundantly clear that if I wanted to build meaningful connections, I would need to look beyond the insular expat community and focus on forging friendships with Colombians. From my very first interactions, I found the Colombian people to be remarkably warm and welcoming. Whether it was because I was a foreigner—a novelty in some circles—or simply because of their natural disposition, I couldn't help but notice how genuine, open, and approachable they were.

Unlike the reserved and somewhat guarded nature of many of the expats I had encountered, Colombians seemed to have a remarkable ability to make you feel at ease. Conversations flowed naturally, without pretence or hesitation, and their smiles felt sincere rather than obligatory. There was a refreshing authenticity to their friendliness, a kind of unspoken invitation to step into their world and share in their culture. It wasn't just politeness—it was a cultural hallmark, deeply ingrained and effortlessly extended.

What struck me most was their willingness to connect on a human level. They didn't seem to view relationships as transactional or superficial; instead, they approached interactions with genuine curiosity and a desire to understand you. Whether it was someone I met at a café, a neighbour, or even a stranger on the street, I often felt like I was being welcomed into a conversation, not just tolerated as a foreigner passing through.

This openness created a sense of community that was hard to ignore. It was clear to me that if I was going to thrive in Colombia, these relationships would be the foundation. The Colombians I met didn't just treat me as a guest in their country—they made me feel like I belonged.

The time flew by, and before I knew it, I was back at work, staring down the mammoth task ahead. My new office was functional, if not exactly inspiring—filled with filing cabinets, maps, and stacks of reports. At the back was a small room that doubled as my bedroom, still crammed with old records and paperwork. It was far from luxurious, but I didn't mind. I had come here to work, not relax.

It wasn't long before I was handed what I'd been waiting for: my very own ride. When I first laid eyes on the Bell 206L-3 LongRanger III, I couldn't help but grin. It was pristine, painted white with sleek blue accents running along the sides, and emblazoned with its registration number, PNC 0921, in bold lettering. While I had secretly hoped for a military green colour scheme to match the gravity of our mission, I couldn't deny that this helicopter was a beauty.

For a pilot, there's nothing quite like the feeling of being handed a new aircraft. It's a moment of pure excitement, filled with the promise of new adventures and challenges. This wasn't just any helicopter—it was mine to command, my workhorse for the missions ahead. I felt like a kid at Christmas unwrapping a shiny new bike, eager to take it for a spin.

Before diving into the heavy operational work, I decided to spend some time getting to know the LongRanger III. Flying it would be second nature soon enough, but every aircraft has its quirks, and I wanted to familiarize myself with its handling and capabilities. I planned a few "recon missions" that were less about gathering intel and more about giving me a chance to stretch the bird's wings, so to speak.

The Bell helicopter felt entirely different from the jets and larger helicopters I'd flown in the past. Climbing into the cockpit, I was struck by its simplicity. The controls were straightforward, the instrumentation largely analog, and the layout intuitive. What stood out immediately was the visibility. The bubble canopy and wide windows gave me an almost panoramic view, which was a godsend for flying in Colombia's challenging terrain.

Take-off was smooth, the Allison 250-C20B turboshaft engine humming confidently as I pulled gently on the collective. The helicopter felt light and responsive, but not in a way that made it twitchy or unpredictable. It climbed steadily, the two-blade rotor providing just the right balance of lift and control. Within minutes, I was cruising comfortably, marvelling at the ease with which the LongRanger handled.

Once I was airborne, I put the LongRanger through its paces. Banking turns were smooth and predictable, and I practiced rapid climbs and descents to get a feel for how it would perform in real-world scenarios. The helicopter's stability was impressive, even at low speeds and altitudes. I tested hovering manoeuvres over imaginary targets, fine-tuning my control inputs to keep the aircraft steady—a skill that would be essential for some of the precision flying we'd need to do on missions.

Flying low and slow over the dense Colombian jungle was both exhilarating and humbling. The terrain below was a vast sea of green, broken only by the occasional river or clearing. It was beautiful, yes, but also unforgiving. I couldn't help but think about emergency scenarios—if the engine failed, there were no good options for landing. The LongRanger's autorotation capabilities were solid, with a glide ratio of 4 to 1, but that would only buy me about six kilometers at 5,000 feet. Out here, six kilometers could still mean nothing but jungle and trees. It was a sobering thought, one I tucked away as I focused on the task at hand.

Despite the risks, there's a certain joy that comes with flying a helicopter like the LongRanger. It's not about speed or altitude—it's about precision, control, and the satisfaction of mastering a machine that feels like an extension of yourself. The LongRanger wasn't flashy, but it was reliable, versatile, and, above all, fun to fly. Every manoeuvre, every turn and hover, reinforced my confidence in the aircraft.

As I flew over the sprawling Colombian landscape, I felt a surge of gratitude. This was what I had signed up for—not just the adventure, but the opportunity to work with a machine like this, in a place as challenging and rewarding as Colombia. The LongRanger wasn't just a tool; it was a partner in this mission, and I knew I could rely on it.

On one of my first flights, I followed the course of a river deep into the jungle, taking in the enormity of the terrain. Below me, the dense canopy seemed to stretch endlessly, broken occasionally by flashes of water or tiny villages tucked into the greenery. It was a reminder of the scale of the task ahead. This wasn't a job for the faint of heart; it was a test of endurance, focus, and resolve.

I also made a point to fly over some of the areas we'd be targeting for fumigation, getting a firsthand look at the terrain and the challenges it presented. The jungle was alive with potential threats—from guerrillas to natural obstacles—and flying low meant constantly staying alert. The LongRanger's excellent visibility and responsive handling made it the perfect aircraft for the job, but I knew I'd need to keep my wits about me on every mission.

Back on the ground, I climbed out of the cockpit and took a moment to admire the LongRanger, its blades still spinning down as the engine whined softly to a stop. It had been a good flight, the first of many, and I felt a renewed sense of purpose as I headed back to my office.

There was a long road ahead—dozens of missions to plan, reports to sift through, and countless obstacles to overcome. But for the first time since arriving in Colombia, I felt truly ready. With the LongRanger by my side, I knew I had the right tool for the job. It wasn't going to be easy, but then again, I hadn't come here looking for easy.

I was eager to get the first operations underway. The reports and satellite imagery piled high on my desk painted a daunting picture: countless probable coca plantations scattered across the vast Colombian jungle. Even those within the range of our aircraft were overwhelming in number. It didn't take long to realize that with our current resources, there was no way we could cover everything. We needed more bases to operate from—there was no avoiding that—but for now, we had to make do with what we had.

The first step was reconnaissance. Before launching full fumigation missions, I needed to confirm the plantations, map their extents, and determine whether they were active or defended. This meant flying over the targets, getting eyes on the ground, and assessing the risks. The intel was solid, but nothing replaced firsthand observation.

Before embarking on my first operational flight, I took no chances with my safety. Drawing inspiration from the modifications the Air Tractor pilots had made, I rigged up my own version of a protective cocoon in the LongRanger. Using thirteen bulletproof vests—two of which were placed beneath the seat cushion and almost an entire roll of duct tape—I created a makeshift armour setup around my seat. It wasn't perfect, but it was better than nothing. The added weight made the seat feel slightly cramped, but that was a small price to pay for the peace of mind it offered.

However, one glaring vulnerability remained: the plexiglass window at my feet. While it provided exceptional visibility of the terrain below, it offered absolutely zero protection against incoming fire. It was a sobering reminder that no amount of preparation could completely shield me from the dangers of flying over hostile territory. Still, I felt a little more confident knowing I had done what I could to improve my odds.

Safety was paramount, and that meant flying with cover. For this mission, my "guardian angel" was an army Black Hawk helicopter armed with a minigun and manned by a crew who clearly knew the jungle and its dangers. Before we got airborne, I gathered the Black Hawk crew—pilots, gunners, and a young corporal named Rodrigues—for a briefing. Rodrigues, a 19-year-old gunner with a wide grin that made him look more like a schoolboy than a soldier, manned the M134 minigun. The contrast between his diminutive 4'10" frame and the oversized helmet perched on his head was almost comical, but the way he cradled the weapon with an easy familiarity left no doubt he knew how to use it.

We worked out the details: flight formations, signals, and the rules of engagement. The ROE was simple but strict—no firing unless fired upon—but we needed a clear system to communicate in the air. A thumbs-up from me meant Rodrigues was cleared to return fire, and I'd point to indicate the direction of the threat. Rodrigues grinned and gave an enthusiastic thumbs-up as if eager to test the plan in action.

With the plan in place, I climbed into my LongRanger and fired up the engine. The helicopter leapt off the hardstanding like a scared cat, its light frame and powerful engine perfectly matched for quick takeoffs. The Black Hawk rose behind me, its imposing bulk and the steady thrum of its rotors a reassuring presence as we headed out over the endless green expanse of jungle.

The scale of the terrain hit me again as I flew over mile after mile of uninterrupted forest. The satellite images and maps hadn't done it justice. From the air, the jungle seemed alive, its dense canopy rolling like waves on a green ocean. Rivers snaked their way through the foliage, their muddy waters glinting in the sunlight, but the rest of the landscape was an unbroken sea of trees.

The first plantation appeared almost exactly where the intel had predicted. From above, the coca fields were easy to distinguish—their lighter green colour stood out starkly against the darker hues of the surrounding jungle. I circled the area at a safe altitude, carefully marking the field's boundaries on the map in my lap with a chinagraph pen. It felt oddly familiar, like déjà vu. Memories of the Falklands came rushing back, of flying reconnaissance missions over Falkland Sound, searching for Argentinian gun emplacements and fortifications ahead of the landings at San Carlos Bay. Back then, it had been rocky, treeless terrain; now it was dense jungle. Different enemies, different landscapes, but the tactics were eerily similar.

I flew in tightening circles, carefully watching for any movement on the ground. My Black Hawk escort kept a respectful distance, its crew scanning the jungle for any signs of trouble. The jungle's thick canopy offered excellent camouflage, making it nearly impossible to spot anything from the air unless someone revealed themselves. I didn't expect the plantation guards to welcome us, but to my surprise, most seemed content to stay hidden. Even when I descended to a few hundred feet above the fields, no one fired.

Despite the lack of immediate hostility, I didn't linger. Flying low over potential enemy territory meant making myself a target, and I wasn't about to make it easy for anyone aiming a rifle at the sky. I maintained a steady speed, presenting a harder target to hit, and kept my altitude just high enough to stay out of easy reach.

Occasionally, I caught glimpses of small shacks nestled in the jungle—rudimentary buildings likely used for processing coca leaves into paste or cocaine. These operations weren't sophisticated, but they were efficient, and their locations were telling. They confirmed the plantations were active, and the size of some of the fields suggested significant production. I marked everything on my map, careful to note any paths or clearings that might indicate access routes or supply lines.

The eerie silence of the jungle was unnerving. The plantation guards rarely showed themselves, and I wondered if they were biding their time, unwilling to risk revealing their positions. The dense foliage was their ally, offering natural cover that made them almost invisible from the air. In the Falklands, the open terrain had made it easier to spot enemy positions, but here, the jungle seemed to swallow everything.

Rodrigues, in the Black Hawk, looked ready for action every time we flew over a plantation. He leaned into the minigun, scanning the ground with an intensity that belied his cheerful demeanour. But there was no need for action, at least not yet. For now, the guards seemed content to let us fly unchallenged, a decision I was happy to accept.

To break the cycle of work and the creeping anxiety that came with it, I decided I needed something to occupy my mind during downtime—something productive, something that would keep me grounded and out of trouble. I had already seen too many men turn to the bottle after hours, sitting in dimly lit bars night after night, losing themselves to whiskey and cheap beer. It was too easy to go that route, and I knew if I wasn't careful, I'd end up the same way. So, I picked up a hobby that felt like a natural extension of my love for aviation: building model airplanes.

It started small. I crafted a simple Huey out of balsa wood, mimicking the iconic shape of its fuselage, its two-bladed rotor, and its sturdy frame. I didn't do it to make money—at least, not at first. I did it because I needed to take my mind off the job: the constant danger, the weight of responsibility, and the nagging fear that I might screw it all up. Imposter syndrome had plagued me since day one. The flying part was easy—that I could handle with my eyes closed. But everything else? The management, the decisions that could mean life or death, the enormous expectations—they loomed over me like dark clouds. What the hell was I even doing here? Why had they hired me, a civilian pilot, to oversee such a massive, high-stakes operation? Shouldn't a Colombian Air Force colonel or some experienced government official be running this? Part of me always wondered if I had been hired to play the role of a convenient scapegoat in case things went catastrophically wrong. It was a thought I couldn't shake, no matter how hard I tried.

But the models helped. With every plane I built, I felt a small piece of that burden lift. It was therapeutic, working with my hands, carving the fine edges of wings and tails, cutting the smallest details into balsa wood, and watching as the lifeless pieces came together to form something recognizable—something real.

The planes turned out to be a hit, not just for me but for everyone who saw them. My first Huey was admired by a few of the guys on base, and before I knew it, I had orders rolling in. Someone wanted a Black Hawk, and then another guy requested a Bell 212 Twin Huey painted in the Colombian police colors—white with green flashes. I painstakingly copied every detail, using maintenance logs from our actual aircraft as my reference. If I didn't have something to go on, I turned to my trusty Revell catalogue, the same one used by plastic model kit enthusiasts around the world.

My workspace soon became cluttered with half-finished models and scraps of material. For the windows and canopies, I'd heat and shape clear plastic bottles over wooden molds until they looked like real glass. It was a fiddly job, but I enjoyed the challenge. I'd source the balsa wood from a hobby store in Bogotá whenever I had the chance to visit. The SR-71 Blackbird was always a crowd-pleaser, with its sleek black design and its mystique as the fastest plane ever built. Fighters like the F-16 and the Mirage—jets flown by the Colombian Air Force—were also in high demand. I even crafted an F-15 once, its wings and missiles meticulously detailed, right down to the tiny fins.

I didn't get rich off my little business. The smaller models fetched about five dollars apiece, while the larger ones brought in more. At most, I made a couple of hundred dollars a month—pocket money, really. But that wasn't the point. For me, it was about the hours I spent hunched over my makeshift workbench, lost in the hum of sandpaper against wood, the smell of paint drying, and the satisfaction of bringing a plane to life. It was about escaping, even if just for a while, from the stress and fear that came with the job.

I liked to imagine the finished models adorning bookshelves, desks, and windowsills across Colombia—tiny testaments to aviation, precision, and the hands that made them. It was a small piece of me, scattered out there in the world.

Looking back, it probably saved me. Building those planes kept me grounded when everything else felt like it might come crashing down. And, if I'm honest, it was cheaper—and far more effective—than paying for therapy.

As the weeks went on, I gained more confidence in the air, navigating the labyrinthine jungle terrain and getting a sense of how these missions played out. The early operations had gone smoothly, and I was beginning to feel a rhythm to the work. But confidence can sometimes tip into overconfidence, and I learned that lesson the hard way on one mission that still haunts me.

The plan was simple: recon a large plantation located in a T-shaped valley deep in the jungle. The intel suggested the area was lightly defended, if at all, and my previous flights had been uneventful. I'd grown accustomed to the eerie silence of the jungle and the lack of resistance from those guarding the coca fields. It was almost easy to forget the stakes, to let the danger fade into the background.

That day, I flew far lower than I should have, descending into the valley to get a closer look at the plantation's extent. The narrowness of the terrain made me feel boxed in, but I didn't think much of it at the time. I focused on the task at hand, mapping out the field's boundaries and noting the signs of activity below. All was quiet—until it wasn't.

Out of the corner of my eye, I caught movement. Instinct kicked in, and I snapped my head around. There, on the valley wall, a man in camouflaged clothing was aiming a rifle at me. My brain registered the details with unnerving clarity: an AK-47, the flash of the muzzle, and the unmistakable jerking motion of someone firing on full auto. He was perched about 100 feet below me and roughly 300 feet to my side—close enough for me to see his face twisted in concentration as he squeezed the trigger.

Almost instantly, I heard the impacts. The sharp metallic *tink-tink-tink* of rounds hitting the aircraft sent adrenaline surging through my veins. My heart raced as I realized I was dangerously exposed, flying low and slow in a narrow valley with no immediate way out. *Aahh FUCK!. This is it,* I thought. *Action—or the end of my days in the Colombian jungle.*

I spun my head toward the Black Hawk, hovering slightly higher and to the side. Its position meant the gunner, Cabo Rodrigues, couldn't see the shooter. My mind raced. If I didn't act fast, the next burst of gunfire might hit something critical—an engine, a rotor, or worse, me. I glared at Rodrigues and gave him the prearranged signal: a thumbs-up, followed by a frantic point toward the shooter now sliding past my side. Rodrigues' face lit up with a grin, and he nodded enthusiastically, giving me a thumbs-up in return. The guy looked like he'd just won the lottery.

I yanked and the collective and the LongRanger shot higher into the air, gaining height and banked sharply to the side, creating an opening for Rodrigues to take the shot. The Black Hawk's minigun roared to life, its ferocious *brrrrrrrrrr* echoing through the valley. The sound was deafening, a deep, mechanical growl that seemed to rip the air apart. I glanced back just in time to see the guerrillero disintegrate in a red mist. One moment, he was there, firing his AK-47, and the next, he was gone, obliterated by the sheer intensity of the minigun's 6,000 rounds per minute.

For a moment, I was frozen in shock. The whole sequence had unfolded in seconds, but the image burned itself into my memory. It was the first time I had seen someone die in this war—truly *seen* it—and the brutality of it hit me like a punch to the gut. This wasn't like the abstract detachment of firing missiles at distant targets in my Navy days. This was up close, visceral, and raw.

The man who had tried to kill me was likely just another young Colombian, caught up in the chaos of the guerrilla movement, probably fed propaganda about fighting for justice or freedom. I couldn't shake the thought that he was someone's son, maybe someone's father. Yet, in that moment, he was my enemy, and his death had been necessary to ensure my survival. I wasn't sure how I felt—relieved, horrified, and oddly guilty all at once.

Rodrigues, on the other hand, was ecstatic. The young corporal practically beamed with pride, giving me a thumbs-up so enthusiastic it was almost cartoonish. "¡Blanco perfecto!" he shouted over the radio, clearly thrilled at having done his job so effectively. There wasn't a hint of remorse in his voice, and I realized that was exactly the kind of person I needed on missions like this—someone who could act without hesitation or second-guessing when things got dangerous.

Over the course of the week, we confirmed six plantations. Each one matched the intel almost perfectly, their locations and extents aligning with the reports and imagery I'd studied. By the time we returned to base, my map was a maze of markings—boundaries, notes, and potential access points carefully sketched out during the flights. The missions had been a success, but they also highlighted the enormity of the task ahead. These six plantations were just a drop in the ocean. There were hundreds, maybe thousands more, scattered across the country's vast jungle.

Once we landed back at the base, I climbed out of the cockpit, still riding the aftershocks of adrenaline from the encounter. Before heading into the operations room to debrief, I decided to check the LongRanger's airframe. It was a routine I'd developed early on—examining the aircraft after each flight for any signs of wear, tear, or, in this case, battle damage.

As I circled the helicopter, I froze when I saw them: three distinct bullet impacts on the underside of the fuselage. My stomach tightened as I crouched down to examine them more closely. One round had hit my seat directly. The others had punched into the cabin just behind me, embedding themselves in the thin metal frame. My throat went dry as I realized how close I had come to being hit.

The bullet that struck the seat had been stopped by my makeshift armor—the layers of bulletproof vests I had rigged up before the mission. Without them, the round would have gone clean through the thin aluminium seat and into my leg. The other two bullets were just as sobering. Had their angles been slightly different, they could have hit me in the back or torso.

I ran my hand over the dented seat armour, feeling a mix of gratitude and unease. The hasty modifications I had made to the seat had earned their keep today. Without them, I might not have been standing there, staring at the damage.

The realization hit me hard. The man who had fired on me wasn't just a faceless threat; he had been inches away from ending my life. I replayed the scene in my head—the flash of movement, the crack of gunfire, the sudden impacts. That guerrillero hadn't been a random bystander taking potshots at the sky. He had seen me, taken aim, and tried his best to kill me. It wasn't luck or chance; it was deliberate, and he had come terrifyingly close to succeeding.

I stared at the bullet marks for a long moment, feeling a strange mix of emotions. Relief, certainly—I was alive, and the helicopter had held together. But also a renewed respect for the danger I was flying into with every mission. The plantation guards might not have military training, but they didn't need it. An AK-47 fired at close range didn't require precision to be deadly.

The scars on the LongRanger were a stark reminder of the stakes. This wasn't a game. Every flight, every pass over a plantation, was a gamble, and the house didn't always play fair. I ran my hand over the airframe one last time, as if trying to imprint the lesson in my mind. The guerrillero was gone, his life snuffed out in an instant by Rodrigues' minigun, but the danger he represented hadn't disappeared. There would be others, equally determined, equally willing to do whatever it took to protect their livelihoods.

This wasn't just about taking risks anymore; it was about understanding those risks and respecting them. The jungle didn't forgive arrogance or complacency, and neither did the men with rifles hidden among the trees.

As I stepped away from the helicopter, I made a mental note to reinforce the armor setup on the seat. It had worked this time, but I wasn't willing to rely on makeshift fixes forever. If I was going to keep flying into hostile territory, I needed to be as prepared as possible. One thing was clear: this close call wasn't going to stop me. If anything, it had sharpened my resolve. I had come too far, invested too much, to back down now.

The following days marked the beginning of the operational phase of our mission. The Air Tractor pilots, armed with precise maps and intel we had gathered, began flying out to spray the plantations we had located. The results came quickly, but so did the realization of the sheer scale of the challenge we were up against.

The operational phase of our mission kicked into high gear as the Air Tractor pilots began their fumigation runs. Armed with the precise maps and intel we had painstakingly gathered, they flew out daily to hit the plantations we had identified. Reports of success came back swiftly, but alongside them came a daunting realization: the scale of the coca cultivation was overwhelming. For every hectare we sprayed, it felt like another two appeared elsewhere, a never-ending battle against an enemy that seemed to have infinite resources.

While I had a commanding role in the operations, there was one restriction that grated on me—I wasn't allowed to fly on actual fumigation missions. The U.S. government and Colombian authorities were adamant that such missions be left to contracted pilots and Colombian nationals, citing concerns about liability, security, and optics. It was frustrating.

I had the skills, the experience, and the eagerness to contribute directly, but I had to respect the rules.

Still, I found a way to stay involved. I managed to tag along on a couple of missions as a passenger in one of the Blackhawks. These observation flights weren't just an opportunity to oversee the operations but also a chance to experience the action firsthand and identify any areas where we could improve.

The first observation flight was exhilarating, even though I wasn't flying. I begged the crew to let me sit in the copilot seat, but they turned me down. "Sorry, Capitán," the pilot said with a grin. "You'll have to enjoy the view from the back." Disappointed but undeterred, I climbed into the cabin, strapping myself into the jump seat by the open door. The contrast between the dark, Spartan interior of the Blackhawk and the blazing Colombian sunlight outside was striking.

As we lifted off, the roar of the twin engines filled the cabin, vibrating through every part of the aircraft. The dense jungle below unfolded in endless shades of green, interspersed with the occasional glint of a river or the dull brown of a remote settlement. Peering out from the open door, the sheer beauty of the country was overwhelming. But I wasn't here to admire the scenery—I was here to see how the missions were executed.

The pilots, were a sight to behold. Watching them operate gave me a newfound appreciation for their skill and professionalism. They flew with a steady confidence that only came from years of experience, weaving through valleys and over jungle canopies with practiced ease. Their timing was impeccable. Every spray run was calculated to maximize coverage, ensuring that no part of the plantation was missed. This precision wasn't just about efficiency; it was about survival. The more thorough they were on the first pass, the less likely it was they'd have to return—an unnecessary risk in hostile territory.

I noted how they coordinated seamlessly with the Air Tractors. The Blackhawk would fly around at a safe altitude, ready to intervene if necessary, while the Tractors swooped low over the fields, releasing their payloads with surgical accuracy. The speed and efficiency were impressive. The cartels might have had the numbers on their side, but they couldn't protect every plantation all the time. Our operations relied on surprise, hitting unprotected fields before they had a chance to react. The intel had been spot on—these fields were undefended, and the mission went off without a hitch.

From my vantage point, I could see the scale of what we were up against. The plantations were like islands of green among the darker, denser jungle, their neatly arranged rows standing out like scars on the landscape. These were just a handful of the thousands of such sites across the country. The enormity of the task ahead was humbling, but it also underscored the importance of getting things right the first time.

As we circled the area, I couldn't help but think of the people on the ground. Somewhere beneath us, farmers and guards might be watching, powerless to do anything as their crops were destroyed. I knew some of them were desperate individuals trying to survive, but I also knew that others were armed and willing to fight back. The Blackhawk's door gunner, a young, wiry Colombian with a perpetual grin, sat ready behind the mounted minigun, his eyes scanning the jungle below. Thankfully, this time there was no need for him to fire.

When we landed back at base, I stepped off the Blackhawk with a mix of exhilaration and respect. Seeing the mission unfold from the air had been invaluable. I was relieved to confirm that the teams were performing at peak efficiency, their precision ensuring that we hit the plantations hard without unnecessary risks. The coordination between the Blackhawks and the Air Tractors was flawless, and the pilots' skill left little to critique.

Still, there was an undeniable thrill in being up there, even as an observer. It wasn't the same as flying the mission myself, but it gave me a deeper understanding of the operation and the challenges we faced. It also reminded me of just how dangerous this work was. Every flight was a calculated risk, and while this one had gone smoothly, there was no guarantee that the next would.

Armed with the insights from these observation flights, I returned to the planning phase with renewed focus. There was so much to do—refining flight paths, coordinating schedules, and ensuring that every mission counted. The enormity of the task was daunting, especially with the limited resources I had available but I was determined to make every hectare sprayed a step closer to our goal. After all, the jungle was vast, but we were making progress, one plantation at a time.

Safety and efficiency became my top priorities. The pilots were flying directly into danger zones, and while they were brave, bravery alone wouldn't protect them. I organized training sessions to improve their flying techniques, focusing on tight turns and minimizing the time spent over target areas—because the moment they crossed into the plantation, they became the targets too.

We practiced emergency procedures relentlessly. Engine failures, evasive manoeuvres, dealing with small arms fire—all of it was drilled until it became second nature. The goal was to reduce exposure and keep everyone alive. Some of the pilots, civilians contracted through DynCorp, didn't have combat experience, and the training proved crucial for building their confidence and resilience.

Back in the office, I worked with the team to refine the maps of the plantations. Each one was carefully annotated with details from the recon flights—plantation boundaries, possible processing sites, suspected defensive positions, and routes in and out. We concentrated on fields within operational range of our aircraft, knowing it was impossible to cover everything.

The Bell LongRanger gave us a decent operational radius, with its range of about 750 kilometers, but it wasn't enough to accompany the Air Tractors on their longer missions. The Tractors had a range of over 1,300 kilometers and flew at cruised at 225 mph—much faster than the LongRanger's top speed of 150 mph. When the Tractors had a BlackHawk escort, they had to slow down to match its cruise speed of 185 mph, but even then, the helicopter's range of 600 kilometers limited how far they could go.

This mismatch in speed and range created operational constraints, forcing us to prioritize targets within reach. It was frustrating, knowing that there were plantations just beyond our range that we couldn't touch. Still, we pressed on, tackling what we could with the resources we had.

By the end of the year, the results were both impressive and disheartening. We had successfully fumigated approximately 9,000 hectares of coca fields, a significant achievement given our limited resources. On paper, it sounded like a lot—until you compared it to the staggering scale of the problem.

A hectare of coca plants, under ideal conditions, could produce up to 2,500 kilograms of coca leaves per year. With efficient processing, that translated to about 1 to 1.3 kilograms of refined cocaine hydrochloride per hectare per year. By fumigating 9,000 hectares, we had effectively prevented the production of about 6,000 kilograms, or 6 metric tons, of cocaine.

That sounded like a win until you looked at the bigger picture. In 1995, Colombia was producing an estimated 350 to 450 metric tons of cocaine annually. Our efforts had barely dented the supply chain, and it was clear that the cartels had the resources to replant and relocate faster than we could eradicate. The scale of the industry was staggering, and the numbers were sobering.

Colombia in 1995 was the undisputed leader in cocaine production, accounting for 50-70% of the world's supply. With an estimated 50,000 to 75,000 hectares of coca under cultivation, the country's coca fields produced millions of metric tons of fresh leaves annually. These leaves were processed into cocaine hydrochloride, the market-ready form of the drug that fueled the global trade.

The Medellín and Cali cartels, though weakened by the deaths of Pablo Escobar and the arrest of the Rodríguez Orejuela brothers, had left behind a well-oiled machine. Smaller, more decentralized groups had stepped in to fill the void, ensuring that the cocaine supply remained steady. The cartels' reach extended far beyond Colombia's borders, feeding demand in the U.S., Europe, and beyond.

Fighting this industry felt like trying to hold back the tide with a bucket. The cartels weren't just rich; they were resourceful, adaptable, and ruthless. The sheer volume of coca fields and the logistical challenges of reaching them made it clear that our mission, while noble, was only scratching the surface.

Despite the odds, we kept pushing. The numbers might have been daunting, but every field we destroyed was a victory, no matter how small. The pilots, both those in the Air Tractors and the Black Hawks, performed their jobs with professionalism and courage, knowing full well the risks they faced on every mission.

One of the most significant challenges was balancing the logistics of the operation with the realities of combat. The jungle was vast, unforgiving, and full of surprises. The plantations we targeted were often defended by armed guards, and while many chose to hide rather than engage, the threat of gunfire was always present. The Black Hawks, with their mounted miniguns, provided critical cover, but the danger never disappeared.

For me, the year was a crash course in navigating this complex and volatile environment. From managing pilots to coordinating with local authorities, every day brought new challenges. I learned to trust my instincts, rely on my team, and adapt to the unexpected. Most of all, I learned to accept that progress would be slow, incremental, and often frustrating.

As 1995 drew to a close, I reflected on what we had accomplished. It wasn't enough—not by a long shot—but it was a start. Every plantation we destroyed disrupted the cartels' operations, even if only temporarily. Every hectare we fumigated meant fewer resources for the traffickers and fewer drugs on the streets.

The numbers told one story, but the people told another. The pilots, mechanics, and ground crews who worked tirelessly to keep the mission going were proof that this fight was worth it. The farmers who had been coerced into growing coca now had a chance to reclaim their land. And for me, this was more than just a job—it was a purpose, a chance to make a difference in a way that felt tangible, even if the results weren't immediate.

The year had been gruelling, but it had also been transformative. I wasn't the same person who had landed in Bogotá months ago, full of nervous energy and uncertainty. I had found my place in this fight, and I was ready to keep going, no matter how long it took. The road ahead was long, but I was committed to seeing it through.

Chapter 4: The Cali Cartel

And speaking of the Cali Cartel, it wasn't just the faceless "enemy." They were a force—an intricate, well-oiled machine that had been built on wealth, fear, and an almost business-like efficiency. They weren't like Escobar's Medellín Cartel, ruling with terror and public displays of violence; Cali was quieter, more methodical. Yet, in 1995, even this empire began to crumble under the weight of relentless pressure from Colombia and the United States.

The takedown of the Cali Cartel was nothing short of a massive, coordinated effort, involving everyone from Colombian law enforcement to the DEA and other U.S. agencies. Watching this unfold was fascinating—and a little unsettling. It felt like witnessing history in the making, knowing that the ripple effects would be felt far beyond Colombia's borders.

President Ernesto Samper's administration had no choice but to act, despite allegations that the cartel had bankrolled his campaign. U.S. diplomatic pressure was unrelenting, with threats of cutting financial aid and sanctions hanging over Colombia's head if they didn't take decisive action. This wasn't just a battle of bullets and raids; it was a war fought in intelligence rooms, courtrooms, and the corridors of political power.

Specialized Colombian task forces, bolstered by U.S. training and equipment, became the spearhead of this operation. The elite anti-narcotics units, supported by advanced surveillance techniques and an extensive network of informants, began closing in on the cartel's top leadership.

The first major blow came in June 1995, with the arrest of Gilberto Rodríguez Orejuela, known as "El Ajedrecista" (The Chess Player) for his brilliant strategic mind. It was fitting that his capture was the result of meticulous planning—a raid on his luxury hideout in Cali that came after months of wiretaps and surveillance.

Two months later, in August 1995, his brother and co-leader, Miguel Rodríguez Orejuela, was apprehended in a dramatic operation. Miguel's arrest shattered the organizational backbone of the cartel. Shortly after, their associate and international distributor, Hélmer Herrera, or "Pacho," surrendered to authorities, further dismantling the cartel's leadership.

For years, the Cali Cartel had seemed untouchable. Their business-like approach—bribing officials instead of blowing them up, operating quietly rather than broadcasting their power—had kept them under the radar. But by 1995, even the most sophisticated strategies couldn't protect them from the relentless pursuit of justice.

One of the cartel's most remarkable aspects was its financial sophistication. Unlike the Medellín Cartel, whose operations were often crudely violent and conspicuous, the Cali Cartel ran a global business empire that included legitimate companies used for money laundering. From their headquarters in Cali, they controlled an intricate network that funneled billions of dollars into everything from real estate to retail chains.

As raids intensified, authorities seized properties, businesses, and bank accounts linked to the cartel. Perhaps most valuable were the financial records uncovered during these operations. These documents provided a roadmap to the cartel's extensive network of bribes, assets, and hidden operations, helping dismantle their empire piece by piece.

By the end of 1995, the Cali Cartel had been effectively dismantled. The arrests of its leaders and the seizure of its assets marked the end of an era. But as I studied the reports coming in, one thing became clear: this was far from the end of Colombia's drug trade.

The fall of the Cali Cartel left a power vacuum that was quickly filled by smaller, more decentralized groups, such as the Norte del Valle Cartel and paramilitary organizations. These groups lacked the sophistication of the Cali Cartel but were no less dangerous. The drug trade adapted, shifting to a more covert model, with smaller operations spread across the country.

In many ways, the decline of the Cali Cartel didn't feel like a victory. It was a necessary step, yes, but it also signaled the beginning of a new phase of the fight. The cartels were learning, evolving, becoming harder to track and dismantle. While the headlines celebrated the downfall of a major player, those of us on the ground knew the battle was far from over.

Reflecting on the year, I couldn't help but admire the scale and determination of the campaign against the Cali Cartel. It was a rare moment of unity between Colombia and the U.S., proof that cooperation could yield results. Yet, it also underscored the complexity of the drug war. Even with their leaders behind bars, the cartels remained a pervasive force. The coca fields we sprayed, the labs we destroyed, the networks we disrupted—they were all pieces of a puzzle that seemed impossible to complete.

And while I was focused on eradicating the source—the coca plantations—it was impossible to ignore the broader implications. The drug trade wasn't just about production; it was about poverty, corruption, and the insatiable global demand for cocaine. For every field we fumigated, another seemed to spring up. For every cartel we brought down, a dozen smaller ones filled the void.

The events of 1995 were a sobering reminder of the scale of what we were up against. The fall of the Cali Cartel was a victory, but it wasn't a solution. As I prepared for the next year of operations, I knew the fight would only get harder. The enemy was adapting, and so would we. The question wasn't whether we could keep up—it was whether we could make a difference.

As the year pressed on, the enormity of the task continued to weigh heavily on me. The successes we had achieved so far were commendable, but they were nowhere near enough. Destroying 9,000 hectares of coca was a drop in the ocean when compared to the tens of thousands still under cultivation. If we wanted to make a meaningful impact, we needed more—more aircraft, more pilots, more bases, more coordination.

I took my concerns to the Colombian government, requesting additional crop-spraying aircraft. The response was blunt: No. Budgets were tight, priorities were elsewhere, and the political landscape was complicated. Frustrated but undeterred, I began asking around about what resources were already available, focusing on aircraft that might be repurposed for our mission. That's when I came across a glimmer of hope: the OV-10 Bronco.

The North American Rockwell OV-10 Bronco was a fascinating aircraft. Originally designed in the 1960s for counter-insurgency (COIN) operations, it had proven its worth in Vietnam and other conflicts. Its twin turboprop engines, central fuselage, and twin-boom tail design gave it a distinctive look, but what caught my attention were its specifications.

The Bronco was a machine built for versatility, and it was clear why it had been chosen. It wasn't just another aircraft—it was a workhorse with a combination of features that made it almost perfect for the job at hand. For starters, its ability to loiter over a target for hours gave it an edge that few others could match. This wasn't just about making a pass and heading home; the Bronco could circle and watch, observe movements below, and strike precisely when and where it mattered. It was persistence in the air, and that persistence could mean the difference between a missed opportunity and a successful operation.

Its payload capacity—up to 3,200 pounds—was another defining advantage. It could carry herbicide tanks for fumigation or swap them out for surveillance equipment, cameras, or even additional sensors to scan the dense jungle for hidden targets. It wasn't flashy, but it was functional, and in our line of work, that mattered far more than anything else.

Then there was the speed. At a maximum of 290 miles per hour, the Bronco sat in a sweet spot between efficiency and precision. It was fast enough to cover vast distances quickly but still slow enough to perform delicate, low-altitude work without sacrificing control. That speed gave pilots the ability to skim tree lines and valleys, hug the contours of rugged terrain, and hit their marks without compromise. This wasn't about brute force; it was about skill and accuracy, and the Bronco delivered both.

Its range was equally impressive. With a ferry range of 1,200 nautical miles, it could push deep into Colombia's remotest regions without refueling—places where other aircraft would be forced to turn back or where bases were too few and far between to offer support. For us, it meant that no plantation, no kitchen, no hidden operation was out of reach. The Bronco's endurance was a game-changer, allowing us to stay in the fight longer and press our advantage over an elusive enemy.

Lastly, there was the altitude. With a service ceiling of 30,000 feet, the Bronco offered unmatched flexibility. It could soar high over mountains, cross dense jungle canopies, and descend low when the mission required precision. The terrain in Colombia was relentless—vast, rugged, and often inhospitable—but the Bronco could handle it all with ease, whether the operation called for a wide aerial sweep or an intimate, close-range strike.

Taken together, these features made the Bronco an irresistible choice. It was fast, efficient, and adaptable, with the strength to carry what we needed and the stamina to go where we pointed it. In a war fought in dense jungles and over sprawling mountains, where persistence and precision were everything, the Bronco felt like the perfect ally.

The Colombian Air Force (FAC) already had a small fleet of 15 Broncos, gifted by the U.S. years ago. These aircraft were mainly used for reconnaissance and light attack missions, but they were underutilized. With some retrofitting, they could become a powerful tool in our arsenal.

Working with the U.S. State Department and other agencies, I helped draft a proposal to retrofit the Broncos for fumigation missions. The plan was ambitious but straightforward: equip the Broncos with spray systems capable of dispersing herbicides over large areas, making them a versatile alternative to the Air Tractors. This would also address the range mismatch between the Air Tractors and the escort helicopters.

The U.S. State Department's Bureau of International Narcotics and Law Enforcement Affairs (INL) was quick to embrace the idea. Their internal assessments painted a compelling picture of its advantages. For one, the Broncos offered something that the existing fleet couldn't—reach. These aircraft, with their endurance and versatility, could extend the fumigation operations into areas that were previously out of range. Remote coca plantations, hidden deep in jungles or scattered across Colombia's unforgiving mountain ranges, would no longer be safe havens. The Broncos could get there, do their job, and return with ease.

There was also the question of personnel. The Broncos were already in Colombia's possession, owned and operated by the *Fuerza Aérea Colombiana* (FAC). This was a significant shift. It meant less reliance on U.S. contractors and pilots—fewer American lives on the line, fewer questions to answer in Washington when missions turned dangerous or tragic. By putting the Broncos in the hands of the FAC, the Colombians would assume full operational responsibility, adding another layer of ownership to the country's fight against narcotics.

And then there was the matter of cost. War was expensive. Aircraft were expensive. But retrofitting the Broncos, converting them for fumigation purposes, would come at a fraction of the cost of purchasing new planes. The U.S. officials, ever mindful of budget allocations and congressional scrutiny, appreciated the practicality of this approach. Every dollar saved on procurement could be funnelled into other facets of the program—better intel, more pilots, more equipment. It was a win-win solution, at least on paper.

As these ideas circulated among the decision-makers, the enthusiasm grew. The Broncos weren't just a stopgap measure; they were a symbol of adaptability, of using what was already at hand to wage a smarter, more cost-effective war. In a conflict where every resource counted and every square mile mattered, the Broncos were more than just aircraft—they were another weapon, a strategic edge.

However, the plan wasn't without challenges. Retrofitting the Broncos would take time and technical expertise. The FAC would also need additional training to safely and effectively carry out fumigation missions. And, as always, there was the bureaucratic hurdle of convincing both the Colombian government and the U.S. authorities to commit the necessary resources.

The State Department, in its meticulous way, drafted a comprehensive report that pulled no punches about the challenges facing the eradication program. It read like a grim inventory of hurdles, each one a roadblock to progress in the war on drugs. The document outlined persistent problems that were as frustrating as they were familiar to those of us on the ground.

Delays in customs clearance for critical aircraft spare parts topped the list. It was maddening to think of grounded planes waiting weeks—sometimes months—for a single component stuck in bureaucratic limbo. Each day lost was another day the cartels gained.

The supply of herbicides, too, was erratic, frequently causing operations to halt midstream. Just when you'd have everything lined up—pilots ready, helicopters fueled, and a target identified—you'd hit the wall of "we're out of glyphosate." It wasn't just disruptive; it was demoralizing.

Then there was the issue of coordination—or rather, the lack thereof. Uncoordinated operations between agencies created inefficiencies that were almost comical if they weren't so costly. Different departments worked at cross-purposes, their goals overlapping but their execution hopelessly misaligned.

Perhaps most troubling was the absence of established search-and-rescue procedures for pilots on risky missions. Every flight was a gamble, and if a plane went down, the odds of a swift rescue were slim. For those of us who flew or knew someone who did, this was a constant weight on our minds.

The report also touched on training gaps among the Colombian National Police pilots. While they were skilled, the restrictions on U.S. instructor pilots participating in operational missions left a noticeable void in their practical education. These gaps were amplified in high-pressure scenarios, where experience often made the difference between life and death.

Despite the grim catalogue of issues, the report wasn't without its optimism. It acknowledged the progress that had been made but emphasized that the program's future success depended on addressing these bottlenecks head-on. One of the proposed solutions stood out: the Bronco retrofit plan. This wasn't just another Band-Aid; it was framed as a transformative step toward enhancing Colombia's self-sufficiency in the fight against narcotics.

The retrofitted Broncos, with their extended range and payload capacity, were more than just aircraft—they were symbols of a potential turning point. The plan wasn't merely about equipment; it was about empowerment, about giving Colombia the tools to take ownership of its skies and its fight. But as with everything else in this war, the devil was in the details, and the road to implementation would be as challenging as the battles we fought every day.

Meetings between U.S. and Colombian officials, including President Ernesto Samper and Defense Minister Fernando Esguerra, were tense. The U.S. wanted more control over the operations, arguing that their pilots and expertise were essential for the program's success. The Colombians, however, were wary of appearing too dependent on American support, especially given the political sensitivities around U.S. involvement in their domestic affairs.

One of the sticking points was the prohibition on U.S. instructor pilots flying operational missions. This restriction hampered their ability to train Colombian pilots effectively, leading to concerns about the long-term sustainability of the program. The Bronco plan, which relied entirely on Colombian resources, was seen as a potential compromise.

Ultimately, the decision rested with the Colombian government. While the U.S. could provide technical support and funding, the Colombians had to be willing to commit their own resources to the fight. The retrofit plan was presented as a way to enhance their capabilities without increasing reliance on American personnel.

The Broncos could be equipped with spray systems, allowing the FAC to take on fumigation missions independently. This would free up the Air Tractors and other resources for more focused operations. It also addressed the growing need for operational flexibility, enabling us to target remote plantations that had previously been out of reach.

While the plan offered a glimmer of hope, it also underscored the enormity of the task. Retrofitting the Broncos would take time, and even then, they wouldn't solve all our problems. The program still faced logistical hurdles, from securing a steady supply of herbicides to improving coordination between the various agencies involved.

Yet, despite these challenges, the idea of using the Broncos felt like a step in the right direction. It was a chance to expand our capabilities, disrupt the cartels' operations on a larger scale, and give Colombia a greater sense of ownership over the mission. For me, it was a reminder that in this fight, innovation and persistence were just as important as firepower.

By the beginning of 1996, the proposal was still under review, but the groundwork had been laid. Whether or not the Broncos would ever take to the skies as fumigation aircraft, the effort symbolized something bigger: the need to adapt, to find new solutions in a war that offered no easy victories.

As I looked at the maps on my desk, marking the locations of plantations still untouched, I felt a renewed sense of determination. The cartels were relentless, but so were we. If the Broncos could give us even a slight edge, it would be worth every ounce of effort. The fight wasn't over—it was just beginning.

Returning to Bogotá always felt like stepping into another world. The bustling streets, vibrant markets, and constant hum of life were a stark contrast to the remote jungle outposts where I spent most of my time. Carolina had seemingly vanished from my life, and while that was disappointing, I didn't let it dampen my spirits. It was time to explore new possibilities—and new company. My Spanish was improving, and the city was full of opportunities to meet people, though my most enduring connection remained Pedro, my baker buddy.

Pedro's bakery became something of a sanctuary for me during these visits. It wasn't just about the bread—it was the nostalgia. The equipment, outdated by European standards, reminded me of my father's bakery in the 1970s. Spending time in the bakery wasn't just therapeutic; it was also fun. I found myself slipping into the rhythm of the work, kneading dough, shaping rolls, and even managing late-night production runs when Pedro had to step out.

Pedro had a contract to supply bread rolls to the local prison, a task that fascinated me more than it probably should have. I volunteered to make the deliveries, relishing the mix of routine and risk. Driving the little van in my white baker's coat, I was an odd sight for the guards. A gringo baker delivering bread rolls to a Colombian prison? It was so absurd it often left them chuckling.

The prison deliveries turned out to be more eventful than I had anticipated. At first, I was escorted by guards, but as I became a familiar face, they let me venture into the yard on my own. The atmosphere was tense yet oddly comical at times. On one occasion, I carried a tray of rolls past a corridor of thick steel bars. Thinking I was clever, I raised the tray high to keep the bread out of reach, only to have hands dart out from bunk beds above and swipe the rolls anyway. It was like being in a zoo, and the inmates howled with laughter at my stunned reaction. After that, I started delivering the bread in boxes instead of trays.

One delivery took me to a special patio where the gay and trans prisoners were housed. As I walked past a worn-out couch, one of the inmates, reclining dramatically, called out, "Doctor, please help me—I'm really sick!" The others burst into laughter, pointing out my white coat and pointing out that I wasn't a doctor but the baker. The embarrassed prisoner screeched and covered his face as I left, grinning at the absurdity of it all.

Then there was the women's patio. Delivering there was straightforward until one day, as I handed over the bread, a woman grabbed my crotch with a bold laugh and declared, "Not bad!" to the cheers of her fellow inmates. Flustered but amused, I quickly finished the delivery and retreated, shaking my head at the audacity.

One evening, while working alone in the bakery, two local toughs walked in. They weren't customers; their swagger and casual disregard for personal space made it clear they were trouble. They sauntered around the bakery like they owned the place, ignoring my polite attempts to shoo them outside. Eventually, I had enough. Carrying a hot tray fresh from the oven, I pointedly suggested they step out before they got burned. They left, slinging insults about the "gringo hueyputa" as they went.

When Pedro returned, he asked what had happened, saying a group of guys was waiting outside, throwing insults. I shrugged it off, assuming it was just posturing. Pedro's next words made my stomach drop: "One of them has a knife."

Still, I had work to do and dismissed the warning. Hours later, when I finished for the night, Pedro had already left. Before stepping outside, I grabbed a long bread knife and tucked it up my sleeve, just in case. I didn't have my Glock yet, and I wasn't about to take any chances.

Sure enough, as I turned the corner into the dark street, trouble found me. The same guy from earlier, the one I had told off, stepped out of the shadows, his unkempt hair and wild eyes giving him an unsettling look. He was stocky and taller than me, with the kind of presence that commanded attention. Worse still, he wasn't alone. Six or seven of his friends emerged from the darkness, surrounding me.

He got in my face, his voice dripping with menace. "What's your problem with Colombians, gringo?"

Keeping my voice calm, I replied, "No problem with Colombians. Just idiots who get in the way when I'm carrying hot trays."

The group erupted in jeers, mocking the cocky gringo. One of them shouted, "He's got a knife!" I let the bread knife slide from my sleeve and into my hand, gripping it firmly. The leader stepped back slightly and revealed his own knife—a much smaller blade. That gave me a small boost of confidence, but I was still outnumbered and terrified.

I did the only thing I could think of: go on the offensive. I raised my voice, shouting wildly, "Yes, I have a knife! You came here with knives, so I got one too. There may be more of you, but I'll kill some of you before you get me!" I pointed my knife at each of them in turn, bellowing, "Who wants to die first? You? You? You?"

The sheer insanity of my outburst seemed to unnerve them. The leader hesitated, his bravado faltering, and the others began backing away. They muttered insults, calling me a crazy gringo, but none of them dared to make a move. A few moments later, the group dispersed, leaving me standing alone in the street, my heart pounding like a drum.

As I walked to the main road and flagged down a taxi, the adrenaline began to wear off. I realized just how close I had come to serious trouble—or worse. My crazy act had worked this time, but I couldn't rely on bravado alone. I needed that Glock, and soon.

Back in the safety of my apartment, I couldn't help but laugh at the absurdity of it all. A pilot turned baker turned prison deliveryman turned knife-wielding lunatic in the streets of Bogotá. Life in Colombia was proving to be anything but dull.

Returning to the base after my time in Bogotá, I was greeted with the news that my long-awaited Glock had finally arrived. "A little late," I thought, recalling the bakery incident and imagining how much safer I'd have felt that night if I'd been properly armed. Nevertheless, the Glock 19 was a beauty—a compact and reliable 9mm pistol, lightweight and perfect for someone constantly on the move.

The Glock's arrival presented a small logistical issue: wearing it with a flight suit and harness. The overalls and the four-point harness left no room for a traditional belt holster, and the last thing I wanted was to be fumbling for my weapon in a crisis. So, I headed into town and sought out a seamstress. I sketched out a rough design for a custom leather holster that would sit against my side, secured with a strap over the shoulder and another around the back to keep it stable during flights.

Three days later, she handed me the finished product. It was perfect—sturdy, functional, and with a touch of flair that made it look damn good. It hugged my side snugly, and the leather was soft enough not to chafe during long hours of flying. It reminded me of the improvised holsters we had made during the Falklands War in 1982. Back then, the Chinese laundry staff aboard the carrier had stitched together holsters for us out of military webbing, crude but effective. This one, though, was a definite upgrade.

While I initially wore it everywhere—feeling like something out of an action movie—I soon relegated it to flight operations. Wearing it around the office all day quickly lost its novelty.

With my Glock ready to go, we set up a small shooting range beside the barracks. Using sandbags for a backstop and carefully ensuring no houses were behind it, we created a safe and practical setup. Ammunition was easy to come by; a simple signature at the army store gave me access to more rounds than I could ever need.

I hadn't fired a weapon since the Falklands, and the familiarity of it came flooding back. The steady weight of the Glock, the firm grip, the sharp crack of each shot—it was almost therapeutic. My aim was rusty at first, but with regular practice, I quickly got back into form. It was comforting to know that if trouble found me again, I'd be ready.

As my Spanish improved, word spread that I was decent with languages, and I was asked to teach English to some of the young soldiers. These were national service recruits, most around 17 or 18, and they were keen to use their service time to better themselves. The problem was, we didn't have a proper classroom, so we improvised. We dragged some benches into a shaded area, found an old-style chalkboard, and got to work.

Without access to teaching materials, I reverse-engineered a Spanish-to-English textbook I'd found in Bogotá. It wasn't ideal, but it worked. The process turned out to be a two-way street: as I taught them English, my own Spanish grammar improved dramatically. Verbs, conjugations, tenses—it all started clicking into place. Before long, I was holding conversations with the locals with far more confidence than my fellow foreigners, especially the Americans.

Some of the Americans had Latin-sounding surnames—Hernandez, Gutierrez, Sanchez—but their Spanish was atrocious, delivered in outrageous accents that made them sound like characters from a bad comedy skit. I suspected they exaggerated it on purpose to make it clear they were Americans, not locals. While I worked hard to blend in linguistically, they seemed content to stand out.

Their Spanish shortcomings aside, they were good company, and we often spent evenings swapping stories at local bars. My tales from the Navy, especially those from the Falklands, always seemed to draw the most attention. There's something about war stories—flying fighter jets, dodging enemy fire—that captures the imagination, even among men who'd seen their own share of danger.

Life on base had its lighter moments, and one of the most surprising was the collective obsession with "Café, Aroma de Mujer," a wildly popular Colombian telenovela. It was the story of a poor coffee farm girl falling in love with a wealthy heir to a coffee empire—a melodramatic, cheesy soap opera that seemed completely at odds with the tough personas of the soldiers and pilots around me.

Every evening, they gathered in the mess hall, riveted to the screen, hanging on every twist and turn of the story. After each episode, they dissected the plot like film critics, discussing the characters' decisions as if they were real people. It reminded me of the British obsession with soaps like "Coronation Street" or "EastEnders," though the sheer drama of Colombian telenovelas took things to another level.

One evening, I was watching "The Good, the Bad, and the Ugly," enjoying Clint Eastwood's stoic badassery, when someone came in and casually switched the channel to "Café." I couldn't believe it. Eastwood was replaced by swooning gazes and over-the-top declarations of love. That was the final straw. The next time I was in town, I bought a TV for my room, ensuring I could enjoy my Westerns in peace.

As I settled into this strange new routine of flying and organising missions, teaching English, practicing my aim, and dodging melodrama in the officer's mess, I began to appreciate the rhythm of life at the base. There was camaraderie, purpose, and even a bit of humour amid the seriousness of our mission. And just maybe, amid the chaos and danger that defined our mission, these seemingly mundane distractions—teaching English, swapping stories at the bar, or debating the twists of a telenovela—became an essential coping mechanism. They grounded us, offering moments of normalcy in an otherwise unpredictable existence. Life on the base was filled with uncertainty; every mission carried the risk of being shot at or worse. The jokes, the camaraderie, and even the absurd arguments about whether "Café, Aroma de Mujer" was better than Clint Eastwood's steely grit allowed us to escape that reality, if only briefly. It was as though these small, everyday routines shielded us from the weight of what we were doing and the stakes we faced. They reminded us that, for all the danger, life was still happening, and finding humour and connection in the mundane was what kept us sane.

Chapter 5: Farmers and Football

1995 brought an unexpected and complex challenge to our mission: a temporary suspension of fumigation efforts due to massive protests from coca-growing communities. What had initially seemed like another step in the fight against cocaine quickly evolved into a bitter confrontation between rural farmers, the government, and international backers like the United States. For me, this was a stark reminder that while our mission targeted the cartels, it had unintended victims—people whose survival depended on the very plants we were trying to destroy.

Word of the protests began trickling into the base through news reports and conversations with locals. Farmers from remote regions, desperate and angry, had started organizing marches and road blockades. Their grievances were clear and deeply personal. The aerial fumigation campaigns using glyphosate had destroyed more than just coca crops—it had wiped out entire fields of legal crops like maize, beans, and plantains. These were subsistence farmers, often living on the edge of poverty, and the loss of their food supply left them with nothing.

The scenes on the news were striking: men, women, and even children carrying placards and chanting slogans against fumigation. Many held up withered plants as evidence of the damage caused by the herbicide. Some brought livestock with skin lesions, claiming the glyphosate had harmed their animals. Others talked about the health impacts on their communities—rashes, respiratory issues, and eye irritation. These weren't just accusations; they were pleas for survival.

At the base, the protests caused an immediate operational halt. The government had no choice but to suspend fumigation in certain regions to ease tensions and avoid escalating the conflict. For us, this was both frustrating and illuminating. Frustrating because it delayed our work and gave the cartels breathing room. Illuminating because it exposed a side of the war on drugs we rarely saw.

As the days passed, I started digging deeper into the situation. Why were these farmers so dependent on coca? The answer was disheartening. Coca was a guaranteed cash crop in these remote regions. It was resilient, grew quickly, and, most importantly, had a steady market thanks to the drug trade. Alternative crops, like coffee or cacao, took years to become profitable and lacked the same market reliability. Without coca, many of these farmers faced outright destitution.

Adding to their plight was the lack of infrastructure. Many of these areas were so isolated that even if farmers wanted to grow legal crops, they had no way to transport them to market. Roads were few and far between, and insecurity from guerrilla and paramilitary activity made travel dangerous. In a cruel irony, the cartels often provided the only "support system" these farmers had, offering quick cash and protection in exchange for their harvests.

The Colombian government, under mounting pressure both domestically and internationally, announced temporary suspensions of fumigation in the most affected regions. This was coupled with promises of alternative development programs. The idea was to provide farmers with the means to transition away from coca cultivation by offering subsidies, technical assistance, and support for infrastructure projects.

On paper, it sounded promising. Programs focused on crops like coffee, cacao, and tropical fruits, which could fetch good prices in legal markets. Plans were drawn up to improve roads, build schools, and offer microloans to farmers. Education campaigns aimed to encourage farmers to embrace legal livelihoods.

But on the ground, the reality was far more complicated. These programs were underfunded and inconsistently implemented. Many farmers never saw the promised assistance. Insecurity in coca-growing regions, controlled by guerrillas, paramilitaries, or traffickers, made it nearly impossible for government officials or international NGOs to operate safely. Even when alternative crops were planted, they took years to yield profits—years these farmers simply didn't have.

During this pause in fumigation, I had time to reflect and talk with locals who were surprisingly open with me. They didn't condone the drug trade, but they saw it as a necessary evil. "What choice do we have?" one farmer asked me. "The government says grow coffee, but coffee takes years. My children are hungry now."

I couldn't argue with that. As much as I believed in our mission, it was hard to ignore the human cost. These weren't cartel bosses or traffickers; they were ordinary people trapped in a system that left them no alternatives. For every hectare of coca we destroyed, a family somewhere lost their livelihood. And with no safety net to catch them, the resentment grew.

The villagers also spoke of their fears. They were caught between two worlds: the government on one side and the cartels on the other. Fumigation left them impoverished, while refusing to grow coca made them targets for violent reprisal. Many farmers told me stories of cartels threatening their families if they didn't plant coca. "It's not just a crop," one man said. "It's survival."

Meanwhile, the United States, which funded much of the fumigation effort, was watching closely. Human rights organizations criticized the campaigns, arguing that they caused undue harm to vulnerable communities without addressing the root causes of the drug trade. Reports highlighted the health impacts of glyphosate and the economic devastation in fumigated regions. Neighbouring countries also raised concerns, fearing the environmental and health effects of herbicide drift across borders.

The U.S. government was in a tricky position. They wanted fumigation to resume—Colombia was the linchpin of their war on drugs—but they also recognized the need for alternative strategies. Pilot programs for alternative development received limited funding, but these were seen as supplementary rather than replacements for aerial eradication. The underlying message was clear: eradication first, development second.

The temporary suspension was a wake-up call for everyone involved in the fight against cocaine. It exposed the limits of our approach and the unintended consequences of focusing solely on eradication. Destroying coca crops was one thing; building sustainable livelihoods was another. Without addressing the root causes of coca cultivation—poverty, isolation, and insecurity—we were treating symptoms, not the disease.

For me, it was a humbling experience. I came to Colombia with a clear sense of purpose, eager to dismantle the cartels and their operations. But the protests, the stories from the farmers, and the sheer complexity of the situation forced me to see the bigger picture. This wasn't just a war on drugs—it was a war on poverty, inequality, and systemic neglect. And that was a much harder fight.

Eventually, fumigation resumed, but the lessons of 1995 stayed with me. I approached my work with a new perspective, understanding that every mission had ripple effects far beyond the jungles we targeted. As I reviewed the maps and planned our next operations, I couldn't help but think about the farmers and families on the ground. We were making progress, yes—but at what cost?

The contractors left for the United States on leave, and I found myself back in Bogotá, still on the payroll but with no immediate work. I didn't dwell on the uncertainty of the situation, but I'd be lying if I said it wasn't on my mind. My bridges with the airline world were well and truly burnt, and while I didn't regret the choices that brought me here, the long-term impact on my career was a gnawing worry. In the airline industry, maintaining currency on large, wide-bodied jets like the Boeing 767 is critical. Spending years flying small aircraft, like crop dusters and helicopters, could seriously diminish my value to major airlines. They need pilots who are up-to-date and experienced on heavy jets, not someone who's been flying single-engine or light twin-engine aircraft in remote jungles. The fact that I'd never qualified on Airbus planes, being firmly a Boeing guy, only added to my concerns. A couple of years away from flying 200-ton jets could make it very difficult to find my way back into the structured, competitive world of commercial aviation.

At the Ministry of Justice, they assured me the suspension of fumigation was only temporary and that operations would resume soon enough. Still, I needed to keep busy and decided I might as well enjoy my downtime. Bogotá, with its sprawling urban life and vibrant culture, was my playground. I was a young, single guy, and in this city, I was exotic—a foreigner with an adventurous streak, a touch of mystery, and a pilot's uniform to boot. The combination was irresistible, and it wasn't long before I found myself juggling the affections of several women.

The women I dated during this period were as varied as they were fascinating. There was Martha, shy and sweet, with an air of quiet intelligence. She was the kind of woman who made you feel at ease with her calm demeanor. Then there was Alba, a voluptuous beauty with a confidence that turned heads wherever she went. She knew how to command a room, and being on her arm was an experience in itself. And lastly, there was Adriana, an exuberant dancer with a passion for life that was as infectious as it was intoxicating. Adriana was energy personified, pulling me into her world of music, dance, and late nights that seemed to melt into mornings.

While Adriana swept me into the vibrant nightlife of Bogotá, I often found myself spending time with Pedro, who had become not only a friend but also my unofficial guide and self-appointed bodyguard. Pedro had an infectious enthusiasm for life, and wherever we went, he took it upon himself to make sure everyone in earshot knew who I was.

Whenever an attractive woman came within range, Pedro would launch into his usual routine. "¡Sí, mi Capitán!" he'd bellow, loud enough to draw attention from half the street. At first, I thought it was just him being over-the-top, but to my surprise, it worked. Heads turned, and many of those heads belonged to beautiful young women who suddenly seemed intrigued by the mysterious "Captain" Pedro was loudly addressing.

"Pedro, you're making me look ridiculous," I said once, embarrassed after he'd shouted it across a crowded café. He just grinned.

"Ridiculous? No, mi Capitán! They love it. You're a hero! A pilot! Who wouldn't be impressed?"

I couldn't argue with the results. Women would smile, and sometimes they'd even come over to ask about my "adventures." It was almost embarrassing how well it worked—almost. I started to notice Pedro seemed to enjoy basking in the reflected glory. As the conversations flowed, he would subtly insert himself into the narrative, emphasizing his closeness to me, dropping lines like, "We work together. Mi Capitán trusts me with everything."

At one point, I found myself involved with all three women simultaneously—a logistical challenge I hadn't quite anticipated. Things came to a head one day at the bakery when, by some cosmic twist of fate, two of them showed up at the same time. My heart stopped when I saw them walk in, and I scrambled to keep them apart. Thankfully, the shopfront had two counters separated by a concrete column. Using this makeshift barrier to my advantage, I managed to keep them from noticing each other. I played the role of the hardworking professional, apologizing profusely for being too busy to chat and promising to see them later. They bought it—for the moment. It was a close call, and I learned to tread more carefully after that.

As the calendar turned to 1996, the suspension on fumigation was finally lifted, and I was called back to duty. The break had been a brief reprieve, but I was eager to return to the skies. The situation on the ground hadn't improved much—if anything, the cartels had taken advantage of our pause to expand their operations. It was time to make up for lost ground.

The real game-changer came a few months later when we finally received the OV-10 Broncos we'd been requesting. These rugged twin-engine aircraft, purpose-built for counter-insurgency missions, added a new level of capability to our operations. The Broncos were flown by Colombian police pilots, while the DynCorp contractors continued to operate the Air Tractors. With the addition of the Broncos, our arsenal now included: 6 Air Tractors and 10 OV-10 Broncos for crop spraying. A couple of Cessnas for aerial surveillance and logistical support plus My trusty Bell helo.

I now commanded two squadrons, a significant step up from where we'd started. Managing the combined operations of 19 aircraft was no small feat, but it was exactly the kind of challenge I thrived on. My days were filled with mission planning, coordinating pilots, liaising with ground forces, and, of course, flying my own missions.

With the expanded fleet, we ramped up our efforts. By the end of the year, we had destroyed 22,000 hectares of cocaine plantations, a significant increase from the previous year's total of 9,000 hectares. The numbers were impressive, but I couldn't shake the feeling that we were still only scratching the surface. Colombia's coca cultivation was vast, and for every field we eradicated, new ones seemed to sprout up elsewhere.

The Broncos proved to be a critical addition. Their ability to loiter over target areas, combined with their larger payloads and extended range, allowed us to cover more ground than ever before. The police pilots quickly adapted to their new aircraft, and I worked closely with them to fine-tune tactics. Meanwhile, the Air Tractor pilots, seasoned contractors with years of experience, continued their precision spraying runs with deadly efficiency.

The Broncos, with their strong construction and being military aircraft from the beginning, were better equipped to handle these threats than the Air Tractors. But even so, every mission carried the risk of enemy fire.

We also faced challenges on the logistical side. Spare parts for the aircraft were often delayed in customs, herbicide supplies ran low at critical moments, and coordination between the various agencies involved was still a work in progress. It was a constant battle to keep everything running smoothly, but the team's dedication never wavered.

By the end of 1996, I felt a mix of pride and frustration. Destroying 22,000 hectares of coca was no small achievement, but the scale of the problem remained daunting. Colombia was producing hundreds of metric tons of cocaine annually, and the cartels showed no signs of slowing down. Every field we eradicated was a victory, but it was hard not to wonder if we were fighting a war of attrition we couldn't win.

Still, I believed in what we were doing. Every hectare we destroyed meant less cocaine making its way to the streets, less money for the cartels, and less power for the criminals who thrived on the misery of others. It wasn't perfect, but it was a start—and for now, that was enough to keep me going.

In 1997, our efforts to combat illicit coca cultivation ramped up to unprecedented levels. We eradicated approximately 43,246 hectares of coca through a combination of aerial spraying and manual removal. This was nearly double the 22,576 hectares we had managed in 1996—a clear indication that our strategies were working, at least operationally. Yet, the total area under coca cultivation paradoxically continued to rise, reaching an estimated 122,500 hectares by the year's end.

This frustrating reality underscored just how deeply ingrained coca cultivation was in Colombia's rural economy. The economic incentives for farmers, the adaptability of illicit networks, and the ongoing struggle to implement sustainable alternative development programs made the task feel like trying to empty a flooding ship with a bucket. For every hectare we destroyed, new ones sprang up, cultivated by communities with little else to sustain them. It was a lesson in the complexity of addressing illicit drug production—it required more than eradication; it demanded a long-term, multi-faceted strategy that combined socio-economic development with institutional reform.

By this time, I felt firmly ensconced in the Colombian way of life. The stark contrast between the lush jungle missions and the camaraderie of the base became my new normal. Among the young soldiers, I wasn't just their commanding officer or the strange foreigner—I had become something of a storyteller and teacher. These were boys of 17 or 18, many on their first real venture away from home, and they hung on my every word.

I would regale them with tales of flying around the world and recount stories from my military days in the Falklands War. My family's history in the armed forces added depth to my anecdotes: my grandfather driving a tank through North Africa and Normandy during World War II, and my maternal grandfather surviving the hell of the Somme in World War I. I'd even pepper in bits of military history from the Spanish Armada to modern warfare, and they listened as if I were narrating a blockbuster film.

The nickname came naturally: "The Oracle."

One day during a break, one of the young soldiers looked at me with wide-eyed curiosity and asked, "Oracle, how do satellites stay in space? How do they not fall back down?"

It was an excellent question, one I was more than happy to dive into. "It's all about ballistics and orbit mechanics," I began, launching into an explanation. I described how a satellite is essentially falling towards the Earth at all times, but because of its speed and the curvature of the planet, it keeps missing the surface.

"Imagine throwing a stone," I said. "If you throw it far enough and fast enough, and the Earth curves away beneath it, it'll keep falling but never hit the ground. That's what satellites do, except at a speed of around 17,500 miles per hour."

I went on to describe the difference between low Earth orbit and geostationary orbit. "In geostationary orbit, a satellite is placed so that it matches the Earth's rotation, making it appear stationary in the sky from the ground. That's why your TV dish points in one direction—it's locked onto a satellite in geostationary orbit."

Their faces lit up with awe as I explained how physics, gravity, and speed combined to create this delicate balance. It was a proud moment; I loved how eager they were to understand the world beyond their immediate surroundings.

Later that evening, while recounting the conversation in the bar, I found myself in a heated discussion with a local school teacher who overheard me. "That's rubbish," he interjected confidently. "Satellites have engines. They use them to stay up there."

I raised an eyebrow and tried to explain. "Engines don't work in space. There's no air for combustion. Satellites rely on their initial velocity and orbit mechanics to stay up. They might have small thrusters to adjust their position occasionally, but they're not using engines to keep from falling."

Unfazed, he doubled down. "No, no. They're nuclear-powered engines. Everyone knows that."

At that, I couldn't help but laugh. "Nuclear-powered engines?" I asked. "Sputnik was a two-foot metallic sphere launched in 1957. Do you really think it had a nuclear reactor on board? And even if it did, where's the thrust coming from? Space doesn't work like that!"

Despite my explanations, he remained adamant, citing some vague, unscientific sources. It was baffling—this was a teacher, someone tasked with educating the next generation. Yet here he was, arguing against basic physics. The soldiers, however, were thoroughly entertained by the exchange and firmly took my side, which only solidified my reputation. "See? The Oracle knows everything!" one of them declared, and I couldn't help but laugh.

Over time, this incident and others like it cemented me as the authority on almost everything, from science and history to international politics. Well, almost everything—when it came to football, I was hopeless.

Being the only European on base gave me a unique perspective. The locals, a few Central Americans, and the Americans brought their own cultural dynamics, but I found my broader world experience made me stand out. I'd already visited over 50 countries by this point—many in Europe, some in Asia and Africa, and of course, the Americas. The Americans, in particular, seemed woefully uninterested in anything outside their borders. Soldiers would often ask me about the world beyond Colombia, and I'd indulge their curiosity with stories of bustling cities, ancient ruins, and desert landscapes.

This rapport led to me being invited to socialize with them, which is how I ended up trying **chicha,** a homemade fermented brew that was both illegal and widely accepted. The young soldiers, earning meagre salaries, relied on this cheap intoxicant, masking its taste with fruit juice to make it palatable.

The first sip was deceptively smooth, but they were clearly watching me for the aftereffects. They didn't have to wait long. Before I knew it, I was not only drunk but experiencing what could only be described as a full-scale gastrointestinal rebellion. I spent a humiliating hour in the bathroom, unsure whether to sit or kneel, as my body purged itself of the chicha. The soldiers found it hilarious, and I became a minor legend on base for my dramatic reaction. I swore off chicha after that, sticking to safer options like Club Colombia and Aguila beers.

As 1998 rolled into view, life seemed to settle into a predictable rhythm. Missions were planned, executed, and evaluated; camaraderie grew stronger with each passing day. Then, one morning, I was summoned to the colonel's office. The tone was serious, and I assumed it was about work—some operational update or directive from Bogota. But when I picked up the phone, the voice on the other end jolted me.

"This is the British Embassy," the man said in clipped, official tones. "We have a letter here from your father."

I was about to ask why the embassy was calling about a letter when he continued, his tone casual, almost flippant.

"Oh, and your mother's dead."

I froze, my breath catching in my chest. "What the fuck?" I said, my voice barely above a whisper. The words hung there, heavy and impossible to process. Then the anger bubbled up. "Are you serious? Is that how you tell someone this kind of news? Are you fucking stupid or just completely insane?"

There was a clumsy shuffle of words on the other end of the line—"Ah, er, sorry… I didn't mean…"—but I didn't wait to hear the rest. I slammed the phone down, feeling a surge of disbelief and fury. Your mother's dead. The phrase reverberated in my mind, drowning out every other thought.

I sat there, staring at the phone, the weight of those words settling on me like a lead blanket. Grief, guilt, and confusion swirled together, a toxic cocktail of emotions I didn't know how to handle. My relationship with my parents had always been… complicated. Years had passed since I'd last seen them. There'd been a falling out over something so trivial I couldn't even remember what it was. But the aftermath had been anything but trivial—my father had disappeared, taking one of my trucks with him. A truck I hadn't finished paying for. Later, I'd almost been arrested when it turned out he'd sold it, leaving me with the bill to avoid criminal charges. It was the kind of thing my dad would do. A "character" was how people politely described him. A rogue, more like.

I hadn't even known where they'd moved to. For years, we'd been completely out of touch. Now, here I was, in the middle of a jungle warzone in Colombia, learning my mother had been gone for two years. Two years. And my father had no idea where I was, no idea what I was doing, no idea about the life I'd built. That would be a hell of a surprise for him.

For the first time since arriving in Colombia, the full weight of my choices hit me. Leaving the structured world of airlines and forging this unpredictable, dangerous life had been exhilarating. But in the process, I'd distanced myself from the people who'd known me longest. And now, it seemed, irreversibly so.

But there wasn't time to sit with my grief. Missions needed planning. Flights needed overseeing. A team depended on me. For better or worse, work didn't stop for loss.

Two weeks later, I found myself in Bogotá, standing at the embassy reception. The clerk handed me the letter, a simple envelope bearing my father's handwriting. My heart pounded as I opened it. The note inside was brief, written in my father's familiar scrawl. He explained he'd been looking for me, going as far as involving the police, who'd come up empty-handed. Eventually, he'd turned to the Foreign Office, who confirmed they knew where I was but refused to divulge my location. They'd agreed to forward his letter instead.

The words hit hard. He explained that my mum had passed away almost two years ago, peacefully in her sleep. She was just 57. He described how they'd returned home from a collector's fair, gone to bed as usual, and the next morning, when he brought her a cup of tea, she wouldn't wake up. Just like that, she was gone.

At the bottom of the note, he'd left his phone number and address: a small town in Yorkshire called Batley, home to Fox's Biscuits, a factory over a century old. A fittingly understated place for my dad to land.

I walked out of the embassy in a daze, clutching the letter like a lifeline. I found the nearest *call shop*—one of those small stores with phone booths for making international calls. Sitting in the cramped booth, I dialed the number with trembling hands. There was a long pause as the call connected, the silence stretching unbearably. Then I heard it—the familiar rasp of my dad's voice, but now different than before, aged and frail.

"Hello?"

"It's me," I said. "Stephen."

There was a beat of confusion. "Who?"

"Stephen. Your son. Remember me? The one who lived with you for 17 years before joining the Navy?"

The silence on the other end was deafening, and then it broke with a flood of emotion. I could hear his voice crack, the sound of tears barely held back. "Holy shit, where are you?" he asked, his voice trembling. When I told him Colombia, he was dumbfounded. "What the fuck are you doing there?"

So I told him. All of it. The planes, the jungle, the missions, the danger. He listened in stunned silence, punctuated only by the occasional gasp of disbelief. Then, in a quieter tone, he told me about Mum. About how they'd spent their last day together at a collector's fair, how he'd gone downstairs the next morning to make her tea, only to find she'd slipped away in her sleep.

It was a raw, emotional conversation, the kind we'd never had before. For the first time in years, I felt the gap between us begin to close. By the end of the call, I'd promised to make arrangements to visit him during my next long leave. It gave me a sense of purpose, something to look forward to amidst the chaos and the bittersweet emotions of reconnecting after so many years. But for the time being, I was still entrenched in my life in Bogotá, and that came with its own set of challenges.

At this time, I was living with Adriana, the dancer. She had recently bought a small, two-bedroom flat in a new building. It had all the charm of freshly poured concrete—barely furnished, with no internal doors and a kitchen that was functional at best. Most of our time together revolved around trips to Homecenter a huge warehouse type of store that sold everything for the home, picking out everything from light fixtures to curtains. Of course, I was footing the bill for all these domestic improvements. Unlike the thrilling indulgences of buying Carolina her high heels and short skirts, there was nothing remotely exciting about purchasing a set of wooden doors or debating over curtain rods. It felt more like a chore than a romantic adventure.

Adriana was still passionate and intoxicating in bed, but I couldn't shake the growing sense that I was little more than a walking ATM. That suspicion was confirmed one afternoon when my credit card was declined while trying to purchase an outrageously expensive set of doors with flashy handles. Adriana's reaction wasn't one of understanding but of visible annoyance, as if my financial limits were a personal affront to her. I felt a strange mix of relief and resentment—relief that the purchase hadn't gone through, and resentment at being reduced to nothing more than a means to fund her aspirations.

Her daughter, Catalina, wasn't helping matters either. At thirteen, she was a precocious and headstrong teenager, brimming with attitude and quick to remind me that I wasn't her father. She usually lived with her grandmother but was staying with us temporarily. I did my best to keep my distance, aware that any attempt at discipline or guidance would almost certainly backfire. Catalina had recently become obsessed with the World Cup, and like nearly every Colombian, she was convinced that their team was destined for glory.

"They're going to destroy England!" she declared with fiery confidence. "Three-nil at least."

I avoided engaging, unwilling to stoke the fire. I wasn't a football fan, but even I knew that Colombia's chances were slim against the heavyweights like Germany, Brazil, or Argentina—let alone England, my home country. Still, the buildup to the game was palpable. The entire city seemed to be holding its breath, draped in Colombian flags and buzzing with national pride.

When the match day arrived, I decided to avoid the inevitable tension at home by going for a walk. Catalina was parked in front of the TV, ready to cheer on her heroes, while Adriana prepared snacks for what she hoped would be a celebratory evening. As I wandered through the complex, I passed a bar where cheers and jeers from about forty men spilled out into the street. The energy was tempting, but I kept moving, preferring the quiet of the small park nestled between the buildings.

As I strolled, a young girl of about seven or eight appeared on a nearby balcony. Tears streaked her face as she wailed, "England have scored!" Her despair was so raw and unfiltered that I couldn't help but feel a twinge of guilt, even though I had no hand in the outcome.

About ten minutes later, she reappeared, now completely inconsolable. "They've scored again!" she screamed, her tiny fists pounding the balcony rail. Colombia's dreams of World Cup glory were officially over, and they had been crushed by my countrymen.

I dreaded returning to the flat. Sure enough, Catalina's glare could have curdled milk. She didn't say anything—she didn't have to. Her silence was louder than any words, and her simmering resentment was palpable. Adriana was more composed, but even she was clearly disappointed, if not at me personally, then at the universe for conspiring against her beloved team.

Still, the match had at least one silver lining: it silenced Catalina. Her fiery proclamations of victory had been snuffed out, replaced by sulky silence. For that small mercy, I was grateful.

I was still in contact with some of my ex-girlfriends, and one Saturday I decided to meet up with Alba, whom I hadn't seen in a while. The plan was casual—no grand date, just catching up. We agreed to meet outside the church in 7 de Agosto, a busy commercial district in Bogotá. It's not the most picturesque part of the city, but it had a certain charm with its bustling streets and small, local cafeterias.

As I stood in the church doorway, blending into the crowd of shoppers and commuters, a young woman walked by. Her head turned, and her eyes widened as she almost shrieked, "Stephen?"

I was momentarily thrown off, her face tugging at the edges of my memory but refusing to fully materialize. I fumbled for a moment, trying to piece it together, when she reached into her bag and pulled out a small artisanal pen holder. She held it up with a shy smile, and there it was—"Martha" embroidered in delicate stitching. Recognition finally clicked into place. Of course, Martha—the shy, quiet girl I had dated briefly months ago.

"Mi amor," I said with a sheepish grin, covering my earlier lapse with a bit of charm. We exchanged pleasantries, the warmth of her presence slowly jogging my memory of just how sweet and captivating she had been. We exchanged pleasantries, and she explained she was working at a nearby sports goods store and was out running an errand. She was genuinely surprised to learn I was still in Colombia, having assumed I'd long since returned to the UK. Our conversation was short and sweet, but as she walked away, I realized I'd forgotten to get her number. She had shown me the pen holder, with her name on it. That gave me a clue—but only her first name.

Martha had left an impression on me. She was a refreshing contrast to Adriana's over-the-top energy. There was a sweetness about her, a grounded charm. I was determined to find her again.

Enter Ruben, my new friend—a street-smart guy who sold knock-off clothes, like "Levi 501"jeans made in Medellin, out of the trunk of his Kia Accent. Ruben loved having me tag along on his rounds, collecting payments and making deliveries. It gave him a certain prestige to have a foreigner riding shotgun. A few days later, when we were in 7 de Agosto, I enlisted his help to track down Martha. She had mentioned working in a sports goods store on the main street, and I naively thought it would be easy to find her.

Little did I know, Bogotá had this peculiar tendency to group similar stores together. The entire stretch of road seemed to be dedicated to sports goods, block after block of shops selling everything from football gear to fishing rods. There must have been at least fifty stores, all crammed into about eight blocks.

Undeterred, I decided to start at one end and work my way back. Each time I walked into a shop and asked for Martha, I was met with blank stares or a curt, "We don't have a Martha here." By the fifteenth store, my patience was wearing thin. At one shop, they finally shouted into the back room, "Hey, Martha! Someone's here to see you!" My heart leaped—until a gruff woman, easily four times the size of "my" Martha, emerged. I muttered an apology and bolted.

Finally, at the second-to-last store, a young woman at the counter grinned knowingly. "Ah, you must be Stephen," she said. Relief flooded through me as Martha appeared from the back room, looking sheepish in her work apron. We laughed off the awkwardness, exchanged numbers, and promised to catch up properly soon.

That evening, Martha called me, but the timing couldn't have been worse. I was still with Adriana, who was sitting next to me on the couch. The conversation was stiff, filled with awkward pauses and one-word answers. I could tell Martha thought I was brushing her off, but I wasn't. I was genuinely interested. Determined to fix things, I showed up at her shop the next day with a bouquet of flowers. She smiled shyly but warmly. Now, I just had to figure out how to extricate myself from Adriana.

My next leave to Bogotá brought things to a head. When I arrived at Adriana's flat, I noticed Catalina was absent, which should have been a relief. But sitting at the dining table, looking far too comfortable, was a younger, good-looking man. He greeted me casually, introducing himself with only his first name, before returning to his meal. When I asked if he was a brother or cousin, Adriana nonchalantly replied, "No, just a friend."

That was the final straw. I calmly went into the bedroom, packed my two suitcases, and called Pedro to come pick me up. He tried to convince me to stay at a hotel, but when he arrived, he insisted I stay at his place—well, technically, his mother's house. In Colombia, it wasn't unusual for men in their 30s to still live with their parents.

Pedro had closed the bakery by then. The prison contract had been a financial disaster, with delayed payments leaving him unable to keep the business afloat. Now unemployed,

Pedro spent his days at home. Despite his own troubles, he welcomed me with open arms, making it clear that his family's home was my refuge.

Living at Pedro's wasn't glamorous, he lived in a working-class area of Bogota, to the south of the city, another one with a date for a name, 2oth of July in this case. I was awoken each day to the sound of a cockerel calling at 5am, but it was exactly what I needed—a fresh start and a chance to sort out my next steps. The chapter with Adriana was officially closed, and a new one with Martha was just beginning, hopefully.

Living at Pedro's may not have been luxurious, but it gave me the reset I needed. With Adriana firmly in the rearview mirror, I started to focus on getting my life back in order. Martha and I were taking things slow, and I was beginning to feel that this fresh chapter might hold something meaningful. But first, I needed a place to call my own.

Ruben, ever the fixer, came through for me. He had a house his family hadn't lived in since they'd upgraded to a much larger place. The location was ideal—a residential area in the heart of Bogotá, close to a park and sports center and just a few blocks from the Autopista Sur, one of the city's main arteries. It felt like the kind of place where I could carve out a semblance of normalcy.

The house itself, however, was a bit unconventional. The front portion was a single floor that led to an open-air patio. Beyond the patio, the rest of the house stretched upward with three floors connected by a narrow, circular staircase. The main bedroom, situated at the back of the patio, felt like an entirely separate house—it was large and private, a perfect retreat. Above that were two smaller bedrooms, and the top floor housed what could only be described as a mini-apartment, complete with a small kitchenette. It was perfect for the new arrangement I had in mind: Pedro would live in the mini-apartment and work as my bodyguard, driver, and all-around helper.

Pedro quickly proved his worth. For instance, when I went into a store to buy a desk, the salesperson would take one look at me and quote an absurdly inflated price—the gringo tax, as I'd come to call it. I would thank them politely and leave, only for Pedro to return later and buy the same item for a fraction of the price. He saved me so much money that he essentially earned his modest salary (plus room and board) several times over.

Pedro's knack for negotiation also came in handy when I decided to buy a car. I didn't want anything flashy or new—just something functional and inconspicuous. With Bogotá's chaotic traffic and a high likelihood of fender benders, I needed a vehicle I wouldn't cry over if it got dinged. Pedro found me a Renault 18 Break, an older but well-maintained station wagon. It was spacious, practical, and cheap—exactly what I needed. The car wasn't glamorous, but it got the job done, whether I was hauling furniture for the new house or groceries for the week.

Moving into the unfurnished house was both exciting and daunting. Furnishing it from scratch on a tight budget was no small feat, but Pedro's resourcefulness turned the process into a manageable challenge. From bedding to kitchen essentials, he knew where to find the best deals, ensuring I stayed within my modest budget.

The house began to feel like a home, albeit a work in progress. I didn't have much time to enjoy it, though, as I had to head back to work shortly after moving in. On my next leave, however, I had a far more significant journey planned—I was flying to the UK to visit my newly reconnected dad. The thought of seeing him after so many years filled me with a mix of anticipation and nervousness. It was a trip that felt both overdue and surreal, a bridge between my past and the unpredictable life I'd built in Colombia.

Pedro had recently added a new tool to his arsenal—a 1911 Colt .45, a veritable "cannon" by most standards. As a civilian now, he couldn't get a 9mm, but oddly enough, a .45 was perfectly fine. Colombian gun laws had their peculiarities, and this was one of them. Pedro was left-handed, and his shoulder holster caused the hefty weapon to push awkwardly against his arm, making it stick out slightly. The sight was far from subtle, but perhaps that was for the best. The sheer size of the firearm, visible even through his jacket, sent a clear message: don't mess with him.

Despite the theatrics of Pedro's cannon, we rarely had to rely on it—or my Glock, for that matter. However, there was one memorable day when the sight of both weapons proved useful. I was driving us home, with Pedro in the passenger seat. We had turned off the main road and found ourselves on a narrow, battered street crawling behind a beat-up bus and a taxi. As the car dipped into yet another pothole, practically coming to a stop, a rough-looking man approached my side of the car. He tapped on my window, and when I glanced over, he opened his tattered jacket to reveal the butt of a revolver tucked into his waistband.

I'd learned enough about Colombian street theater by now to read between the lines. If he truly had a working gun, he would have pulled it out and shown the whole thing, not just the handle. Flashing the butt of a revolver likely meant it wasn't operational—or worse, it wasn't even a full firearm, just a bluff to intimidate someone like me. Still, I wasn't about to take any chances. Smiling faintly, I opened my jacket to reveal my Glock, now tucked at my waist for ease of access while driving. Pedro, ever the dramatic one, let out a grimace, adjusted himself, and opened his jacket as well, exposing his oversized Colt .45. The man's face turned ashen. He took a step back, then another, and before I knew it, he vanished as quickly as he'd appeared. Pedro and I exchanged a knowing look before continuing down the road.

Living in Colombia demanded a constant awareness of your surroundings and some creative security measures. For example, whenever I withdrew cash from an ATM, I immediately stuffed the notes down the front of my trousers. I figured that no mugger would have the nerve to search there. My wallet only carried the bare minimum—just enough cash for immediate needs, plus some expired cards. I even carried a fake wallet with a few outdated credit cards and a small amount of cash, around 7 dollars, as a decoy in case of a robbery. It was a minor inconvenience I was prepared to lose.

Not all encounters required firearms or elaborate precautions, though. Once, while walking along a relatively quiet sidewalk, a young man dashed past me and snatched my cap—a cherished Fleet Air Arm cap from my time in the Navy, and one not easily replaced. Instinctively, my reflexes kicked in. As he grabbed the cap, I seized his wrist and kicked his legs out from under him. He tumbled to the ground, still clutching the cap, but I maintained my grip on his wrist and wrestled the cap free. Realizing he'd lost his prize, the would-be thief turned to me with an incredulous grin and, to my utter disbelief, asked if I could spare some change. I shook my head, gave him a light nudge with my foot—not hard, just enough to remind him who was in charge—and continued on my way, cap firmly back on my head.

These incidents were a reminder of the unpredictability of life in Colombia, but also of the resilience and adaptability I'd developed since moving here. Each day brought its own challenges, but I was learning to navigate them with a mix of caution, humour, and the occasional firm hand.

Chapter 6: Homecoming

On my next long leave, I made the journey back to the UK. Flying out of Bogotá to Amsterdam on KLM—my old airline—felt surreal. It was strange to be a passenger on a route I'd once worked. From Amsterdam, I could only secure a flight to Liverpool, not Manchester, which meant my dad had to drive a bit further to pick me up.

When I landed at Liverpool's Speke Airport, the smallness of the terminal struck me. It felt like stepping back in time. At immigration, there was just one officer behind a podium, and as I handed over my passport, I saw my dad waiting in the terminal beyond. I did a double take. The man I saw was not the robust, larger-than-life figure I remembered. His hair had turned completely white, and his posture was hunched. His face was pale, and he looked frail, every bit of his 63 years—and then some. It was like seeing a shadow of the man he used to be.

As I walked through, we locked eyes. There was a moment of hesitation as we both took in the changes in each other, but then he broke into a smile. We hugged—longer than I can ever remember us doing before. My dad wasn't one for big shows of affection, so this gesture spoke volumes. It felt like a bridge being built between us, repairing years of distance.

Once the bags were in his car—an almost new Ford Escort—he suggested I drive. I learned the car had been given to him for free by the government as part of his disability benefits. Ever the schemer, my dad had apparently faked a heart attack to escape a terrible job and managed to qualify for a disability pension. "Working the system," he called it with a wink.

Driving down the motorway felt like a dream. After the chaos of Colombian roads, this was a revelation. No potholes, no erratic motorbikes weaving in and out—just smooth tarmac and orderly drivers. The car almost drove itself, compared to the constant vigilance required back in Bogotá. I found myself relaxing behind the wheel, something I hadn't done in years.

Dad directed me to the small Yorkshire town of Batley, winding through narrow streets until we reached his house. It was a typical working-class terraced house, with a tiny patch of garden at the front. Inside, it was clear the place hadn't been touched since Mum's passing over a year ago. The air felt heavy, like the house itself had stopped moving forward. Dust covered every surface, and the once cozy interior was now tired and grimy. My dad confessed he hadn't cleaned since she died.

The next few days were spent giving the house a much-needed overhaul. It was no small task. Dust and grime had accumulated to a level his ancient vacuum cleaner couldn't handle. I ended up scrubbing every inch of the place, hauling out old furniture, and cleaning behind items that clearly hadn't been moved in decades. In the bedroom, I discovered my mum's clothes still hanging in the wardrobe, untouched.

It took eight large bin bags to clear them out, and I loaded them into the Escort. Dad didn't argue when I suggested donating them, so we took them to a local hospice shop in Huddersfield. I think he felt relieved seeing them go—an unspoken step in letting go.

The real challenge came when I tackled the spare room and cellar. These were crammed full of boxes and bags of random items my parents had accumulated over years of doing flea markets and collectors' fairs. Net curtains, porcelain figurines, household knickknacks—it was a hoarder's paradise. To me, it looked like junk, but Dad insisted it was worth something. So, we made a plan to sell the lot.

Over the next couple of weeks, we hit every flea market and car boot sale we could find. My strategy was simple: sell everything at rock-bottom prices to get rid of it. Dad struggled with this at first, arguing that certain items were worth much more. I had to send him off for a walk while I manned the table, selling pieces for pennies on the pound. By the time he returned, the cash box was full, and the clutter was gone. That seemed to ease his objections.

One collectors' fair turned out to be particularly lucrative. We sold porcelain figures, including a few that had belonged to Mum, and walked away with nearly £2,000. Dad's eyes widened when he saw the money. "You're a natural born salesman," he said, half-joking.

The last haul was the net curtains. At an indoor market, we were approached by a man who owned a curtain shop. He wasn't happy about how cheaply we were selling. "You're ruining my business," he complained. I struck a deal with him: he could buy the entire stock, along with the table and tablecloth. We drove home with an empty car and a full cashbox.

The selling spree continued for a week, and by the end of it, we had cleared out nearly everything. Dad, who had always insisted this so-called "crap" was worth money, was now vindicated—but even he was surprised by how much we'd made. Over the course of just a few markets and fairs, we had turned all the clutter into over £5,000.

The transformation was almost magical—what had once been dusty, forgotten boxes crammed into every corner of the house was now a small fortune in cash. Dad couldn't stop grinning, counting the money over and over as if it might disappear. For someone who had been scraping by on his disability pension, this was a huge windfall. "See?" he said, with a triumphant look. "I told you it was worth something!"

I couldn't help but laugh. It had been hard work, but watching his joy made it worthwhile and I could see the relief and pride in his face. It was like a weight had been lifted, and for a brief moment, life seemed lighter.

For Dad, this was a windfall. Living on his modest disability pension, he was used to budgeting down to the penny. He kept coins piled up on the mantlepiece, each stack allocated to bills: gas, electric, food, and, of course, beer. His social life consisted of two visits a week to the local working men's club, where his budget allowed him exactly four beers per visit.

To celebrate his newfound wealth, we headed to the club—but this time, I was paying. Seeing him enjoy himself, laughing and telling stories over a pint, was worth every penny. For the first time in a long time, he seemed genuinely happy, and I felt like I'd helped give him a fresh start.

The working men's club, nestled in an old brick house just a short walk away, was a quintessential relic of another era. As we approached, Philip insisted we walk, grinning mischievously, "No point risking the car; we're getting plastered tonight." The club's name felt ironic to me, given that nearly all the members were retired or unemployed. As Philip signed me in with a flourish, I noted the average age of the crowd—it had to be pushing 60, if not older.

Stepping into the bar, I felt like I had entered another world. The place was alive with chatter, laughter, and the smell of beer-soaked wood. Philip, energized in a way I hadn't seen in years, immediately began introducing me to everyone. "This is my lad, Stephen, back from Colombia!" he announced proudly, buying drinks for anyone who would listen. I watched as he brandished his newly earned cash with the kind of delight that only came from years of scraping by. He paid for the rounds with a theatrical flourish, his pockets lined with the small fortune we had made selling his "crap."

As I settled into conversation with his friends, I quickly realized I was a curiosity. They leaned in, their weathered faces etched with scepticism, as I spoke about my work in Colombia. When I mentioned helicopters, aerial eradication, and the drug war, their expressions turned from interest to outright disbelief. One man, nursing a pint and leaning heavily on the bar, chuckled and muttered to Philip, "Your son's a right Walter Mitty, eh?"

Philip laughed heartily, slapping the man on the back. "No, mate. He's telling the truth. You wouldn't believe half of what he's done!" But the scepticism persisted. In Batley, great adventures happened on TV or in novels, not in real life. The most excitement anyone around here had seen was a factory supervisor retiring with a gold watch from Fox's Biscuits. The idea that someone from their town was out there fighting a literal drug war seemed too fantastical.

When I casually spoke a few sentences in Spanish, their response was even more incredulous. "That could be anything!" one of them snorted. They couldn't fathom why anyone would learn a foreign language, let alone speak it fluently. The strong Yorkshire accents made me smile—though I had been born just a few miles away, my years abroad had softened my own accent, and they immediately teased me for sounding "posh." "Southern bastard," one man quipped. I laughed, correcting him, "I was born right near here in Huddersfield, mate." That earned me a grudging nod of approval, although I don't think he even believed that.

Amid the ribbing, I noticed two women taking a keen interest in Philip. They fluttered around him, chatting and giggling like schoolgirls. "You've still got it, Dad," I teased later, but he waved it off. "Fuck off," he muttered. "She's a fuckin' old bird." Despite his protests, I could tell he was enjoying the attention.

While in Batley, I was determined to maintain my Spanish. I signed up for an advanced class at a college in Huddersfield, my birthplace. Initially, I tried a local school, but during the first session, the instructor confidently taught that the word for "to drive" was *dibujar*—which actually meant "to draw." That was enough to send me looking for something more credible.

The advanced class was no better. The students, mostly in their twenties and thirties, had been studying for three years but spoke slowly, haltingly, and with constant mistakes. When it came to my turn, I rattled off a passage in fluent Spanish, my Colombian accent drawing puzzled looks. During the break, I tried conversing with them in Spanish, only to be met with blank stares. Realizing I was wasting my time, I didn't return after the second class.

As my time with Dad wound down, we spent our evenings talking late into the night. He shared stories of his younger days, and I told him about life in Colombia. When I suggested he move out there with me, his initial reaction was pure shock. "What, leave Batley? Fuck off," he said, leaning back in his chair with a smirk. Swearing had become second nature to him since Mum had passed; the absence of her disapproving glances seemed to have liberated him to use the F-word at every opportunity. It punctuated nearly every sentence he spoke now, almost like a verbal tic.

But as I painted the picture—warm weather, a large house with a patio, friendly locals, and the allure of being an exotic Englishman in a country where age didn't matter as much—he began to waver. "You're telling me I could pull a fit 40-year-old?" he asked, his eyes lighting up. "Absolutely," I replied, holding back laughter. "And you'd have a driver and bodyguard too."

Slowly, the idea began to take root. His life in Batley was a shadow of what it once was, and I could see he was lonely. The memories of Mum lingered in every corner of the house. Moving to Colombia offered a fresh start, a new chapter filled with possibility. By the end of the week, Philip had made up his mind. "Fuckin' hell, all right," he said, grinning like a man with a secret. "Let's fuckin' do it."

I arrived back in Bogotá with a suitcase bursting with gifts for Martha. She had never asked for anything, which was a stark contrast to Adriana, and I wanted to show her how much I appreciated her. Among the treasures were a cuddly bear dressed as a pilot, an ornate bracelet with sapphires and emeralds, a Shakira CD—my growing appreciation for Latin music was starting to take root—and a handful of other trinkets. Martha was a hardworking shop assistant earning a meager wage, and she deserved to be spoiled a little. Besides, her job wasn't just underpaid; it came with the risk of having to reimburse the store for stolen goods, which made her already challenging days even tougher.

I'd heard one story from her that both amazed and terrified me. One afternoon, she noticed a man stuffing a tracksuit under his jacket and hastily walking out of the store. Without hesitation, Martha dashed out from behind the counter and into the street after him. She spotted him boarding a bus just as it was pulling away. Most people might have let it go at that point, but not Martha. She ran straight to a nearby Police Kiosk, flagged down an officer on a motorbike, and explained the situation. The officer, who casually slung a mini Uzi over his shoulder, waved her onto the back of the bike. Together, they sped off after the bus, weaving through Bogotá's chaotic traffic until they managed to get in front of it and force it to stop.

The cop and Martha climbed aboard, and Martha immediately pointed out the thief. The man, feigning innocence, claimed he didn't have anything. Martha wasn't having any of it. She demanded he open his jacket, and sure enough, there was the tracksuit, still in its shop wrapping. The officer hauled the man off the bus, and Martha returned to work after filing a report, tracksuit in hand. It was just one example of her fierce determination, and it made me admire her even more.

On the following Sunday, the only day she didn't work, Martha and I decided to spend the day at the water park. I loved swimming—always had—and the idea of splashing around in pools and enjoying water slides sounded like the perfect break from our busy lives. Martha, on the other hand, admitted she wasn't just a bad swimmer—she was a non-swimmer. I wasn't deterred; I figured she'd stick to the shallows, dip her toes in, and enjoy herself anyway. The water park was impressive, housed in a massive building that felt like a tropical paradise tucked inside a concrete shell. There were multiple pools of varying sizes, two giant water slides twisting like orange serpents, and even a sprawling artificial beach complete with a wave machine. The sound of water splashing, kids screaming in delight, and laughter echoing off the walls set the tone for the day.

We started off simple. I coaxed Martha into the shallow end of one of the pools, where the water barely came up to her waist. She clung to the edge, cautiously stepping forward as I swam a few gentle strokes nearby, showing her it wasn't so bad. "See? Easy," I teased. She splashed me playfully, but I could tell she wasn't ready to venture deeper. That was fine—at least she was in the water.

Then, I spotted *it*: the towering water slide. It was at least four or five stories high, an orange tube spiraling down to a plunge pool below. "We *have* to do that," I said, grinning like a kid. Martha eyed it warily. "You go first," she said, hesitating. I nodded, undeterred.

We climbed the endless flights of stairs, Martha grumbling under her breath as young kids sprinted past us, giggling and dripping with water. At the top, I surveyed the scene—the long line of boys, the slick entry into the rushing water of the tube—and turned back to Martha. "Ready?" She shook her head but gave me a nervous smile.

"See you at the bottom!" I called, throwing myself feet-first into the tube.

The water pushed me violently, swirling and slamming me around each bend at what felt like breakneck speed. Parts of the tube were open to the air, and for a fleeting moment, I swore I might fly out altogether. The sensation was pure exhilaration—a feetfirst plunge into chaos. The kids did it headfirst, but I wasn't up for that, yet. Before I knew it, I shot out of the tube like a torpedo, splashing into the pool below. I surfaced, laughing, and waded through the three feet of water to stand near the exit, waiting for Martha to follow.

Seconds later, I heard a high-pitched scream echo down the tube. I turned with a grin, ready to catch her. But instead of Martha, a small boy shot out like a rocket, landing with a splash and blinking up at me in confusion. "What the...?" I mumbled, realizing Martha must have let him go ahead. I looked up toward the top of the slide. Sure enough, she was still standing there, peering nervously down the pipe.

Another shriek. Another splash. Another kid.

By now, I was laughing so hard I could barely stand. I waved at her from below, motioning for her to come down. Finally, Martha shook her head vigorously and started walking back down the stairs, wagging her finger at me as if to say, "Absolutely not."

After the slide fiasco, we made our way to the imitation beach. The water was shallow at first, with a soft sandy bottom leading into the deeper section. Martha was content to stand near the shoreline, dipping her toes into the gentle lapping waves, while I ventured further out. Then, the wave machine kicked on.

I felt a surge of excitement as the first wave rolled toward me, lifting me up and crashing over my head. I dove into the next one, relishing the force of the water, the way it tossed me around like I was weightless. For me, this was bliss.

I surfaced, shaking the water from my hair, and scanned the area for Martha. She'd been right near the edge a moment ago. Then I heard it—

"Steeeeeveeeeeeen!"

The scream cut through the noise of the waves, high-pitched and panicked. I spun around to see Martha clinging to the edge of the pool for dear life. The waves were lifting her up with every swell, dragging her downward as they crashed onto the fake beach. Her face was a mix of fear and exasperation, her knuckles white from gripping the ledge.

"Stev—*eeeeeeen!*" The upward rise elongated the first half of my name, while the downward crash stretched the second into a desperate wail.

It was a ridiculous sight—almost cartoonish—but I knew she wasn't enjoying herself. I swam toward her, fighting the pull of the waves, and reached her side. "Let go!" I shouted over the roar of the water. "I'll guide you out!"

"No!" she yelped.

"Yes! Trust me!"

Reluctantly, she released her death grip on the edge, and I grabbed her hand, pulling her gently toward the shore. I stayed close, keeping her steady as the waves tried to sweep her away again. When we finally reached the shallows, she stood dripping and panting, glaring at the water as if it had personally insulted her.

"That was awful!" she declared, brushing wet hair out of her face.

"You weren't in danger," I reassured her, trying to hold back a smile.

"I felt like I was going to die!"

I couldn't help but laugh, which earned me another glare. "Okay, okay," I said, raising my hands in surrender. "No more waves. I promise."

We sat on the edge of the fake beach for a while, her hand tucked in mine, watching kids and couples dive into the waves I had so thoroughly enjoyed. "It's a pity you don't love the water as much as I do," I said softly.

She glanced up at me with a smile that was all warmth and love. "I might not love the sea, but I love *you*."

That was all I needed to hear. I may have loved the water, but Martha had always been my anchor, steady and unwavering no matter how rough the waves got. I wrapped an arm around her and kissed her damp hair, silently vowing to leave the wave pools behind—at least for her sake.

A few weeks after my return, I was back on leave in Bogotá, eagerly preparing for Dad's arrival. He'd bought his own ticket, determined to find the cheapest option, which meant a marathon journey: Manchester to Amsterdam, Amsterdam to Toronto, Toronto to Miami, and finally, Miami to Bogotá. It took him nearly a day and a half to make the trip, all in economy class, but he arrived at El Dorado airport safe and sound, albeit exhausted.

When he emerged from the final security checks, he waved his hands in the air like a triumphant conqueror, a broad grin lighting up his face. Despite the long journey, his spirits were high. Pedro was with me, and I made the introductions. "Pedro, this is my dad, Philip."

Pedro, ever respectful, greeted him with a deferential "Hello, Don Felipe."

Dad's face lit up even more at the title. "Don Felipe?" he repeated, savouring the sound of it. "Fuckin? hell, I sound like a fuckin' mafia boss!" He laughed heartily, clearly relishing his new moniker. I also knew I would have to work on his "colourful" language, at least until I could get him to speak Spanish and I wouldn't teach him the swearwords.

I decided to tackle one of Philip's more colourful habits—his relentless use of swear words, particularly his tendency to "fuckin'" his way through nearly every sentence. It wasn't that I didn't enjoy his sharp humour or the wit that often accompanied his expletives; it was more that I feared his vibrant language might not go over so well in polite Colombian society.

One evening, as we sat in the living room with cups of tea—Philip insisted on tea, no matter how hard I tried to sway him toward Colombian coffee—I broached the subject.

"Dad," I started carefully, "you might want to tone down the swearing a bit."

He frowned, genuinely puzzled. "I don't fuckin' swear that fuckin' much."

"You're doing it now," I said, raising an eyebrow.

"No, I'm fuckin' not. Oh, wait, I fuckin' well am. For fuck's sake!"

I couldn't help but burst out laughing at the absurdity of it. "See what I mean? It's like you don't even realize you're doing it."

Philip scratched his head, clearly trying to process the idea. "Maybe it's 'cause your mum's not here anymore," he mused after a pause. "She'd never let me fuckin' swear. Every time I so much as said 'fuck,' she'd give me a clip round the ear."

That made sense. Mum had always been the disciplinarian in their marriage, the one to rein in Philip's wilder tendencies. With her gone, it was as if he'd been let off a leash, and now the words flowed freely, unchecked. It wasn't malicious or vulgar in intent; it was just... Philip.

"I get it," I said gently. "But maybe try cutting back a little? You don't want to shock everyone here."

He shrugged. "I'll fuckin' try, but don't expect fuckin' miracles. I'm too fuckin' old to stop now."

True to his word, Philip did make an effort. Over time, the constant string of expletives began to diminish. He'd catch himself mid-sentence, muttering something like, "Oh, fuck, there I go again," which was its own sort of progress. But it was clear that eradicating the habit completely was a lost cause, and honestly, I wasn't sure I wanted him to. His swearing was part of his charm, a reflection of his unfiltered personality and the life he'd lived.

By the end of it, he was swearing less, but the occasional outburst still slipped through, especially when he was caught off guard or particularly excited about something. It was Philip in a nutshell—rough around the edges, unapologetically himself, and utterly endearing.

Philip hadn't come empty-handed. In typical Dad fashion, he'd gone all out. Before leaving the UK, he'd accepted a credit card offer from his bank that he'd previously ignored, securing a £5,000 credit limit. Now, he was determined to spend every penny of it, and over the following days, he threw himself into the task with gusto.

He bought furniture, bedding, kitchen supplies, and anything else he thought the house needed. Being a baker and a cook for most of his life, he took particular pleasure in equipping the kitchen. He even splurged on ingredients to whip up spectacular meals and desserts. Cooking was one of Dad's great joys, and it showed. Within days, he was turning out elaborate dishes and cakes that could have rivalled anything from a professional bakery.

One evening, as we sat down to a meal he had prepared, I couldn't help but recall the wedding cake he'd made for my ill-fated marriage to Karen. It had been a masterpiece, layered and decorated with incredible precision with what looked like an outpouring of delicate flowers, except these were edible. The marriage, on the other hand, had lasted a grand total of two years and nine months, including six months of separation. I couldn't help but chuckle at the irony of that memory while biting into one of Dad's creations.

Having him in Bogotá felt surreal but wonderful. His energy, humour, and endless swearing filled the house with life. Watching him adapt to Colombia, I realized just how much I'd missed this side of him. Don Felipe, indeed.

Philip was absolutely thrilled with the house. He claimed the ground-floor bedroom, which came with a small toilet and sink, though it lacked a shower. He used the one in my bathroom across the indoor patio, which suited him just fine. With his newly outfitted kitchen, he was in his element, cooking up elaborate meals that would have impressed even the toughest critics. To make the most of his culinary enthusiasm, I started inviting Martha over for dinner nearly every night after her shift at the store.

Martha didn't drive, so she'd take the bus, which often meant an hour-long journey to reach us. After dinner, I'd arrange for a taxi to take her home to Soacha, a city just outside

Bogotá. The trip was about 45 minutes by car, but taxis were cheap, costing just a couple of dollars—a small price for her comfort and safety. I offered to drive her, but it would take me about 2 hours there and back and meant me driving back quite late in poorly lit streets, she insisted she would be fine in a taxi. Philip adored Martha, and they got along wonderfully, though he struggled with her name. In Spanish, Martha is pronounced "Mar-ta," with a silent "h," but for reasons unknown, Philip insisted on calling her "Mat-ra." Martha took this in stride, laughing at his repeated mispronunciations.

One evening, as he watched the two of us together, Philip mused, "I wish I had my own Matra." And so, the matchmaking began.

This was the mid-90s, long before the advent of online dating, so we resorted to the old-fashioned way: placing a lonely hearts ad in the local newspaper. We described Philip as a "Mature English Gentleman," exercising some creative license, and stated that he was looking for someone lively between the ages of 40 and 50. To my surprise, the responses poured in—letters sent to the newspaper for us to collect. Each contained basic details with their likes, eating out, travel, long romantic walks etc, the usual, I thought, and phone numbers.

Philip sifted through them, narrowing the pile to five prospects. Then, the next task fell to me: calling on his behalf. None of the women were guaranteed to speak English, so I had to handle the initial conversations. "You can't be my son," Philip instructed, "they'll think I'm old" which was met with a sharp look from me, "you are old". "Fuck off," he contested, "I'm your younger brother. Tell them I'm fuckin' 49."

With his newly dyed light-blond hair, Philip looked a little less his age, maybe not 49 but not too bad. Martha, who found the entire situation hilarious, sat beside me as I made the calls. The women were polite, and some even flirted with me outright. When I explained that I was calling for my "brother," a few chuckled in disbelief, teasing me for being shy. "it's for you really isn't it?" when the conversation got a little "warmer" I got a dig in the ribs and a glare from Martha.

Philip managed to secure five coffee dates, all scheduled at nice cafés in upscale shopping malls. Since his Spanish was non-existent, I had to accompany him as a translator, creating some truly bizarre scenarios. Conversations ping-ponged awkwardly: the women spoke to me, I translated for Philip, and he replied, often with his signature swearing edited out. More than once, I accidentally spoke Spanish to Philip, earning only confused looks, followed by laughter from all three of us.

While the dates were pleasant enough, none clicked. The women were charming and reasonably attractive, but they didn't match Philip's personality. Most were too mature, bookish, or reserved, likely drawn to the idea of an "English Gentleman." What Philip truly wanted, though, was an "English Rogue."

After one of these mismatched dates, Philip and I found ourselves wandering the aisles of Éxito, the massive supermarket chain that was as much a symbol of Colombian modernity as it was a magnet for whispers about its murky origins. Stories about Éxito's potential links to drug money during its early days swirled like urban legends. While allegations against the influential Gaviria family, who had spearheaded the chain's growth, made the rounds, no concrete evidence ever emerged. Still, in a country where the shadow of the drug trade touched everything, such suspicions clung stubbornly to success stories.

Philip, however, was uninterested in the chain's questionable history. He had other things on his mind as we perused the neatly stocked shelves. Out of nowhere, he began speaking loudly in an exaggerated, almost theatrical voice.

"What are you doing?" I asked, stopping in my tracks and narrowing my eyes at him.

"I'm making sure everyone knows we're English!" he declared, his tone making it clear he thought this was a stroke of genius.

I sighed, rolling my eyes but unwilling to argue. Philip, oblivious to my exasperation, continued his performance. The melodic tones of his Yorkshire accent carried across the aisles, a stark contrast to the hushed murmur of Spanish around us.

In Colombia, hearing someone speak English was rare enough to turn heads. And while most locals might automatically assume any English speaker was American—a "gringo"—Philip's clipped British vowels and colorful delivery were unmistakably different.

Sure enough, his antics had the desired effect. Female employees began peeking curiously around the shelves, their faces lighting up with smiles as they caught sight of the source of this loud foreign voice. Philip, dressed in his signature light blue suit and his ever-present Panama hat, looked every inch the "Don Felipe" he aspired to be. He basked in the attention, standing a little taller and tilting his hat just so, projecting an air of colonial-era charm.

I couldn't help but chuckle despite myself. This was one of the quirks of Colombia—someone like Philip, a man from a modest northern English town, was suddenly perceived as exotic, intriguing, *somebody*. And Philip, never one to shy away from an opportunity, seized it with both hands. Here, he was not just a retiree or an aging romantic; he was a character, a persona, a living novelty.

Watching him revel in this newfound identity, I thought about how much he seemed to thrive in this setting. Colombia, with its open warmth and sense of possibility, had given Philip a stage. And he intended to live it up, playing the role of the quintessential English rogue to perfection.

Philip needed to return to the UK every three months to collect his pension checks, a bureaucratic hassle that barely justified the cost of the flight. He insisted it was about principle—he had earned that money, and he wasn't about to let it go unclaimed. The trips weren't entirely unwelcome, though, as they gave him a chance to visit old haunts and catch up with his few remaining friends in Batley.

After one such trip, we decided to throw him a surprise welcome-home party. The guest list was small but lively, consisting mostly of Pedro's family, Martha, and a few of my friends. We even had a banner strung across the living room that read *Bienvenido a Casa Don Felipe!* Everyone huddled in the darkened house, waiting for the grand reveal.

I went to the airport with Martha to pick him up, leaving Pedro behind to coordinate the guests. As Philip came through the arrivals gate, his first question was, "Where's Pedro?" Pedro had become something of a personal bodyguard for Philip, and their bond was clear. "He's not feeling well," I replied, watching his face drop slightly in disappointment.

We pulled up to the house around 9 p.m., and I made a show of unloading the car, slamming the doors and fiddling with the luggage to give the partygoers a cue. "Get the door, Dad," I said, gesturing toward the house. As he stepped inside, the lights snapped on, and twenty voices yelled, "¡Bienvenido a Casa!" and "Welcome Home!"

Philip froze, his eyes wide with surprise, and then broke into a grin that could have lit up the room on its own. He threw his arms into the air and shouted, "Well, I'll be damned!" He took a moment to take it all in—the colorful banner, the beaming faces of friends both new and old, and the table laden with Colombian dishes and bottles of aguardiente.

As he went around shaking hands and giving hugs, I mentioned casually, "Oh, by the way, one of the women from the newspaper ad decided to meet you after all."

That was when things went off the rails.

Philip turned to the next woman in line—a striking, dark-haired beauty—and with a mischievous grin, he swept her into his arms, bent her back like a scene from an old Hollywood film, and planted a long, theatrical kiss on her lips. It was a kiss with such gusto that the entire room erupted into laughter and gasps.

It wasn't until I felt a tap on my shoulder that I realized something was amiss. Pedro's brother stood behind me, looking equal parts amused and concerned. "Uh, that's my wife," he whispered.

"Oh, crap! Dad, let her go—that's not her!" I blurted out, waving my hands like an air traffic controller.

Philip pulled back immediately, a sheepish grin spreading across his face as if nothing out of the ordinary had happened. To my relief, both the woman and her husband laughed it off, much to the delight of the crowd, who clearly enjoyed the spectacle.

When Philip finally met the intended woman from the ad, he was the picture of decorum, bowing slightly and kissing her hand like a true gentleman. However, their connection was lukewarm at best, and by the end of the evening, it was clear there wasn't going to be a second meeting.

Despite the mix-up, the party was a roaring success. Philip was in his element, swapping stories, raising toasts, and revelling in the attention. By the time the last guest had left, he leaned back in his chair with a satisfied sigh and declared, "I don't need to go back to fuckin' Batley. This—this feels like home." But he was still feeling like a third wheel he needed a girlfriend, and my way seemed not to be working.

Pedro came to the rescue once again. When I explained the situation, he jumped at the chance to help. Pedro was dating a woman named Marie—a no-nonsense type with a fit physique but not much warmth or beauty, and she sported a prominent moustache that was hard to ignore. However, Marie had a flatmate who, Pedro suggested, might be a good fit for Philip and she was "Hot" he said but I was sceptical, to say the least.

I wasn't overly optimistic. Based on Marie's demeanour, I expected her flatmate to be much the same—stoic and underwhelming. But Pedro was determined, and Philip, ever the optimist, decided it was worth a shot. With Pedro orchestrating the introduction, we waited to see what this new prospect might bring.

Pedro had arranged a double date, and the evening promised to be an event. I handed him the car keys, and he set off to pick up the ladies before returning to collect Philip. As the car pulled up outside, we lined up in anticipation—me in the centre, with Philip on one side and Martha, holding my arm protectively, on the other. Pedro stepped out first, followed by his girlfriend, Marie. Then, from the other side of the car, emerged Jacqueline.

Jacqueline was striking. She looked about 30, slightly taller than Martha at 5'3", with a slim yet curvaceous figure. She wore tight shorts and a fitted top that accentuated her ample cleavage, paired with high heels that showcased her shapely legs. Her blonde hair, though streaked with visible dark roots, framed her pretty face perfectly, and not a sign of a moustache like Marie. Philip's reaction was instant—his eyes lit up, and he elbowed me several times, whispering, "Fuckin' hell, look at that!" Martha noticed, smirking sardonically as she squeezed my arm possessively and leaned closer, silently staking her claim on me.

Philip, however, was already enchanted. He puffed out his chest, straightened his posture to its maximum, and beamed a broad, slightly goofy smile. He was smitten.

The four of them headed off to a nightclub, and though I was mildly concerned, I knew Pedro would ensure Philip's safety. They returned around 2:30 a.m.—Philip looking slightly drunk but happier than I had seen him in years.

The next morning, he recounted his adventures with the enthusiasm of a teenager. "It was fuckin' fantastic!" he said, grinning from ear to ear. He described dancing wildly under a foam fountain, even undoing his shirt as foam cascaded over him. He had bought roses for the ladies and begged Jacqueline—"Jacky," as he now called her—for more dances. At one point, when she refused and sat down to rest, Philip admitted he snuck behind a column to catch his breath, grateful for her break. He ended the night with what he called a "proper passionate kiss" goodbye, one that, to his delight, was returned. "I think I'm fuckin' in love," he declared with a sheepish grin.

Their romance blossomed quickly. Soon, Jacqueline was staying over at the house regularly. She told us she was 29 and had a four-year-old child, something Philip accepted without hesitation. On his next trip to the UK to collect his pension, he returned with a suitcase packed full of gifts—mostly for Jacqueline. Perfumes, jewellery, and even a teddy bear dressed as a pilot (identical to the one I'd bought for Martha) filled the house. His credit card limit, however, didn't stretch as far as his enthusiasm. He began maxing it out and continued spending freely, buying duty-free items on every leg of his convoluted flight routes, justifying it as "beating the system." But eventually, the card reached its limit. One day, while buying bedding at Homecenter, the manager was instructed by the bank to cut the card. Philip was devastated—no more "freebies," as he called them.

Meanwhile, my relationship with Martha was flourishing. She moved in while I was away at work, and I phoned Philip constantly to check on her arrival. The day he confirmed she had moved in, I felt over the moon. Martha was everything I had ever wanted—hardworking, lively, and full of warmth. At 26, she was younger than me by over a decade, but her maturity and grounded nature belied her age. Unlike my ex-wife, Martha was sweet as hell, easygoing and unassuming also very pretty and petit. She seemed perfectly content with quiet evenings at home, enjoying meals cooked by Philip or watching TV together. She was "the one," and I couldn't have been happier.

After just a few months of living together, I decided to propose. She said yes without hesitation, and we began planning the wedding. Initially, I thought getting married in Colombia would be straightforward, but bureaucracy proved otherwise—I needed several documents from the UK, and the process seemed overly complex. I suggested we marry in the UK instead. That way, we could obtain a visa for Martha and ensure the marriage certificate would be valid anywhere. She agreed, and so began the next chapter of our lives together.

I helped Martha complete the visa application forms and delivered everything to the British embassy, along with copies of all my required documents. However, a snag quickly emerged—because I was divorced and we were applying for a visa to get married, the embassy required a copy of my divorce certificate. Luckily, this coincided with one of Dad's trips back to the UK, so he was able to retrieve the necessary document for us. Once we handed that in, we awaited the next steps.

The embassy scheduled an interview, and we arrived promptly, though I wasn't allowed into the interview room. Martha was met by a dour-faced employee who, from what she later described, seemed more intent on intimidation than understanding. They asked her detailed questions about me, our relationship, and even my income. Martha explained that I worked for the Colombian government, but when they inquired about my income in the UK, she had no answers—because, of course, I didn't have any. The interview didn't go well, and being stuck outside, I couldn't intervene or clarify anything.

A week later, we received their decision: the visa was denied. To make matters worse, they also rejected her for a residency visa. This was absurd because we hadn't applied for residency in the first place. When I confronted them about the mix-up, they responded dismissively, saying, "Well, most people applying to marry want residency, so we assumed you did too." Assumed? It was clearly marked on the application that we were requesting only a tourist visa. I was furious, but arguing with bureaucracy proved futile.

Determined not to let this setback ruin our plans, I began considering alternatives. Then it hit me—Jamaica. I had flown there a few times during my KLM days and knew it was a popular destination for British couples seeking a picturesque and hassle-free wedding. As a former British colony, Jamaica's marriage certificates were valid in the UK. A bit of research confirmed that getting married there would be straightforward. I booked a civil marriage officer in Montego Bay to officiate the ceremony and began making arrangements.

The one challenge was obtaining visas for the women to travel. Fortunately, this was relatively easy. All that was required was a letter from me or Philip guaranteeing responsibility for their expenses, along with our passports and theirs. However, there was a slight hiccup—Jacqueline didn't have a passport. She applied immediately, and within a week, it was issued. Naturally, before handing it over to the Jamaican consulate, I took a look.

"Dad," I said, unable to hide my amusement, "do you know your girlfriend isn't 29? She's 34."

Philip shrugged, completely unbothered. "So what? She's still fuckin' 30 years younger than me." He had a point.

A week later, we had the visas in hand. I booked flights for all of us: Martha, Jacqueline, Dad, and me. It was now 1999, and in July, we would all fly to Montego Bay, Jamaica. Our unusual little family was going on a tropical adventure, and this time, the bureaucracy couldn't stand in our way.

We landed in Montego Bay after a somewhat convoluted journey: Bogotá to Panama, then onward with Copa Airlines to Kingston, and finally to Montego Bay. The moment we stepped out of the airport, the Caribbean heat hit us like a wall—summer in Jamaica was no joke. The air was thick and sweltering, and even Philip, who usually claimed not to mind the heat, muttered something about needing a drink as soon as possible.

We piled into a taxi that took us to the El Greco Resort, a charming little property perched on a hill about a block from the sea. The accommodations were beautiful—a whitewashed house that felt airy and bright, with an open-plan living room, dining area, and a small but functional kitchen downstairs. Upstairs, two spacious bedrooms awaited, each with tall windows letting in streams of sunlight. The furniture was a mix of bamboo and light-coloured wood, and the whole place had a fresh, breezy charm that made us feel like we were on a proper holiday.

As soon as we dropped our bags, I rushed off to meet the marriage officer at his office. I had arranged a 4:00 p.m. appointment to deliver our paperwork, and I arrived with five minutes to spare. The officer, a cheerful man with an easy demeanour, seemed genuinely impressed by my punctuality—a rarity in the relaxed rhythms of the island.

Over the next few days, we explored as much of Jamaica as we could. We visited Negril, with its famed seven-mile beach, where we lazed on the sand and dodged the constant offers of "Ganja." One particularly persistent vendor kept hovering around us until I jokingly said, "Hey, we're from Colombia. We can get a kilo of cocaine for about $1,500." His eyes lit up, and instead of backing off, he leaned in conspiratorially, asking, "Can you bring me a couple of kilos, man?" Needless to say, I laughed it off and walked away.

In Ocho Rios, the bustling port city that welcomed cruise ships daily, we found ourselves mingling with curious tourists. One particularly nosy man struck up a conversation, asking if we were enjoying our holiday. When I mentioned we were there for our honeymoon, he gave me a stunned look and said, "I thought she was your daughter!" Martha, clad in shorts, a T-shirt, and a floppy straw hat, did look much younger than her 26 years. Lifting her hat to reveal her elegant features, I replied, "Nope, she's my wife." That shut him up.

The persistent offers from taxi drivers and street vendors became something of a running joke. At one point, I joked about buying a T-shirt we saw everywhere, emblazoned with the words: "I don't want Ganja, I don't want a taxi, and I don't want a woman. What part of 'no' don't you understand?"

Jacqueline, always the instigator, would point to jewellery stores and teasingly ask Philip, "Shall we make it a double wedding?" His nervous laugh and quick dismissal made it clear he wasn't keen on the idea. Later, he confided in me that he could never remarry—Mum would always be his wife, no matter what.

The wedding itself was perfect in its simplicity. It took place in the gazebo of the marriage officer's home. I wore a suit far too thick for the weather and spent most of the ceremony sweating profusely. Martha, however, was breathtaking in her off-the-shoulder white dress, her long gloves, and a sparkling tiara that held her dark hair elegantly in place. Philip, in a light blue suit and Panama hat, looked every inch the mafia don, while Jacqueline wore a pale blue dress that matched her tan perfectly.

The ceremony proceeded smoothly, though I had to translate every word for Martha. We signed the documents with Philip and Jacqueline as our witnesses, took a few quick photos, and raced back to the house to change into cooler clothes. And just like that, we were married. It was simple, intimate, and absolutely perfect.

The rest of our stay was spent soaking up the sun, drinking Red Stripe beer, and swimming—or trying to. I was the only one in our group who could actually swim. Jacqueline's "swimming" consisted of waving her arms around while secretly walking on the pool's floor. One day, while the girls were splashing in the shallow end and I was preparing to dive in, Jacqueline waved to me. It took me a moment to realize that her bikini top had slipped, revealing far more than intended. I motioned for her to fix it, but she didn't seem to understand. Martha, however, caught on quickly and sharply told her to "put it back in." Martha was unimpressed and later muttered that Jacqueline was flirting with me.

By the time we left Jamaica, Philip was sunburned to a crisp and slathered in aloe vera, Jacqueline was regretting her braided hairstyle, and Martha and I were happier than ever. We arrived back in Bogotá tanned, tired, and officially husband and wife. It was a trip to remember, full of laughter, love, and the occasional hiccup—everything a wedding adventure should be.

Chapter 7: Going to prison

Despite my growing workload when away, my time off in Bogotá often felt like a slow march of boredom. I wasn't built to sit idle, and twiddling my thumbs only made me restless. I even pestered the airline for work during my leave, but the best they could offer was sporadic emergency replacement flights—usually for sick or vacationing pilots. These were rare and almost always on weekends, leaving the weekdays stretching endlessly ahead. By the time my next six-week leave rolled around, I was practically climbing the walls.

Determined to find something more meaningful, I walked into the operations office and asked the director if there was any work for me. To my astonishment, he immediately said, "Actually, yes. Can you teach?" Having taught math in the navy and English at the airfield, I was quick to agree. "What and where?" I asked. His response stunned me.

"La Modelo National Prison," he said, matter-of-factly.

I blinked, my mind racing to process what I'd just heard. This was no ordinary prison. La Modelo was infamous, one of the most dangerous facilities in the world, where paramilitaries, guerrillas, and common criminals were housed together in chaotic, overcrowded conditions. But I didn't want to appear rattled. "Sure," I said casually, even as I wondered if I'd lost my mind.

"They won't pay extra—you're already on the payroll," he added, as if that might be the dealbreaker. He had his secretary draft a short letter on Ministry of Justice letterhead, complete with official seals, instructing the prison director to welcome me. As I tucked the letter into my pocket, a thought flashed in my mind: How am I going to explain this to Martha?

Predictably, Martha thought I was insane. "You want to work in a prison? In La Modelo? Are you out of your mind?" she exclaimed. Her eyes widened with a mix of concern and exasperation. I tried to reassure her that I'd be in a controlled environment with armed guards and layers of security, but she remained unconvinced. Still, she reluctantly acquiesced, though her face betrayed her lingering doubts.

Monday morning, I set off for the prison, which turned out to be less than ten blocks from our house—a detail I conveniently hadn't mentioned to Martha.

La Modelo was an unimposing structure, its dirty white walls only about 3 metres high, topped with barbed wire and guard towers casting long shadows. I was ushered in to meet the director, Gustavo García, a civil servant who looked weary and overburdened by his responsibilities. His appearance was that of a man harried by the demands of his job, clearly overwhelmed by the pressures that came with his position. As he explained the myriad problems he had to tackle, it was evident that he was at the end of his rope, his demeanour almost warning, "this is what you are letting yourself in for."

He laid out the grim realities of the prison. "We have over 5,500 inmates in a facility designed for 2,000. Two guards for every thousand prisoners," he said, his tone blunt. "There's no classification system here. You'll find guerrillas, paramilitaries, kidnappers, rapists, and petty criminals all mixed together. We lose around 150 inmates a year to violence, and hundreds more are injured. You'll be taking a risk every time you step through these gates."

I nodded, determined to appear unfazed. But inside, a knot tightened in my stomach.

Next, I was introduced to a young INPEC lieutenant, the head of the prison guards. INPEC was the department of the MOJ dealing with the prisons, Instituto Nacional Penetenciario y Carcelario (National Institute for penitentiaries and prisons). A jail being for those not yet sentenced and a penitentiary being for those who are sentenced. His cheerful demeanour was a sharp contrast to the colonel's grimness. He seemed genuinely pleased to meet me, shaking my hand enthusiastically before leading me on a tour of the facility.

The entry process alone was an ordeal. I surrendered my ID, had my fingerprints taken, and passed through a metal detector before enduring a quick frisk. We walked down a narrow corridor with a thick security mesh separating us from the prisoners, who were lined up on the other side to speak with their attorneys through small holes in the wire.

At the end of the corridor, we passed through a fortified area with two massive sliding metal doors each with a small window in it. One led to the southern wing, controlled by paramilitaries, while the other opened to the northern wing, dominated by guerrilla factions. Between these areas was the "maximum security" block, reserved for the most dangerous inmates.

We continued through another passage that opened onto a courtyard. The central yard was dominated by a makeshift football pitch, bordered by the imposing outer wall, where guards patrolled the watchtowers with military rifles. Halfway down, we entered a room off to the side. This was the education department—a surprisingly well-maintained area with classrooms, a library, and two small offices.

I was introduced to Ramón, the head of education, a man who exuded calm in the midst of chaos. Ramón welcomed me warmly and explained the department's mission: to provide basic education and vocational training to inmates. "We try to keep them occupied," he said with a wry smile. "It's better than leaving them to their own devices."

I was shown my assigned classroom—a stark but functional space with rows of wooden desks and a battered chalkboard. The students, I learned, would be a mix of inmates from both factions. "And they'll all be armed with pencils, not knives," I joked internally.

I left the prison that day with a swirl of emotions. Excitement mingled with trepidation as I considered what lay ahead. One thing was certain: I had no intention of telling Martha just how dangerous this truly was.

The next day, I arrived bright and early at La Modelo, navigating the now-familiar security procedures with a brisk efficiency. The guards greeted me with casual nods, and I waited in the courtyard outside the education department for Ramón, the head of the program. It didn't take long to realize that Ramón's work ethic left much to be desired. He strolled in about an hour late, looking unbothered, jingling the keys to the department as if he were doing me a favour by showing up. Over the coming days, I noticed a pattern—Ramón consistently arrived late, took long lunches, and often left early. It was clear he wasn't overly invested in his role, but he had no one to hold him accountable.

I also met another teacher, Natali. She was a slight woman, about 45, with a nervous tic that caused her to blink hard several times every few seconds. It was almost hypnotic, and I found myself trying not to mimic her blinking during our conversations. Despite her nervous demeanour, she was friendly and helpful, giving me a rundown of the daily routine. She warned me that classes rarely started on time because of the morning headcount, a chaotic process that rarely tallied correctly.

"It's never accurate," she explained in a quiet voice. "Some escape, some are killed and... disappear." She left the rest to my imagination.

By the time the prisoners were finally allowed into the education block around 10 a.m., the day already felt half gone. They entered from two passageways—one leading from the south wing, where the paramilitaries were housed, and the other from the north, controlled by the guerrillas. An INPEC guard, barely 18 and armed with nothing but a flimsy baton, stood at the doorway while Ramón checked their names on a list. Each prisoner was frisked before entering, though the process seemed more ceremonial than effective.

In my classroom, I took roll call, ticking off names on a register. Attendance wasn't motivated by a thirst for knowledge but by the incentive of reduced sentences—two days of class equalled a one-day reduction. It didn't take long to figure out who was there for the discount versus those genuinely interested in learning.

The classroom was a motley mix of 64 inmates. Guerrilla fighters sat on one side, paramilitaries on the other, with unaligned criminals—murderers, thieves, and the like—in the middle. It was a tense but orderly setup, with each group maintaining a fragile peace.

Despite their rough appearances and colourful histories, the men were surprisingly well-behaved. I had expected chaos, but most were in their 30s and 40s and treated the class with a surprising level of respect. A few younger ones seemed eager to learn, though others stared blankly, clearly counting the minutes until they could leave.

I introduced myself, explaining my background and why I was there. The fact that I was British fascinated them, though it quickly became clear that many had no real concept of what that meant. Some thought England was part of the U.S., while one even asked what language we spoke there. When I replied, "English," he nodded knowingly and said, "Ah, like America." It wasn't a joke—he was entirely serious.

I started the lesson with some basic geography and history, weaving in English words and phrases as I went. Most of the class had limited formal education, and even simple concepts like world maps and historical timelines were new to them. I kept the English lessons rudimentary: letters, numbers, and the days of the week. We went around the room, each inmate reciting the next letter or number. Some refused outright, waving me off with a disinterested shrug a few said "dejame sano profe" which is basically "leave me be" so someone only here for the discount then. I left them alone, after all what could I do, give them detention? Some of these people were looking at 50 years or more in prison.

What really captured their attention, however, were my stories. I talked about my travels to over 50 countries, weaving in tales of historical battles and events, which they seemed to love. When someone asked which country had "liberated" us, like Colombia had from Spain, I found myself giving an impromptu lecture on Britain's history, going back to the Romans and Vikings.

The more I shared, the more they warmed to me. Eventually, word got out about my aviation background, which led to a barrage of questions about flying and airport security. It didn't take long to realize that some of these inquiries weren't out of idle curiosity—they were fishing for potential loopholes in drug transportation. I quickly shut down those conversations, redirecting them back to geography or English vocabulary.

At the end of each class, I often had the chance to chat one-on-one with some of the inmates. Strangely enough, I rarely thought about the precarious position I was in—a closed classroom with 64 of Colombia's most dangerous criminals. Despite their reputations, I was always treated with respect, even deference, and never once felt in danger.

These conversations were unexpectedly candid, often surreal in their honesty. Some inmates spoke openly about their crimes, delivering their confessions in a matter-of-fact tone that would have been jarring in any other setting. One man casually explained, "Well, I had to shoot him—he was being disrespectful." Another admitted, with a wry grin, "I didn't rob the house they said I did, but I couldn't give an alibi because I was robbing a different one at the time." It was the kind of twisted logic that only made sense in La Modelo.

What struck me most was the rarity of the classic "I'm innocent" claim. Very few tried to convince me they were wrongfully imprisoned. Perhaps this was because those in the education department were already resigned to their circumstances and focused on earning sentence reductions. In a place like this, hope often took the form of practical steps—like attending class for time off their eventual sentences.

These moments of connection, as odd as they were, humanized them for me. Beneath their hardened exteriors, many of them had stories that went beyond their crimes—tales of poverty, desperation, and survival. Some were undeniably dangerous, yet others seemed like ordinary men who had made catastrophic decisions in extraordinary circumstances. While I was never naïve enough to forget where I was, I found myself increasingly able to see them as individuals rather than just inmates.

Despite the challenges, I found myself enjoying the classes. These men, hardened by lives of crime and violence, were often disarmingly curious, even humorous. Teaching them wasn't just a job—it was becoming an unexpectedly rewarding experience. Still, every evening as I left the prison and stepped back into the world outside, I couldn't help but breathe a sigh of relief. La Modelo might have been a place of learning during the day, but it never stopped being one of the most dangerous places on Earth.

In October, the prison underwent its seemingly annual shakeup as Garcia, the director, was replaced.

The reason for Colonel Villamizar's arrival might have been tied to a series of disturbing incidents that rattled the prison just before his appointment.

One morning, I was sent home almost as soon as I arrived. A dead body had been discovered in one of the patios on the paramilitary side. "No classes today," I was told bluntly as I watched the forensic team arrive to begin their investigation.

The following day, during a conversation with some inmates, I learned the grim details. The victim, nicknamed *Conejo* ("Rabbit") for his prominent front teeth, had been a low-level paramilitary leader. Apparently, Conejo had been conducting extortion operations on his own without informing the AUC leadership and pocketing the profits. This was a grave offense in the eyes of the *Autodefensas*, and as a lesson to others, they had executed him with two shots to the head.

The official report, however, claimed it was a suicide. I couldn't help but shake my head at the absurdity of the explanation. "Suicide?" I said incredulously to one of the inmates. "How does someone shoot themselves in the head twice?" He shrugged with a smirk, as if to say, "Welcome to Colombian justice."

Another incident, not long after, was even more grotesque. One afternoon, the prison was locked down due to a significant discrepancy during the inmate count. These counts were rarely accurate, but this time the gap was larger than usual, prompting a series of recounts. I found myself stuck near the guards' control center, an area located at the end of the corridor leading to the football pitch. This area also served as a temporary dumping ground for trash, with piles of refuse stacked up waiting for removal.

As we waited for the recount to be resolved, the south wing's unofficial mascot, a scruffy black-and-brown mongrel named *Para* (short for paramilitary), trotted in from the football pitch. *Para* wasn't much to look at—skinny and unkempt—but he was friendly and well-liked by the inmates and guards alike. His tail wagged furiously as he carried something in his mouth—a long, dirty bag, caked in dried blood and grime. At first glance, I assumed it was some old meat or trash he'd scavenged from the pile outside.

But as *Para* strolled closer, proudly dragging his find across the floor, the shape of the bag became disturbingly clear. It wasn't trash. It was a human arm. The fingers hung limply from one end, dried blood staining the skin.

Para sauntered up to the guards, dropped the arm at their feet, and sat down happily, his tail still wagging as though expecting praise for his discovery.

The room fell silent as everyone stared in horror. One guard muttered a curse under his breath before ordering someone to shut the door to the pitch. Moments later, I was sent home again, the excuse being the need for a "thorough investigation."

The next day, the grim findings continued. The *ordenanzas*—inmates trusted to do odd jobs around the prison due to their low-risk status—were tasked with sorting through the mountain of trash outside. Their efforts uncovered two legs, a left arm that matched *Para*'s find, and then, inexplicably, another right arm. I didn't even bother asking how the body parts didn't match up. The less I knew, the better.

The new Director, Colonel Laureano Villamizar, was a stark contrast to his predecessor—a no-nonsense man with a commanding presence and an air of unyielding discipline. His firm handshake and sharp gaze during our first meeting left no doubt about his military roots.

"I'm here to bring order," he said bluntly, before adding, "If you need anything to ensure the success of your work, don't hesitate to ask." It was the kind of standard welcome I'd come to expect from new directors, who typically lasted only as long as it took for the next crisis to unfold. I wondered how long Villamizar would hold the reins before he too became a scapegoat for La Modelo's inevitable turmoil.

Classes continued to go well, though there were moments when my students reverted to behaving like schoolboys. They were endlessly fascinated by English swear words and sexual slang, constantly interrupting lessons to ask for translations. Rather than let it disrupt every session, I decided to tackle it head-on.

One day, I filled the blackboard with every profanity and obscenity I could think of, turning it into a crash course on curses. The inmates were thrilled, jotting down notes with the intensity of scholars preparing for an exam. By the end of the session, the board looked like something out of a sailor's notebook. I realized that if anyone from INPEC walked in, my teaching career would likely come to an abrupt and unceremonious end. Fortunately, the students were delighted, and the lesson seemed to purge their curiosity—for a while, at least.

One morning, as I passed the guardroom on my way to class, I noticed a figure standing behind the barred gate that led to the maximum-security block. Stocky but unassuming, with a clean-shaven face and a military-style haircut, he was dressed far better than most inmates. The man exuded a sense of confidence and familiarity that made me pause.

Then it hit me: I recognized him from countless news reports. It was Jhon Jairo Velásquez Vásquez, better known as "Popeye" or "JJ," Pablo Escobar's notorious hitman. This was a man allegedly responsible for over 300 murders, a figure so entwined with the dark legacy of the Medellín Cartel that his very presence seemed to cast a shadow over the corridor. He was serving a thirty-year sentence—the maximum under Colombian law—for terrorism, drug trafficking, extortion, conspiracy, and murder.

"Hey, aren't you the professor?" he called out, his voice strong and unflinching.

I hesitated for a moment but walked over, stopping a safe distance from the gate. "Yes, I am," I replied evenly.

"I've heard about you," he said, nodding. "Teach me English."

The casualness of his request was startling. It was as though he were asking me to pass the salt at dinner.

"No," I said simply.

His expression shifted, a flicker of surprise breaking through his composure. "Why not?"

"I don't want to," I replied, my voice steady.

He frowned slightly, his tone growing more insistent. "Why not?"

I met his gaze steadily, the kind of look that cut through the pretence. "Because I don't want to teach a person like you," I said, each word deliberate and firm.

There was a moment of silence, a charged pause as the weight of my words settled between us. His expression remained unreadable, a flicker of surprise perhaps, but nothing else. Without waiting for a reply, I turned on my heel and walked away, my heart pounding against my ribs. Despite the adrenaline coursing through me, I kept my stride steady, refusing to let any hint of uncertainty show as I headed back to the classroom.

The moment lingered in my mind long after I left the corridor, a stark reminder of the unpredictable encounters that came with working in La Modelo. It wasn't every day that you turned down a request from one of the most infamous criminals in the world—a man whose name alone once commanded fear.

Later that evening, over a quiet drink with a colleague, I recounted the incident. He looked at me incredulously, shaking his head. "Weren't you afraid there'd be repercussions? This is *Popeye* we're talking about. You know, the guy who worked for Escobar?"

I shrugged, swirling the liquid in my glass. "Not really," I replied. "He's in jail, isn't he? No cartel, no drug lord to back him up. Just a pathetic inmate now, with zero power or influence. A leftover from a time that's long gone."

The words felt true even as I said them. He was a ghost of his former self, a man who had traded his empire of terror for a cell and a shadow of infamy. For all the bravado he might have had left, here in La Modelo, he was just another prisoner—contained, irrelevant, and powerless. And that, I realized, was the difference between the myth of Popeye and the reality of the man who'd stood before me.

As I was leaving the prison that day to go home, as I was passing the thick, metal-grilled passageway where inmates met with their lawyers, a voice called out in heavily accented English, "Hey! Do you speak English?" I turned to see a large black man crouched down, his face pressed against the small postbox-like gap used to pass documents. His accent was unmistakably Nigerian.

Curious, I walked over and nodded. "Yes, I do."

Relief washed over his face. "Can you help us? We don't even know why we are here!"

I explained that I wasn't a lawyer, but he quickly thrust a wad of paperwork through the gap, pleading, "Please, we can't read it."

I agreed to take a look, flipping through the stack of legal documents. I was familiar with Colombian court processes, so I knew where to start—at the section titled *Hechos* (The Facts). I read them aloud.

"Number one: The individuals arrested are Africans."

He nodded eagerly and rather redundantly added "Oh yes, we are Africans. I am from Nigeria."

"Number two: Africa is a long way from Colombia."

He tilted his head, considering this. "Yes, it is far. We flew by South Africa and Brazil because we couldn't go through the U.S.—visa restrictions."

This wasn't helping much. So far, these "facts" were just observations. Although it was a fact they WERE indeed Africans and Africa IS a long way from Colombia, undeniably.

"Number three: They were staying in a cheap hotel."

He confirmed, "Yes, Hotel Bogotá. It's not very nice. Only $8 a night."

I frowned, feeling no closer to understanding why they had been arrested. "Okay, let's see the final fact," I said, hoping it would shed light.

"Number four: They did not have any money."

I paused. That was it. That was the final *fact*. They were Africans staying in a cheap hotel without money. Hardly the smoking gun I expected.

Puzzled, I asked more questions and pieced together the story. There were 20 Nigerians in total, traveling together. One of them was caught at El Dorado Airport carrying two kilos of cocaine. Under interrogation, the man admitted where he was staying. The police responded with a full-scale raid on the hotel, descending with about 50 officers armed to the teeth. They stormed the place and asked the receptionist where the "Africans" were staying. Then they arrested every African in the building—19 of them.

The man caught with the drugs pled guilty, earning himself a reduced sentence. With good behaviour, including attending my English classes, he was released after just 19 months. The other 19, however, were never convicted of anything. They languished in prison on remand for 21 months before being released without charges. It was a chilling illustration of how Colombian justice worked—or didn't.

Another case was even stranger. An Italian man, thin and wiry, approached me one day. A pleasant fellow of about 40, he handed me his process papers and asked for help understanding them. As I scanned the documents, I was stunned by the sole reason listed for his imprisonment: *"For walking in a funny manner."*

I stared at the paper, baffled. "Walking in a funny manner?" I asked him. "Is this a joke?"

"No joke," he replied, shaking his head.

Prodding for more details, I finally got the full story. He had been walking down a street with a Colombian friend when a car pulled up. The driver started chatting with his friend—nothing unusual. After a brief conversation, the driver drove off. Unbeknownst to them, the driver was a person of interest under police surveillance. The police, apparently not wanting to miss any connections, arrested everyone the driver had spoken to that day—including the Italian and anyone who happened to be standing nearby.

The story sent a chill down my spine. It underscored how perilous it could be to be a foreigner in Colombia. We seemed to be instant suspects in drug trafficking cases, and the threshold for suspicion was shockingly low. From that day on, I made sure to carry multiple forms of ID and contact numbers that could be verified quickly. I wasn't about to take any chances.

Another day, in the same passageway, I met an Italian man who caught my attention with his friendly demeanour and animated gestures. He was a wiry fellow, probably in his early forties, with a thick accent and a knack for dramatic storytelling. He handed me his paperwork and asked, "Could you read this and tell me why I am here?"

I flipped through the legal documents, searching for the *Hechos* section to uncover the facts of his case. When I finally found it, I couldn't believe my eyes. The main justification for his arrest was summarized in one perplexing line: *He was walking in a funny manner.*

I looked up at him in disbelief. "Walking in a funny manner?" I asked, barely able to suppress a chuckle. "That's all it says?"

"Yes!" he exclaimed, throwing up his hands in exasperation. "Walking funny! Like this is a crime now?"

Digging deeper, I discovered the bizarre backstory. While he was strolling down a street in Bogotá with a Colombian friend, a car pulled up beside them. The driver, it turned out, was under surveillance by the police as a suspected drug trafficker. After a brief conversation between the driver and his friend, the car sped off. The police, following their suspect, decided to arrest anyone who had spoken to him that day.

"They just grabbed me and my friend," the Italian explained, shaking his head. "Next thing I know, I'm here, and they say I'm guilty by association—or because of my *walking*! Can you believe this?"

His story made my skin crawl. It was becoming clear just how arbitrary and fragile life could be as a foreigner in Colombia. With little more than hearsay or suspicion, one could find themselves locked away indefinitely. I resolved to be even more cautious about my movements and interactions, always carrying proper identification and avoiding any situation that might raise an eyebrow.

On another occasion, I met a man who introduced himself as Rodrigo, a fellow pilot. Unlike many of the others I encountered, Rodrigo seemed genuinely interested in learning English—specifically aviation English. His knowledge of aircraft, including the Cessna 208 Caravan, was impressive, and I could see that he was well-versed in aviation. But as we spoke, I learned that his company, a small aviation business, had been a front for laundering cartel money. While Rodrigo claimed he just wanted to fly and own his own business, his involvement had landed him squarely in prison.

Rodrigo was housed in Patio 3, an exclusive area of the prison reserved for wealthy inmates. To gain entry, prisoners had to pay an initial "donation" to the paramilitary group controlling the patio, typically around $1,500. Then there were ongoing expenses: either a weekly rental of $200 for a cell or a one-time payment of $10,000 for permanent rights to a more luxurious space.

Rodrigo invited me to teach him aviation English in Patio 3, insisting it was a safe area. "They wouldn't dare kidnap me or hold me for ransom here," he said confidently. "The paras run this place. You'll be fine."

His confidence was reassuring, but I wasn't fully convinced. To enter the patio, I would need the prison director's permission. I approached Colonel Villamizar with the request. He agreed, but only on the condition that I sign a waiver absolving the prison of any responsibility for my safety. The implication was clear: once inside, I was on my own.

Despite the unsettling nature of the arrangement, curiosity got the better of me. I signed the waiver, collected my new identification badge, and returned to the guard station at the entrance to the south wing.

"Are you sure, profe?" one of the guards asked, looking at me with concern.

"Yes," I said, doing my best to sound confident, though my heart was pounding.

As the massive steel door rolled open, I stepped into the patio. Behind me, the door closed with a heavy clang, and I was alone in the passage. Bullet marks dotted the inside of the door—a grim reminder of the violence that had occurred here.

At Patio 3's entrance, a scruffy inmate sat on a chair, casually cradling a revolver on his lap. He stopped me as I tried to enter.

"Where do you think you're going?" he sneered.

"I have permission from the director," I replied, showing him my badge.

"Yeah, but do you have *our* permission?" he shot back, smirking.

My stomach dropped. It was clear that official clearance meant little in this part of the prison. Before I could respond, the man called for the "Comandante" on a walkie-talkie. Moments later, a sharply dressed inmate arrived. Comandante Diego Alvarez, as he introduced himself, greeted me with a surprisingly polite demeanour.

After explaining my purpose, he granted me entry and offered to give me a tour. To my amazement, the patio resembled a bustling small town. There was a restaurant run by two

Italian inmates, a hot dog stand, a video rental store with VHS tapes, and even a sauna. The cells for wealthier inmates were like mini-apartments, complete with wooden furniture and plush bedding. It was surreal.

Over a steak lunch at the patio's restaurant, Alvarez shared more about life inside. The paramilitaries controlled every aspect, from cell rentals to taxes on the businesses. It was a self-contained world with its own economy and hierarchy.

As I left Patio 3 that day, I couldn't help but marvel at the stark contrasts within La Modelo. The sheer disparity between the lives of inmates was both surreal and deeply unsettling. In one corner of the prison, I had seen cells that defied every preconceived notion of what incarceration meant. These personal "apartments," remodelled with care and precision, featured fitted wooden furniture that would not have been out of place in a well-appointed home. Thick curtains draped across small windows, blocking out the harsh realities outside. The bedding was luxurious, far removed from the threadbare mattresses or concrete slabs I had expected. These lavish setups came at a steep price: a $10,000 upfront payment, a sum that secured the inmate their small slice of comfort in a place otherwise defined by deprivation.

But as I toured the other patios, the differences were painfully evident. In these overcrowded spaces, a single cell intended for three housed up to five people. Here, everything came with a cost. A bunk on the lower level, the most coveted spot, fetched $25 a week. The top bunk was slightly cheaper at $20, and for those who couldn't afford even that, the floor was the only option—$10 a week for the privilege of sleeping under the lower bunk or squeezed into a cramped corner. The starkness of these arrangements painted a grim picture of survival, where money dictated not just comfort but dignity.

In both worlds—luxury and squalor—power and wealth were the currency that determined an inmate's reality. For those with money, life in La Modelo could almost resemble a warped version of freedom, complete with restaurant meals, private quarters, and even recreational facilities. For the rest, survival meant navigating the crushing weight of overcrowding, deprivation, and the constant threat of violence.

As I left the South Wing that day, I couldn't help but marvel at the stark contrasts within La Modelo. The luxurious lives of some inmates stood in sharp relief to the grim reality faced by others. And yet, in both worlds, power and money dictated everything. It was a lesson I would not soon forget.

As we continued the tour, Comandante Alvarez escorted me through various patios, each with its own unique characteristics. Some were bustling with activities, while others seemed quieter but carried a tense undercurrent. The disparities between wealthier and less privileged inmates were stark, with certain areas resembling functioning mini-societies and others barely scraping by. It was an unsettling but eye-opening experience that shed light on the layers of power and control within La Modelo.

As we approached one of the gates separating the sections, a guard inmate stopped me with a condescending glare. "Who the hell are you?" he asked, his tone dripping with disdain.

Comandante Alvarez intervened, his voice authoritative yet calm. "Open the gate for the Captain."

The guard sneered and asked, "Captain of what?" his voice thick with scepticism.

Without missing a beat, I straightened my posture, meeting his gaze directly. "Captain of a 200-ton Boeing 767 and currently two squadrons of aircraft for fumigation," I replied, my tone measured but firm.

The response seemed to take him aback. His sneer faded, replaced by a grudging respect as he swung the gate open without further question. The moment cemented my status among the paras in the south wing, earning me a measure of impunity and even respect. This tour, while risky, proved essential in establishing my position and ensuring that I could move freely in the patios without facing undue challenges—a necessity for the unique work I was doing in this unpredictable environment.

I told Martha only the sanitized version of what had happened in the patios that day. But with Dad, I spared no detail. His eyes lit up as I recounted the experience, and he leaned forward eagerly, practically buzzing with excitement. "I have to see that for myself," he declared, as though I had just described some exclusive country club. At first, I hesitated. The risks were real, and I wasn't entirely sure how safe it would be to bring him along. But after mulling it over, I decided it was doable—provided we stuck to Patio 3 and only visited as regular guests, not as "Captain" and tourist.

Saturday was designated for male visitors, with Sundays reserved for females, so I made arrangements for Rodrigo to invite Dad. Rodrigo readily agreed and provided the necessary information for the visitor's application. I went to the justice office at the prison, filled out the paperwork, and obtained a visitor's pass for Philip. The visit was set for the following Saturday.

We arrived at the prison around 7:30 a.m., as visiting hours ran from 8 a.m. to 5 p.m. The scene outside was chaotic, with a line of visitors snaking around two walls of the building. Hundreds of people waited patiently, carrying bags of food, clothing, or other items to bring to their loved ones inside. But being staff had its perks. I walked straight up to the guard at the entrance, flashed my ID, and discreetly slipped him 20,000 pesos (about $10 at the time). In no time, we bypassed the queue and were ushered inside.

The security checks were thorough—frisking, emptying pockets, and passing through metal detectors. I had anticipated this and had instructed Dad to bring only money and his passport. However, we hit a snag at the ID station. My staff ID had a fingerprint for verification, but Dad's British passport didn't. The guards insisted on a fingerprint for both entry and exit. Thinking quickly, we slipped out a side door to a nearby shop that offered photocopying and other services. Dad rolled his finger on an ink pad with the precision of someone who had done this before, leaving a clear print that we affixed to his passport. After retracing our steps and clearing security a second time, we finally made it past the ID checkpoint.

Entering Patio 3 was like stepping into a parallel universe. Dad's jaw dropped as he took in the scene: the bustling market-like atmosphere, the restaurant in the middle of the patio, and the Italian inmates running their café with a level of finesse that rivalled professional establishments. There were video stores, a hot dog stand, and even a tennis court tucked away in a neighbouring patio. "Bloody hell," he muttered, wide-eyed. "This is nicer than where I lived in Batley."

I introduced him to some of the inmates I had gotten to know. They greeted him warmly, addressing him as "Don Felipe" and shaking his hand with respect. We settled down for a meal at the restaurant—steak for Dad and salmon for me. The quality of the food and the attentiveness of the service left him utterly amazed. "I could do time here," he joked, though I suspected he wasn't entirely kidding.

Before leaving, I gave him a quick tour of the less glamorous patios. These were worlds apart—overcrowded cells, grimy corridors, and the palpable tension of survival in close quarters. The contrast hit Dad hard. "Fuckin' hell, this is a fuckin' slum," he said, visibly uncomfortable. It was a sobering reminder of how starkly money dictated the quality of life even within prison walls.

As 4 p.m. approached, the exodus began, and the queues to leave were as daunting as the ones we'd bypassed that morning. Spotting a guard I knew well, I called him over and asked for assistance. Without hesitation, he led us to the front of the line. We retrieved our documents after a fingerprint check, breezed through another frisk, and stepped outside into the fading afternoon light.

Nobody in the line complained about us skipping ahead; they knew the rules—or lack thereof. In this system, money and connections always spoke louder than fairness. Dad, for his part, was ecstatic. "Best day out I've had in years," he declared, practically glowing with satisfaction. It was an adventure for him, one he would recount endlessly with the kind of enthusiasm reserved for tall tales. For better or worse, it had been an unforgettable experience, and I had no doubt he would be talking about it for months to come.

By the time the holiday season rolled around, it was clear that we were no longer just a loosely connected group of individuals under one roof. We had become a family. Philip, Martha, Jacky, and I settled into a rhythm that made the house feel alive and warm. This would be our first Christmas together, and I wanted it to be memorable.

Martha, ever the organizer, took charge of decorating. She transformed the house with festive lights, garlands, and a tree adorned with ornaments she'd carefully selected. Philip, seeing her enthusiasm, got swept up in the holiday spirit too, though he had a somewhat gruff approach to it. "Fuckin' hell, are we decorating a house or a fuckin' palace?" he grumbled while stringing up lights outside. But the twinkle in his eye betrayed how much he enjoyed being involved. Jacky added her own flair, insisting on draping every chair with ribbons and even braiding some into her hair. The house looked like something out of a Christmas card—festive, chaotic, and full of life.

Christmas Eve was a major event in Colombia, more significant than Christmas Day itself. Martha prepared a traditional Colombian feast, with *lechona* (roast pig stuffed with rice and peas), *buñuelos* (fried cheese dough balls), and *natilla* (a creamy pudding-like dessert). Philip, wanting to contribute in his own way, insisted on making a Christmas pudding, a tradition he refused to abandon even in the tropics. He had somehow smuggled suet and raisins back from England, and with much fanfare, he unveiled the dense dessert after hours of steaming. To everyone's surprise, it was a hit, though I suspect the copious amounts of brandy he poured over it and then flambéed might have been the main attraction.

On Christmas Day, we exchanged gifts. Philip had gone overboard, as usual, maxing out his credit card to shower Jacky and Martha with perfumes, jewellery, and clothes. "You only live once," he said, shrugging off my raised eyebrow when I pointed out he was now deeply in debt. Martha and I had agreed on simpler gifts for each other. She gave me a leather-bound notebook embossed with my initials, perfect for jotting down thoughts or notes for work. I gave her a delicate gold bracelet, which she wore immediately and admired in the light.

As the year came to an end, the city of Bogotá erupted into celebration. New Year's Eve was unlike anything I'd experienced before—a massive street party that seemed to involve the entire neighbourhood. We joined the crowds, stepping out into a sea of music, laughter, and fireworks. Vendors sold street food, drinks flowed freely, and everyone seemed to be in a jubilant mood. Philip, ever the life of the party, bought a bottle of aguardiente, Colombia's potent anise-flavored liquor, and declared it his mission to toast every single person he met.

As midnight approached, the energy reached a fever pitch. Fireworks lit up the sky, their explosions reverberating through the city. When the clock struck twelve, strangers hugged, danced, and celebrated as if they were lifelong friends. Philip danced with Jacky, spinning her around dramatically, while Martha and I shared a kiss under the glow of the fireworks. It felt like a perfect moment, a culmination of everything we'd built together that year.

The new millennium had arrived, and with it came a sense of hope and possibility. Standing there with my family, I couldn't help but feel that despite the chaos and challenges of our lives, we were heading into the new century stronger and more united than ever.

Chapter 8: New York, New York

In January 2000, U.S. Secretary of State Madeleine Albright visited Colombia, a moment that underscored the growing partnership between the U.S. and Colombia in addressing the dual challenges of drug trafficking and internal conflict. Her two-day visit to Cartagena included meetings with President Andrés Pastrana and senior Colombian officials to discuss the progress and future of the soon-to-be-signed Plan Colombia. The initiative, born out of cooperation between Pastrana and U.S. President Bill Clinton, aimed to combat drug cartels, insurgent groups, and the pervasive instability that had plagued Colombia for decades.

During her visit, Secretary Albright toured the bustling Cartagena port, observing customs inspection procedures designed to disrupt narcotics smuggling. While her presence was meant to signify the U.S.'s unwavering commitment to Colombia, for those of us directly involved in the fumigation and eradication efforts on the ground, her visit was a distant event. She didn't venture into the regions where we worked, nor did she meet with the personnel facing the challenges of executing this ambitious initiative. It was clear that the policy was being shaped at the highest levels, far removed from the realities of the field.

By February, I received an unexpected request: to attend a high-level meeting in New York City with representatives from the U.S. Department of Defense (DOD), Drug Enforcement Administration (DEA), and State Department. No Colombians were invited to this meeting, which I found curious. Perhaps they thought my perspective, unencumbered by political ties, would offer a more candid assessment of the eradication program's successes and its shortcomings.

I arranged my travel via Panama, taking the opportunity to explore Panama City during a day-long stopover—a city I hadn't seen since I sailed through the Panama Canal as a young officer in the Royal Navy in 1979. However, my arrival in Panama was less than smooth.

The customs officials in Panama seemed to have a singular fixation: I had arrived from Bogotá, which instantly made me a suspect in their eyes. My suitcase was seized and flung onto the inspection table with an enthusiasm that bordered on hostility. Layer by layer, my belongings were yanked out and tossed aside. I watched silently, thinking to myself, *That's never going to fit back in.*

The search continued until the customs agent reached the navy-blue uniform I'd brought along. I'd packed it thinking I might need to present myself formally, especially if other uniformed personnel were present at the meeting. The agent froze upon seeing the four gold stripes on my jacket sleeve. "Pilot?" he asked, his tone shifting from suspicion to deference.

"Yes," I replied calmly.

"Civil or military?" he pressed, squinting at me.

"Both," I said, anticipating a barrage of questions about how that was possible. To my surprise, none came. Instead, the agent gently replaced my belongings in the suitcase, draped the lid over the top, and offered a sheepish nod. Lesson learned: from now on, my uniform would sit at the very top of my suitcase, visible as soon as it was opened.

Landing in New York, I checked into the Gramercy Park Hotel, which, I was told, had once been the epitome of luxury. But time had clearly taken its toll. The carpets were worn, the furniture creaked with age, and the overall atmosphere was one of faded grandeur. It didn't matter much—I was only there for a couple of nights.

The meeting was scheduled at the DEA's New York headquarters on 10th Avenue, a nondescript building overlooking the Hudson River. I donned my uniform, a decision I didn't take lightly but one I believed would lend me credibility in a room filled with representatives from some of the most powerful agencies in the United States.

Walking into the room, I immediately felt the weight of the moment. Representatives from the DOD, DEA, Department of Justice, U.S. Customs, ATF, and the State Department's Bureau of International Narcotics and Law Enforcement Affairs (INCLE) were gathered, along with other key stakeholders. Absent, however, were environmental or social organizations—groups that might have advocated for the broader humanitarian components of Plan Colombia. Also absent were the contractors DynCorp Aerospace Technologies.

The session began with me giving a detailed overview of our eradication efforts. I highlighted successes while also being upfront about the challenges we faced. Questions came at me rapid-fire:

"How effective is the spraying program in reducing coca cultivation?"

"Are we seeing evidence of drift into neighbouring Ecuador?"

"What's your assessment of the security risks posed by guerrillas and paramilitaries?"

The questions were relentless, and I answered them all to the best of my ability. When asked what resources we needed to improve the program, I didn't hesitate to present a detailed list: more aircraft, additional support for pilots and mechanics, increased funding for infrastructure closer to target areas, and streamlined bureaucratic processes to allow for quicker operational decisions. I also pointed out the need for greater investment in alternative development programs to provide coca farmers with viable livelihoods—though I could see that this suggestion landed with lukewarm interest in the room.

By the end of the day, I felt both exhausted and reflective. Plan Colombia was undoubtedly ambitious, with the potential to reshape Colombia's future. But it was also clear that its success depended on more than just military aid and eradication efforts. Without addressing the root causes of coca cultivation—poverty, lack of infrastructure, and the absence of viable economic alternatives—it risked being a temporary fix to a deeply entrenched problem.

As I left the meeting, the cold New York air hit me, and I realized the stark contrast between this city and the places where these policies would play out. In Bogotá, farmers didn't care about high-level meetings or diplomatic jargon. They cared about feeding their families, staying safe, and finding a way to survive in an unforgiving landscape. Plan Colombia's architects would do well to remember that.

Plan Colombia, at this stage, was more than just an ambitious policy—it was a vision. It was conceived as a lifeline for a country drowning in decades of violence, narcotrafficking, and crippling internal conflict. Spearheaded by Colombian President Andrés Pastrana, with strong backing from U.S. President Bill Clinton, it aimed to bring Colombia back from the brink. The plan wasn't yet in motion, but the gears were turning, the blueprints laid out with expectations soaring high on both sides of the partnership.

The heart of Plan Colombia lay in its bold mission to slash coca cultivation and cocaine production in half within six years. To achieve this, a strategy was crafted with military precision. Aerial fumigation would form the spearhead of the offensive, targeting coca fields with herbicides from the air. The hope was that choking off the raw material would deal a devastating blow to the cocaine trade, cutting off revenue to guerrilla groups and cartels alike. The logic was simple, though the execution promised to be anything but.

But this wasn't just a war against coca plants. It was also a battle for the hearts and minds of rural Colombians. The architects of Plan Colombia recognized that coca farmers weren't villains; they were often desperate individuals with no other means of survival. The plan promised programs to help farmers transition to legal crops, offering subsidies and technical support to replant fields with coffee, cacao, or other marketable produce. Roads would be built, markets opened, and villages once forgotten by the state would finally find themselves connected to the rest of the country. In theory, this would offer these farmers a way out of the vicious cycle of coca dependence.

Military support would come in tandem. Colombian forces would be bolstered with new equipment, modernized training, and intelligence sharing. Helicopters like Black Hawks and Hueys, icons of counter-insurgency warfare, would fly missions deep into the jungles, ferrying troops and supporting the fumigation teams. Colombian soldiers and police, trained by U.S. advisors, would take the fight to the insurgent groups that had carved out their own territories in the hinterlands. The security objectives were clear: dismantle the FARC and ELN guerrillas, weaken the paramilitary groups, and bring law and order to areas long ruled by the barrel of a gun.

In this phase, there was hope—idealistic and unblemished by the realities that would come later. Diplomats and planners spoke of revitalized communities and economic rebirth, of a Colombia that would rise from the ashes of its own history. Yet, even then, cracks in the plan's foundations were evident to those who chose to see them.

The fumigation strategy, for all its military efficacy, promised collateral damage. Entire communities would find their food crops destroyed alongside the coca. Health concerns over the herbicides would inevitably spark outrage, and already whispers of resistance were reaching Bogotá. What would happen to a family whose livelihood was uprooted overnight? The alternative development programs, though noble in intention, would face monumental logistical hurdles. Many of the coca fields lay deep in guerrilla-controlled zones where government representatives couldn't tread without armed escorts. How could you offer help to a farmer when they couldn't even meet you safely?

And then there was the question of money. Most of the funding—over $1.3 billion in its initial phase—would come from the United States. While the lion's share of this aid would go toward military efforts, only a sliver was earmarked for social programs. Critics whispered that this was less about saving Colombia and more about securing American interests, about waging a proxy war on drugs and insurgency.

For all these concerns, the political will on both sides of the partnership was undeniable. Pastrana spoke of Plan Colombia with the fervour of a man trying to sell salvation to a country on its knees. In Washington, officials talked of measurable successes—coca hectares destroyed, guerrilla camps dismantled, drug routes disrupted. The plan was set to be a bold experiment in international collaboration, blending the firepower of the United States with Colombia's resolve to reclaim its sovereignty.

As the months inched toward implementation, I found myself tangentially drawn into the orbit of this grand scheme. The scope of it all was breathtaking, a sweeping campaign to alter the very trajectory of a nation. But even as the wheels began to turn, I couldn't help but wonder how it would feel on the ground, in the coca fields and the guerrilla strongholds, where policy met reality. Would it be as transformative as the glossy presentations promised? Or would it, like so many ambitious plans before, leave more questions than answers in its wake? Only time would tell.

Seeing the Hudson River the day before had reminded me of something I'd been meaning to do—the visit to the USS *Intrepid* Museum. An old aircraft carrier turned museum, it was moored just off Manhattan, and I couldn't resist the opportunity to tour its decks and relive memories of my days in the Royal Navy. The ship, a testament to naval engineering of its time, loomed large, its steel hull now a tribute to history rather than an instrument of war. Stepping aboard brought back a flood of memories, the scent of old oil mingling with the tang of the sea air.

I wandered through the aircraft display, marvelling at the icons of aviation history. The SR-71 Blackbird loomed sleek and menacing, a pinnacle of Cold War technology. Nearby, the F-14 Tomcat stood proudly, a symbol of American air superiority, while a Harrier jump jet rested on an aircraft elevator—a sight that felt closer to home. But what truly struck a nerve was the Super Étendard. Its streamlined design belied its infamous role in the Falklands War, where it carried the Exocet missiles that had sunk HMS *Sheffield* and the MV *Atlantic Conveyor*. Standing before it, I felt a complex twinge of nostalgia, respect, and sorrow for those harrowing days.

Across the pier, a World War II destroyer, the USS *Edison*, caught my eye. It had its own story to tell, but what truly drew my attention was the modern warship berthed alongside—a sleek Oliver Hazard Perry-class guided missile frigate. A nearby sign identified it as the USS *Samuel B. Roberts* (FFG-58), fresh from anti-drug patrols off the Colombian coast. Unlike the museum ships, this frigate was still an active-duty vessel and open to public tours. There was no chance I was passing that up.

Joining a small group of tourists, I climbed aboard, trying not to regret that I wasn't in uniform. As we were led through the ship, various sailors were stationed at key points to share details about its capabilities. On the forecastle, below the towering bridge, we stood near the missile launcher as a sailor proudly recounted their latest mission: three months patrolling the Colombian coast. With evident pride, he mentioned that during the deployment, the ship's efforts had resulted in the confiscation of 40 kilos of cocaine.

I couldn't help it. A laugh burst out of me before I managed to stifle it. Forty kilos? I thought about the scale of their operations—this massive warship, bristling with advanced weaponry, a crew of nearly 200, armed helicopters, radar, sonar, and missiles. Millions spent over months at sea, and for what? Forty kilos. I tried to compose myself as the sailor shot me a sharp look, while the other tourists turned to me in confusion. I bit my tongue for the rest of the tour, but the absurdity stayed with me. I couldn't help comparing their efforts to ours in the fumigation program. One air tractor could wipe out 40 hectares of coca in a few hours, putting a far larger dent in production. It struck me as yet another example of how costly and inefficient the "War on Drugs" could be when approached the wrong way.

I decided to do a bit of shopping. I wanted to bring back something special for Martha, so I wandered into a store near Madison Square Park, not far from the iconic Flatiron Building. Browsing through dresses, I tried to guess her size, keeping in mind her petite frame. As I deliberated over lengths and styles, a woman interrupted, holding up a dress and asking me, "Do you have this in a size 6?" Apparently, I looked like I worked there. When I explained I didn't, she flushed with embarrassment and scurried away, leaving me to laugh quietly to myself.

Before leaving New York, I made one final stop to take in another iconic sight. While on board the *Intrepid*, I had snapped a selfie with the New York skyline behind me, the twin towers of the World Trade Center standing tall and proud in the background. Inspired by the photo, I decided to see them up close. At first, I thought I could walk there, but I quickly realized it was farther than I expected, so I hopped on the subway, getting off at the World Trade Center stop.

Emerging onto the plaza, I found myself face-to-face with the twin towers. The sheer magnitude of their height was overwhelming. I tilted my head back to take it all in, and the dizzying perspective of the buildings towering into the sky sent me spinning. I couldn't keep my gaze fixed for more than a few seconds at a time without feeling as if I might fall over. It was a surreal, almost disorienting experience to stand at the base of such marvels of engineering. They were, without question, impressive—monuments to human ambition and ingenuity.

After soaking in the scene, I realized this would be my last act of playing tourist in New York.

That evening, I packed my bags, reflecting on the whirlwind of meetings, museum visits, and observations from the past few days. The following morning, I boarded my flight back to Bogotá, prepared to debrief the Colombian authorities on my experience with the "big boys" in the U.S. Plan Colombia, with all its ambition and complexity, loomed on the horizon, and I had no doubt that I'd soon find myself in the thick of it once again. Upon landing, I made my way to the Colombian Antinarcotics Directorate (Dirección de Antinarcóticos, DIRAN), headquartered at the El Dorado Airport Police Complex in Bogotá.

The El Dorado Police Complex, a sprawling facility adjacent to the airport, served as the nerve center for DIRAN's operations. From here, the Colombian National Police coordinated interdiction efforts, managed intelligence-gathering activities, and provided logistical support for anti-narcotics campaigns across the country. It was a place where strategy met action, a critical hub in the fight against the drug trade. Walking through its bustling corridors, filled with uniformed personnel, intelligence officers, and logistics experts, I could feel the weight of the challenges ahead. This was where the fight against Colombia's narcotic underworld took shape.

In April 2000, I was back in Bogotá, settling into my usual routine of teaching at La Modelo prison. The walk from my house to the prison was uneventful at first—a short stroll across the main road and two blocks further. The sight of the prison's looming structure was familiar, almost mundane by now. But this day was different. The air was heavy, tense, and the streets surrounding the facility were crawling with soldiers. A military truck with an anti-aircraft gun mounted on its flatbed sat ominously near the entrance, its barrel pointing skyward like a silent sentinel.

I approached the main gate, as casually as one could in such a surreal scene, nodding at the soldiers as if their presence was perfectly normal. As I reached the entrance, an army captain hurried toward me, his expression a mix of disbelief and urgency. "Where the hell do you think you're going?" he barked.

"To work," I replied, holding up my ID and gesturing toward the gate.

He stared at me, incredulous. "Have you seen the police surrounding this place? There's a battle going on inside!". It turned out they were not the army but special armed police wearing green army style uniforms.

A battle? For a moment, I thought he meant a riot, the kind of chaos that prisons are infamous for. But his tone made it clear that this was something else entirely. He leaned closer, his voice low and grim. "It's a full-scale confrontation battle between the paramilitaries and the guerrillas. You don't want to go in there today."

I took his advice, turned around, and walked back home. Watching the events unfold on the evening news was harrowing. The battle wasn't a simple prison uprising; it was a war within the prison walls, fought with grenades, firearms, and raw hatred.

It was a few days before I was allowed back in. When I finally returned, the atmosphere inside was charged with a heavy, oppressive silence. Walking down the familiar passageways, I noticed gaping holes in the walls—remnants of the explosions that had torn through the prison. The once-intact corridors were now marked by scorched stone and twisted metal. The destruction was a brutal testament to the carnage that had taken place.

As the count was completed, the surviving inmates filed into the classroom. The mood was tense, sombre, and palpably different. For the first time, I was acutely aware of the danger of sitting in a room with both paramilitaries and guerrillas, men who had been at each other's throats just days before.

I called the roll, a routine task that felt profoundly heavy now. Seven names went unanswered. Seven of my 64 students had been killed. As I read their names, the surviving inmates filled in the grim details:

"Pedro Sánchez—shot in the head." "Alberto Vázquez—killed by a grenade in the dining area." "Raúl Vázquez—his brother—same grenade."

The list went on, each name a casualty of the prison's war.

The inmates explained what had happened. The violence had been ignited by a breach of a fragile peace pact. The dismembered corpse of a paramilitary leader named Carlos Alberto León had been found in late March, sparking outrage among his comrades. On April 26, the tensions exploded into an armed confrontation between the paramilitaries of the Autodefensas Unidas de Colombia (AUC) and the guerrillas.

The battle began when members of the paramilitary faction learned that one of their spies, Yema Ospina Flórez, had been killed by the guerrillas. The paramilitaries, led by a figure known as Cadavid, launched a coordinated assault. Walls were blown apart with grenades, and the prison echoed with gunfire for twelve hours. The AUC fighters wore black armbands emblazoned with their insignia as they demanded the guerrillas' surrender. Those who complied were spared; those who resisted were executed on the spot.

The aftermath was horrifying. Over 100 were confirmed dead, with dozens more injured or missing. The bodies of 17 inmates were unaccounted for, rumoured to have been hidden in tunnels or disposed of through the prison's sewer system. The official investigation uncovered an arsenal of weapons buried in the walls—pistols, grenades, and even a submachine gun.

The scale of the violence was staggering. Much of the fighting was carried out not by hardened paramilitary soldiers but by young, impressionable inmates who had been offered rusty pistols and false promises of glory. The guerrillas, by contrast, were well-prepared and entrenched. They used sniper positions, created by removing bricks from walls, to devastating effect. It was a massacre. In total over 100 lives were lost, many of them those same naïve young men who had sought to prove themselves.

Standing in that classroom, surrounded by the surviving inmates, I felt a pang of doubt about my work here. The risks were becoming increasingly evident. I had always known La Modelo was dangerous, but this—this was something else entirely. It was a battlefield masquerading as a prison, and I couldn't shake the thought that maybe it was time to rethink how often I came here.

Chapter 9: Plan Colombia

Plan Colombia was signed into law by President Bill Clinton on July 13, 2000. It marked a decisive step in a comprehensive effort by the United States and Colombia to combat the deeply entrenched problems of drug trafficking and insurgency, while also aiming to promote economic development and strengthen governance. This ambitious initiative received bipartisan support in the United States and was accompanied by a dramatic increase in funding, particularly for counter-narcotics operations and military aid.

The scale of U.S. involvement was unprecedented. In 2000 alone, the United States nearly tripled its assistance to Colombia, with Congress approving more than $1.3 billion in aid under the Clinton administration. This included a significant boost in funding for aerial eradication, which rose by nearly 50% from $50.9 million in fiscal year 1999 to $73.4 million in 2000. The funds poured into the program were a testament to its importance in the broader framework of the U.S. global war on drugs.

The resources allocated to Plan Colombia were both vast and diverse. Military equipment formed the backbone of the initiative, with the provision of helicopters such as the Black Hawk and Huey facilitating rapid troop deployment and aerial fumigation. The Colombian National Police and military forces underwent extensive training in counterinsurgency and counter-narcotics operations, provided by U.S. advisers. Economic aid was also a component of the plan, intended to fund alternative development programs to offer coca growers other viable livelihoods. However, these social programs, while well-intentioned, were often criticized for their limited reach and questionable effectiveness.

Plan Colombia, envisioned to last until 2005, would evolve over the years, with its impact extending well beyond the initial timeline. By the time I was back on the ground, the program had already transformed Colombia into one of the largest recipients of U.S. foreign aid outside the Middle East, with over $10 billion allocated to the effort over two decades. This infusion of resources was designed to deliver on multiple fronts: reducing coca cultivation, combating insurgent groups, and bolstering Colombia's institutions. The plan was pivotal but controversial, leaving an indelible mark on Colombia's socio-political landscape and its relations with the United States.

From my perspective, the arrival of Plan Colombia promised to change everything. For the first time, it felt like we had the financial and logistical backing to seriously undermine the cocaine industry. We were promised planes, equipment, people, bases, and funding on a scale that could truly make a difference. There was optimism in the air—at least initially. The prospect of having the resources to carry out our mission effectively was thrilling, and

I believed, perhaps naively, that we could finally turn the tide in this seemingly endless war.

Yet, in those early days, we were energized. The idea of finally having the tools to dismantle the cocaine trade seemed within reach. For me, it meant stepping into a new chapter of my work—one with higher stakes, greater risks, and, potentially, a much more profound impact. Little did I know that the complexities of Plan Colombia would soon reveal themselves, testing not just our resources, but our resolve and our ability to navigate the murky waters of geopolitics and deeply entrenched local dynamics.

The arrival of new helicopters was like a scene out of a military movie. One day, a C-5 Galaxy transport aircraft—the largest plane in the Western world—touched down at El Dorado Airport. This beast of the skies was a marvel, a flying fortress capable of swallowing tanks, trucks, and in this case, eight UH-1H Hueys. As the massive rear ramp lowered, revealing the cavernous hold, a ripple of excitement went through our crew. There they were, two neat rows of Hueys, lined up like soldiers awaiting deployment.

The Hueys were a newer, longer model than the ones immortalized in Vietnam War footage, and we welcomed them like long-lost comrades. These were the cavalry of the skies, legendary machines with a storied past. But as I approached them, my excitement dimmed slightly. Their olive-green paint was chipped, their fuselages scuffed and worn. When I opened the logbooks, I realized why—they had all been built between 1968 and 1970. Over 30 years old. These were flying relics, veterans in their own right.

The Colombian mechanics were miracle workers, diving into the maintenance with a fervour that rivalled battlefield medics. They coaxed life back into these tired airframes, and within weeks, all eight Hueys were airworthy. But it didn't last. Spare parts were scarce, and the supply chain was agonizingly slow. By the end of the first year, we were cannibalizing the less-fortunate helicopters to keep the others in the air. Out of eight, only three were still flying.

The first time I climbed into the cockpit of one of these Hueys, I felt a sense of reverence. This wasn't just a helicopter; it was a legend. Starting the Lycoming T53 engine was like awakening a sleeping giant. The deep, throaty rumble resonated through the airframe, a sound that carried the weight of history. The controls were heavy, deliberate. This wasn't the nimble, agile LongRanger I was used to. Flying the Huey demanded respect; it wasn't a machine to be trifled with.

Hovering the Huey was an entirely different beast. The LongRanger had been like a precision instrument—light, responsive, almost playful. It made flying feel effortless, like gliding on a cushion of air. The Huey, on the other hand, was a brute. The feedback through the controls was raw, unfiltered. You had to fight for every manoeuvre, wrestle with its weight and power. But there was something deeply satisfying about it, a connection to the machine that felt primal.

As I lifted off for the first time, the blades kicked up a whirlwind of dust and debris, and the roar of the engine drowned out every other sound. I felt the weight of the Huey's history pressing down on me—the medevac missions, the troop insertions, the rescue operations it had been designed for. This wasn't just flying; it was stepping into a legacy.

The LongRanger might have been sleek and modern, but the Huey had character. Its imperfections, its quirks, its sheer presence made every flight an event. I felt safer in the Huey despite its age—it was a machine built for war, rugged and reliable in the worst conditions. Whenever the LongRanger was down for maintenance, I seized the chance to fly the Huey. I couldn't help but hum "Ride of the Valkyries" from *Apocalypse Now* as we roared over the jungle, the sound of the blades echoing the heartbeat of the machine.

Each flight in the Huey reaffirmed something I thought I'd left behind: the military pilot in me. There was no denying it—I belonged in the cockpit of a machine like this, commanding the skies with raw power and purpose. Every flight was a reminder of the dangerous, vital work we were doing, and in those moments, I felt unstoppable. The Huey wasn't just a helicopter; it was a symbol of resilience, of grit, of the unrelenting fight against the odds.

The success of Plan Colombia's initial funding surge had energized the entire operation. With resources finally flowing in—helicopters, personnel, and logistical support—the scale of our efforts expanded dramatically. Gone were the days of piecemeal missions with limited scope; we were now coordinating large-scale operations that targeted entire regions, aiming to cripple the cartels' operations at their very roots.

In August 2000, a significant shift in the Colombian legal framework regarding aerial eradication gave all of us in the field a renewed sense of purpose. Through our channels, we learned that the Colombian government had established the Interinstitutional Technical Committee (ITC)—a body designed to oversee and advise on the aerial eradication program. This development, though administrative in nature, brought a welcome structure and clarity to the process, addressing many of the concerns raised by critics. It reassured us that there was now a more formalized system to balance the demands of our mission with the need to mitigate its unintended consequences.

The ITC, we understood, was headed by DNE (Dirección Nacional de Estupefacientes) and included representatives from key agencies such as DIRAN (Colombian National Police's Anti-Narcotics Directorate), PLANTE (Colombia's Alternative Development Agency), and both local and national environmental organizations. These were not just figureheads but people who were tasked with examining the real-world impact of our efforts on health, the environment, and legal agricultural crops. Importantly, while the ITC could make recommendations on areas to be sprayed, the ultimate decision rested with the

Colombian government. Still, knowing that a body was reviewing the data provided us with a sense of accountability and fairness.

News of how complaints were being handled trickled back to us, and it was both fascinating and reassuring. Complaints—whether about damage to legal crops or alleged health problems—could now be routed through various agencies, including DIRAN, the DNE, the Attorney General, or the Environmental Ministry. There was a process in place, a methodical system for investigating claims, which stood in stark contrast to the chaos often associated with Colombia's drug conflict.

The first step in addressing a complaint involved consulting SATLOC computer records, the very data we pilots relied on to precisely guide our spray operations. SATLOC tracked every flight, every spray path, ensuring there was a reliable record of exactly where glyphosate had been deployed. Hearing that these records immediately invalidated around 50% of the claims was satisfying; it underscored the precision of our work. Those claims that passed this initial filter were then subjected to field investigations, where teams would examine the alleged damage on-site.

What came back through our channels was clear: in nearly every case, damage to legal crops was due to their being deliberately interspersed with illicit coca fields—a tactic growers used to make it harder for us to spray. This wasn't just hearsay; these were facts gathered from thorough investigations. As for human health complaints, not a single claim had ever been substantiated. It became apparent that many of these reports were linked to the illicit growers themselves, who used highly toxic chemicals like paraquat and parathion on their fields—substances far more harmful than glyphosate.

For those of us in the air, this was more than a bureaucratic update—it was a moral boost. We were often on the receiving end of criticism from environmental activists, human rights organizations, and even sceptical farmers. To know that there was a robust mechanism in place to vet complaints and separate fact from fiction made our work feel more validated. It confirmed what we had long believed: that our efforts were not only precise but necessary.

The establishment of the ITC also gave the operation a sense of legitimacy on the world stage. It was no longer just about flying missions and spraying fields—it was about being part of a larger, structured strategy to combat a deeply entrenched problem. The fact that our efforts were monitored, investigated, and ultimately upheld as effective and ethical added a layer of professional pride to what we were doing.

This shift helped many of us reconcile the inherent difficulties of our job. It wasn't easy being part of something that often faced such harsh scrutiny. But knowing that our work was being carefully examined and consistently found to be both precise and justified allowed us to push forward. It wasn't just about eradicating coca fields; it was about doing so responsibly, ensuring that we were making a difference in a way that respected the people and the land of Colombia.

The first major initiative on the calendar was "Operation Manglar," set to take place in September 2000. This wasn't just a mission; it was a statement—a bold declaration that we now had the means and the will to take the fight directly to the coca fields in one of Colombia's most entrenched drug-producing regions. For me, it was the start of a new phase, one where the stakes were higher, the risks greater, but the potential impact was enormous. We were no longer chipping away at the problem—we were gearing up to strike at its heart.

The planning for "Operation Manglar" began weeks in advance. The target: a vast expanse of coca fields near Barbacoas in the Nariño province, a region notorious for its coca cultivation. The operation was ambitious, aiming to eradicate 5,000 hectares of coca plants, and it represented the largest coordinated effort I'd been involved in since joining the mission. With Nariño's proximity to the Pacific coast, these fields fed directly into the drug trafficking routes, making this area critical to the cartels and equally vital for us to dismantle.

The tension at the base was palpable on the morning of September 12, 2000. The operation required a fleet of helicopters and Air Tractors, each playing a crucial role in the synchronized assault. The helicopters, including our newly acquired UH-1H Hueys, a Blackhawk, and a sleek Little Bird, were armed and ready. The Little Bird, with its reputation for precision in special operations, added an edge to our arsenal. Seeing it there, perched like a predatory hawk, gave the operation a sense of gravity. This wasn't just fumigation—this was a battle.

As the final checks were completed, I stood on the tarmac, relegated to the role of observer for this mission. I wasn't allowed to fly on these operations, a regulation that frustrated me endlessly, especially on a day like this. The scene unfolding before me was nothing short of cinematic. The Hueys roared to life, their rotors kicking up clouds of dust. The Blackhawk and the Little Bird followed, their engines a deep, resonant thrum that vibrated in your chest.

It was impossible not to think of *Apocalypse Now* as the fleet prepared to take off. The ground crew scurried between the aircraft, securing gear, loading ammunition, and making final adjustments. I half-jokingly asked someone, "Where's *Ride of the Valkyries*?" but no one laughed—they were too focused. The Hueys lifted off first, their slower speeds dictating an early departure, while the Air Tractors remained poised to follow. It was all meticulously timed to ensure they arrived at the target simultaneously. As the helicopters ascended and banked toward the horizon, the Air Tractors revved their engines, their distinct whine filling the air as they lined up for takeoff.

The sight of the entire fleet rising into the sky, silhouetted against the morning sun, was awe-inspiring. It was an image of raw power and precision, the embodiment of Plan Colombia's might. I stood there, both proud and frustrated, watching as they disappeared into the distance, leaving me behind.

The operation was a showcase of tactical coordination. The helicopters would reach the fields first, providing cover for the Colombian drug enforcement police as they moved in on the ground. These officers would patrol the fields, marking areas for fumigation and securing the perimeter against potential threats.

Nariño was a volatile region. The dense jungle and mountainous terrain made it a haven for both the FARC and local paramilitary groups, who often clashed over control of the coca fields. The police weren't just combating plants—they were walking into hostile territory. That's where the Little Bird came in. Agile and deadly, it was designed for inserting forces into tight spaces and providing precise aerial support. It would hover over the field edges, ready to unleash its firepower if needed.

As the helicopters secured the area, the Air Tractors swept in, their spray nozzles releasing a fine mist of herbicide over the coca plants. These aircraft were the workhorses of the operation, each one capable of covering vast swathes of land in a single sortie. Flying low and fast, they painted the fields with their deadly cargo, leaving a trail of dying greenery in their wake. The contrast was stark—lush, vibrant plants turning brown and withered within days.

The pilots had to be precise. Nariño's fields weren't isolated—they were interspersed with legitimate crops. A single miscalculation could ruin a farmer's livelihood and add fuel to the local resentment against these operations. The pilots were well-trained, but the stakes were high.

While the operation was a tactical success, it wasn't without its challenges. Nariño wasn't just a strategic hub for coca cultivation—it was home to thousands of impoverished farmers who depended on coca to survive. For many, it was the only crop that could thrive in the region's conditions and fetch a price high enough to sustain their families. Destroying these fields without offering viable alternatives created a cycle of resentment and desperation, one that the cartels were all too eager to exploit.

There were also the environmental concerns. The herbicides used in aerial fumigation were effective but controversial. Critics argued they contaminated local water sources and harmed surrounding ecosystems. The government insisted the methods were safe, but the debate raged on, casting a shadow over the operation's successes.

Back at base, I followed the progress of Operation Manglar through radio updates. Reports trickled in throughout the day: hectares destroyed, ground secured, minor resistance encountered but nothing the team couldn't handle. The Air tractors arrived back first, being faster than the helos, but they soon poured in and landed in true military style, one by one, their rotors chopping through the humid air as they settled back on the tarmac. The pilots looked weary but triumphant. They'd eradicated a significant portion of the coca fields, dealing a blow to the cartels operating in the area.

Yet, as I debriefed with the team and reviewed the operation's outcomes, my thoughts returned to the USS frigate I'd visited in New York. Their proud claim of confiscating 40 kilos of cocaine in three months now seemed almost laughable compared to the scale of what we were achieving here. In a single day, Operation Manglar had destroyed the raw material for thousands of kilos, cutting deep into the cartels' supply chain. But the work was far from over. This was just one battle in a war that seemed to have no end.

As I walked back to my quarters that night, the sound of helicopters still echoed in my ears. The operation had been a success, but I couldn't shake the feeling that we were fighting a hydra—cut off one head, and two more would take its place. Still, for today at least, we had made a difference. And sometimes, that was enough.

The momentum from Operation Manglar carried us into the final months of 2000 with a renewed sense of purpose. These large-scale missions became the cornerstone of our efforts, showcasing the newfound capacity and coordination brought by Plan Colombia. Though I was primarily involved in the planning phase and not on the ground for the operations themselves, the sense of accomplishment after each successful mission was undeniable. The scale of these endeavours was staggering, and their execution required meticulous strategy and seamless collaboration between Colombian forces and their international partners.

One such mission, Operation Paramillo, unfolded on November 30, 2000, in the rugged terrain of Caucasia, Antioquia. It was another ambitious push to dismantle the cocaine supply chain at its core. The operation aimed to fumigate approximately 7,000 hectares of coca fields and take out several cocaine processing labs concealed deep within the wilderness. Caucasia, with its fertile land and proximity to critical transport routes, had long been a hotbed for the cultivation and trafficking of coca.

Adding weight to the significance of the operation was the presence of U.S. Ambassador Anne Patterson at its launch, a move calculated to showcase the strategic partnership between Colombia and the United States in their shared fight against drug trafficking. Her arrival was marked with the kind of diplomatic precision that underscored the operation's importance. Flanked by Colombian officials and military leaders, Patterson exuded a calm yet authoritative presence as she addressed a small gathering of press and local dignitaries, emphasizing the steadfast commitment of the United States to combat the narcotics trade and its associated violence.

Her speech highlighted the resources and expertise the U.S. was bringing to the table. From state-of-the-art equipment to rigorous training programs for Colombian forces, the American contribution extended beyond financial aid. The helicopters taking off that morning—the Black Hawks, the Littlebirds

and Hueys laden with guns and troops—were emblematic of U.S. military aid under Plan Colombia. Patterson made it clear that these missions were not only about targeting the coca fields but also about strengthening the institutional capabilities of Colombia's military and police forces.

Behind the scenes, her presence was equally significant. It wasn't just a matter of optics. Ambassador Patterson's attendance symbolized the diplomatic weight and political stakes tied to these operations. Her role as a bridge between the two nations went beyond rhetoric; she was deeply involved in ensuring the alignment of goals and resources, acting as a key figure in managing the complex dynamics of U.S.-Colombian relations. Her words to the Colombian officials that day were not just about solidarity but about accountability. The U.S. was heavily invested, and there was an unspoken understanding that results were expected.

Her participation also brought media attention to the operation, ensuring that its scale and intent were broadcast far and wide. For the Colombian government, this was an opportunity to showcase its commitment to tackling one of the country's most entrenched problems. For the United States, it was a chance to demonstrate the tangible application of Plan Colombia, a program that had already faced criticism and scrutiny in Washington. The ambassador's presence was a statement in itself: the U.S. wasn't just funding the fight; it was actively engaged in it.

On the ground, her involvement was a morale booster for the Colombian forces and a stark reminder of the international dimensions of their mission. Police and civilian contract pilots alike took pride in showcasing their readiness and professionalism before such a high-profile audience. They knew the stakes weren't just national but global; the success or failure of these missions would ripple far beyond Colombia's borders.

Through her actions and presence, Patterson made it clear that the United States viewed the war on drugs in Colombia as an essential front in its broader international strategy. The mission in Caucasia that day wasn't merely an anti-drug operation—it was a symbol of the collaboration between two nations bound by a shared goal, albeit one that carried immense challenges. Patterson's presence wasn't just ceremonial; it was a reminder of the resources, expectations, and international scrutiny that accompanied this fight. The stakes had never been higher, and for those on the ground, her presence underscored just how much was riding on their success.

The mission's scale demanded the use of many of our force of helicopters, which played a dual role in this operation. They were deployed not only for fumigation runs over the vast fields of coca plants but also for logistical support, allowing troops to access the remote, heavily forested areas where the labs were hidden. These helicopters—alongside the resilience of the Colombian anti-narcotics forces—were pivotal in overcoming the challenges of the harsh terrain, ensuring the mission could target both the agricultural and production stages of the drug trade.

Antioquia's reputation as a critical region in Colombia's drug trade meant that operations like Paramillo were not merely tactical but symbolic. By targeting such an integral hub of the coca supply chain, the mission aimed to send a clear message to the cartels: no region was beyond the reach of Colombia's forces. Beyond eradicating crops, the destruction of processing labs was a direct strike at the cartels' ability to convert raw coca leaves into marketable cocaine, further disrupting their operations.

The day the operation commenced, I watched from afar, reflecting on the months of planning and preparation that had gone into it. Knowing that my contributions helped shape these monumental efforts was immensely rewarding. However, even amid the satisfaction of a successful mission, the challenges remained clear. Operations like Paramillo often sparked debates about their long-term impact on the local environment and communities. Aerial fumigation, while effective in the short term, raised concerns about the health of local populations and the unintended consequences for subsistence farmers caught in the crossfire.

Still, the eradication of coca fields and the dismantling of cocaine labs were critical steps in curbing the flow of drugs and weakening the cartels' grip on the region. Operation Paramillo stood as a testament to what could be achieved through determination, collaboration, and the resources provided by Plan Colombia. As I reflected on its success, I couldn't help but feel a mix of pride and anticipation for what the coming months would bring. This was only the beginning of a long and arduous fight, but for now, it was a victory worth celebrating.

Chapter 10: New Surroundings

By the end of 2000, life in Bogotá had taken on a new shape for me. What had begun as a solo journey in an unpredictable and often dangerous world had evolved into something more settled, more rooted. I was originally taken on with a 2 year contract which had annual extensions but with Plan Colombia rolling out my contract was extended for five years. It now felt like the right time to put down firmer roots. I wasn't just a single guy anymore—there were three of us now, Martha, myself, and of course, Philip. It was time for a bigger, better home.

The new house wasn't far from our old one, still in a decent residential area with a bustling main road nearby lined with shops and conveniences. It was a corner property, two stories tall, and much larger than what we were used to. Four bedrooms upstairs provided ample space for all of us, while downstairs featured a spacious sitting room and dining room separated by an open, dramatic staircase. The parking area was vast, perfect for my growing family and any guests. The garage, which had the potential for a small business, was an added bonus.

The house wasn't perfect, though. The kitchen, Martha pointed out immediately, was tiny—far too small for her liking. I assured her we'd make do, and we all agreed the rest of the house was more than enough compensation. With the extra space came extra responsibility, and we hired a young woman to clean twice a week. Martha, however, quickly grew restless when I wasn't home. Having quit her job at the sports store six months prior, she longed for something to occupy her time.

The garage, with its business potential, became the answer. Martha decided to open a laundry. We bought four large washing machines and two industrial dryers and installed them in the garage. A bright yellow sign soon adorned the front: **"Lavandería Harrison"**. It didn't take long for the neighbourhood to take notice. Customers poured in, bringing bundles of clothes that Martha worked tirelessly to clean.

I admired her strength and resilience as she carried heavy loads of wet laundry from the machines to the dryers. For someone so small in stature, Martha was formidable. Pedro occasionally stepped in to help with the heavier tasks, but even he found it exhausting. This from a young, fit ex-soldier. "She's tougher than she looks," Pedro muttered one day, shaking his head in disbelief. And he wasn't wrong.

Pedro's other role—making purchases—remained vital. He was our secret weapon against the infamous "gringo price." On one occasion, I asked about the cost of a wooden work table at a local store and was quoted $40. Pedro went in a few hours later and returned with three tables—for $30 total. It became an ongoing joke in the household that I wasn't allowed near negotiations unless I wanted to pay triple.

Philip, meanwhile, continued his lively romance with Jacky, though it wasn't without its hiccups. One night, he had a date with her at a popular bar in the city's nightlife district. By midnight, with no sign of him and his phone forgotten at home, Martha and I grew worried. We stayed up late, pacing the house. At 2 a.m., the doorbell rang. Through the small window, I saw a taxi driver standing there, holding a scrap of paper with our address.

"Yes, this is the right house," I said, relieved. I handed him a generous tip—far more than the fare. It wasn't uncommon in Bogotá for taxi drivers to drug and rob their passengers, and I wanted to show our appreciation. Philip stumbled in, muttering incoherently, "I love you, son. I love you, Mat'ra. Why can't I find someone like Mat'ra?" We laughed, helping him upstairs and putting him to bed.

The next morning, the story emerged. Jacky hadn't shown up, so Philip had drowned his disappointment in whiskey—first at one bar, then another when the first ran out. By morning, all was forgiven, though the incident became a running joke in the house. Jacky's apology seemed to smooth things over, and their relationship continued, albeit with its quirky moments.

One day, as he waited for Jacky to visit, Philip asked me, "How do you say 'Suck my dick' in Spanish?"

"Dad, I'm your son. Don't ask me that."

"Just tell me!" he pleaded.

I relented, and he scribbled it down on a piece of paper, muttering "Chupame la verga" under his breath as he climbed the stairs. Unfortunately for him, Martha overheard.

"What's he saying?" she asked, raising an eyebrow.

"Nothing important," I replied quickly, hoping to defuse the situation.

A few minutes later, the doorbell rang, and Jacky arrived, her usual cheerful self. "Hi, Stephen. How's Philip?"

"Oh, he's fine," I replied, grinning. "He's been practicing his Spanish."

"Isn't that sweet?" she said, oblivious to what exactly he'd been practicing. Philip, hearing her voice, bounded down the stairs like an eager teenager, greeted her with a dramatic "Hola, mi amor," and whisked her back upstairs.

I couldn't help but smile at this situation. Life in our house was never dull.

Philip had always been a man of bravado, a trait that made him larger than life in so many ways. But behind the twinkle in his eye and his endless charm, there were cracks beginning to show. He had been smoking since the age of eleven, a habit that had now stretched across more than fifty years. It was catching up with him. Over the past few months, I had noticed how he tired easily and was often overcome by violent coughing fits that left him short of breath.

"You need to see a doctor," I told him one evening as he slumped into the armchair, his chest heaving after another coughing spell.

He waved me off with his usual bravado. "I don't need some fuckin' foreign doctor I can't even talk to. What's he gonna do? Talk to me in fuckin' sign language?" He laughed, but it was half-hearted. The truth was, he hated feeling vulnerable, and the thought of seeing a doctor who didn't speak English only added to his discomfort.

"Fine," I relented. "See your doctor when you go back to the UK for your pension."

He nodded. "Yeah, yeah. I'll get it sorted." But his tone was dismissive, as though the issue could simply wait.

In July, Philip flew back to England to collect his pension. He was excited, as always, about the trip and had already made plans to see old friends and visit his usual haunts. A week after he left, I received a call. It was Philip, and his voice, though familiar, carried a strange edge of weariness.

"Son, I've had a bit of a scare," he began, his tone uncharacteristically subdued.

"What happened?" I asked, immediately on edge.

"Almost passed out on the fuckin? plane," he admitted. "They had to take me off under supervision. Can you believe that? Fuckin' embarrassing."

"Did they take you to a hospital?" I pressed, already dreading the answer.

"Yeah, they did," he admitted reluctantly. "They've got me in now, running all sorts of bloody tests. I feel fine now, though. Nothing to worry about."

But it was clear to me that there was something to worry about. Philip's dismissive attitude wasn't reassuring, and the fact that he was calling from a hospital bed, admitting to tests, only heightened my concern.

"What kind of tests?" I asked, trying to keep my tone neutral.

"Eh, the usual. Fuckin? tests, X-rays, fuckin' prodding me here and there. They've got all the time in the fuckin' world, these doctors. You know what the NHS is like—don't fuckin' rush for anything." He chuckled, but there was a hollowness to it.

I could hear the strain in his voice, the way he tried to downplay everything, as though by minimizing it, he could will it into being less serious. But I wasn't convinced. The image of him, taken off the plane under supervision, stuck in my mind. This was not a man who fainted or admitted weakness easily. For him to have landed in a hospital after such an episode—it was serious.

"Dad," I said, my voice firm, "I need you to let me know the results of those tests as soon as you get them. No messing around."

He sighed, a long exhale that told me he understood my concern even if he wouldn't admit it outright. "Alright, alright. Don't worry yourself. I'll let you know. But I'm fuckin' fine, really."

I hung up the phone, trying to shake off the sense of unease that had settled in my chest. Despite his words, I couldn't ignore the facts. Philip wasn't the indestructible man he'd always seemed to be. Something was wrong, and I could only hope the doctors would find it in time. For now, I had to wait—and hope he wasn't hiding the truth from me.

When I learned we were moving our central operations to Larandia in the department of Caquetá, I felt a mix of anticipation and nostalgia. This wasn't just another relocation—it was a step toward establishing a more professional and centralized operation. Larandia, officially known as El Fuerte Militar Larandia, was a sprawling joint military base shared by the Colombian Air Force, the National Army, and the Navy. Situated in the rural outskirts of Florencia, Caquetá's capital, the base embodied a unique blend of strategic importance and rugged charm.

The story behind Larandia added to its mystique. It had once been a grand hacienda belonging to the Lara family, who donated the land to the Colombian Army. The resulting base was a sprawling military town divided by a wide, fast-moving river, with the airstrip positioned to the north. Soldiers' barracks, officer accommodations, workshops, and even casinos (the Colombian term for military mess halls) dotted the landscape. An armoured brigade was stationed there, complete with jeeps and compact six-wheeled tanks that gave the base an atmosphere of readiness.

When I first arrived, the scene transported me back to my days in the Royal Navy. Young soldiers bustled about, saluting officers as they passed. Some even saluted me, likely unsure of who I was or whether they were required to. I never corrected them—I wasn't entirely sure myself—but I always returned the salutes crisply, in proper Royal Naval fashion. There was something immensely satisfying about stepping into a world that felt structured and disciplined, even if it wasn't quite my own.

My quarters in the officer's accommodation were modest but comfortable. I was given a senior officer's room, spacious enough for my needs and conveniently close to the mess hall. My new office, located in the admin building, was another source of pride. For the first time, it felt like we were running a professional operation. The chaotic days of makeshift setups in Bogota or Tumaco were behind us. Here, we had structure, resources, and, most importantly, respect.

Larandia also became the headquarters for the newly created Brigada Contra el Narcotráfico (Counter-Narcotics Brigade). Established on December 8, 2000, the brigade was a specialized unit composed of three battalions, each trained to combat the ever-evolving tactics of drug traffickers. Its creation underscored the escalating war against cocaine production, and Larandia was now at the heart of it.

While Larandia served as our central hub, we maintained active operations from two other critical bases: Tumaco and Santa Rosa. Each was strategically located to cover the vast regions where cocaine fields thrived. Tumaco, on the Pacific coast, provided access to the sprawling coca plantations hidden in the dense jungle terrain of Nariño. Santa Rosa, in Bolívar Department, was roughly 720 kilometers north of Larandia and offered a foothold in the northern regions of the country. Its proximity to strategic waterways and trafficking routes made it a key location for interdiction efforts.

With these three bases—Larandia, Tumaco, and Santa Rosa—we had the reach to conduct operations on a truly national scale. The logistics were daunting, but the prospect of coordinated, simultaneous missions across Colombia was thrilling. It felt as if the years of groundwork were finally coming together.

Living on base had its perks. The sense of camaraderie was strong, and the daily rituals of military life brought a comforting routine. Soldiers moved with purpose, the roar of helicopters became a constant backdrop, and the sight of armoured vehicles rumbling across the grounds reminded me of the high stakes we were dealing with.

I found myself drawn to the energy of the place. The salutes, the hierarchy, the drills—it all brought back memories of my own military career. Though I was technically a civilian contractor, my rank of O-6, equivalent to a colonel, afforded me certain privileges. And while I never demanded respect, it was clear that the soldiers regarded me as one of their own, even if only unofficially.

Larandia wasn't just a base—it was a symbol of what we were trying to achieve. It represented the fusion of military precision, international cooperation, and national determination to dismantle Colombia's cocaine empire. The move marked a turning point, not just for our operations but for me personally. It felt like a homecoming of sorts—a return to the structured, disciplined life I had once known, but with a new and urgent purpose.

As we settled into Larandia and began planning our next operations, the possibilities seemed endless. For the first time, I felt we had the tools, the strategy, and the infrastructure to make a real difference. This wasn't just another chapter—it was the beginning of a new era in the fight against Colombia's most pervasive enemy.

Chapter 11: Hitting back

At the beginning of 2001, we faced our first casualty—a stark and sobering reminder of the dangers we were dealing with. The incident happened during a routine aerial eradication mission deep in the jungle, in an area heavily contested by the Revolutionary Armed Forces of Colombia (FARC). One of our Air Tractors, those steadfast workhorses we relied upon to spray the coca fields, was shot down by the FARC during a mission near El Tarra, a small town in the Catatumbo region of Norte de Santander in northeastern Colombia. The pilot, one of the originals from our Tocuma days, a seasoned veteran who had been with us through the early, chaotic missions, didn't survive.

The Catatumbo region was notorious, a rugged expanse of dense jungle and mountainous terrain that had long been a haven for armed groups like the FARC. Its strategic location, close to the Venezuelan border, coupled with its sprawling coca plantations, made it a focal point for both insurgent operations and government eradication efforts. It was an area where the stakes were always high, and the risks even higher. The FARC's presence here wasn't just significant—it was entrenched. They controlled much of the lucrative coca trade and had no intention of relinquishing it without a fight.

The mission had launched from our newly established northern base in Santa Rosa del Sur, Bolívar. The pilot, a steady and reliable man who had been with us since the early days in Tocuma, was among those who had helped shape our operations. He knew the dangers, as did we all, but his calm demeanour and unwavering dedication made him a cornerstone of our team. This was supposed to be a routine mission—another step in our relentless campaign against coca cultivation.

But nothing in Catatumbo was ever routine. Intelligence reports had warned of increased FARC activity in the region, but the exact threat level had been unclear. As the Air Tractor descended low over the fields to release its payload of herbicide, the ambush came. Hidden deep in the jungle, the FARC had positioned themselves with automatic weapons and possibly even an anti-aircraft gun. Witnesses from the escort helicopters described a barrage of gunfire erupting as the Air Tractor flew over. Smoke billowed from its engine, and the plane lost altitude rapidly. The pilot fought valiantly to regain control, but the jungle canopy swallowed the aircraft in a final, terrible descent.

The aftermath was chilling. Efforts to recover the wreckage and the pilot's remains were fraught with danger. The FARC's control of the area meant the recovery team, composed of police and soldiers, faced the constant threat of ambush. The thick jungle, treacherous terrain, and the looming presence of armed guerillas turned what should have been a straightforward operation into a perilous mission. Despite these obstacles, the team succeeded in bringing back what they could, ensuring our fallen comrade wouldn't be left behind.

The loss hit us hard. This was more than just a reminder of the risks we faced—it was a harsh awakening to the brutal reality of our work. The pilot wasn't just a colleague; he was a friend, a mentor, a brother-in-arms. He had been there in the early days, flying from Tocuma when our operations were still finding their footing. He had been a steady hand, a voice of reason, and a symbol of the resilience that defined our team. Now, he was gone, and his absence was a void we all felt deeply.

Back at Larandia, the mood was somber. We gathered in the mess to share stories, raise a toast, and honour his memory. Even in the sadness, there was a shared resolve—a determination to carry on the work he believed in. For many of us, the danger was part of the job, but this loss made it deeply personal. We weren't just fighting a war on drugs; we were fighting for each other, for the team, and for the lives touched by the devastation of the cocaine trade.

The loss of the aircraft and its crew sent ripples far beyond the jungles of Catatumbo. The incident forced immediate and long-term changes, touching everything from our operational procedures to international diplomacy. It wasn't just another casualty of war—it was a flashpoint, underscoring the dangers we faced and the broader implications of our mission.

In the days following the crash, the security measures for eradication flights were placed under intense scrutiny. The ambush had exposed vulnerabilities in our planning, particularly in high-risk areas like Catatumbo. Conversations in Larandia and Santa Rosa turned to how we could prevent such tragedies in the future. Enhanced air support and reconnaissance quickly became priorities. Helicopters equipped with advanced surveillance equipment were integrated more closely into eradication missions, and the timing of operations was adjusted to include real-time intelligence updates. Escort helicopters were ordered to stay closer to the spray planes, and our pilots received additional training in evasive manoeuvres to handle hostile fire.

The loss also triggered diplomatic ripples, especially because the fallen pilot was an American citizen. The United States, a critical partner in Plan Colombia, was drawn deeper into the controversy surrounding its role in Colombia's internal conflict. Media coverage in both countries amplified the narrative, with some praising the bravery of the crews and others questioning the cost—both human and financial—of America's involvement. The incident became a lightning rod for critics of Plan Colombia, fueling debates about the ethics and effectiveness of the aerial eradication program. In Washington, there were murmurs about whether enough was being done to protect the crews risking their lives.

Some questioned if the strategy itself needed re-evaluation, as the growing backlash called into question the balance between the program's objectives and its human toll.

Amid this heightened scrutiny, operational reviews were ordered. Discussions about the effectiveness of aerial fumigation resurfaced, alongside concerns about the risks to crews. The method, while efficient in covering vast areas of coca cultivation, faced renewed criticism. Environmental groups pointed to the potential harm caused by glyphosate on local ecosystems, while human rights organizations raised alarms about its impact on communities living near sprayed areas. The tragedy of losing a crew member became a symbol for both sides—those advocating for the continuation of the program and those demanding a shift toward less confrontational methods.

The broader context of the war on drugs in Colombia only added layers of complexity. The FARC's grip on regions like Catatumbo was a stark reminder that aerial eradication missions were never just about spraying coca fields. These areas were battlegrounds where powerful armed groups defended their lucrative drug trade with military precision. The incident brought to light the high-risk nature of our work. The dense jungles, the hidden snipers, and the unpredictable terrain made every mission a gamble. Even with the best technology and meticulous planning, the danger was omnipresent.

As these debates raged on, we in the field faced the stark reality of our mission. The risks were not theoretical; they were painfully real. And yet, the work continued. The loss of a plane and its pilot served as a somber reminder of what was at stake, but it also strengthened our resolve. Each eradication flight, each destroyed coca field, was a blow against an industry that fuelled violence and instability. We knew we were fighting a hydra, and every head we severed seemed to grow another, but we also knew the alternative—doing nothing—was unthinkable.

For us, the tragedy became both a lesson and a rallying point. The adjustments we made in the aftermath didn't just aim to safeguard the crews; they reaffirmed the commitment to the mission. We were there to make a difference, and the sacrifices made by those who had come before us, including the fallen pilot, only deepened our resolve. The battle against coca cultivation wasn't just about statistics or hectares sprayed—it was about the lives caught in the web of a deadly trade. And we owed it to our fallen colleagues to see it through.

As I stood in the hangar looking at the aircraft readying for their next mission, I couldn't help but think of him. The work would go on, the planes would keep flying, but his loss was a stark reminder of what we were up against. In the end, it wasn't just about eradicating coca fields or disrupting drug routes—it was about the people, the lives we saved, and those we lost along the way.

As operations were temporarily suspended, I found myself summoned to Bogotá for meetings with DIRAN. The lull in the aerial missions left me restless, and I decided to return to the prison to continue teaching. It was a familiar setting that allowed me to keep my mind occupied during the pause in eradication flights. The morning I arrived, the prison was its usual cacophony of sounds—the clang of metal gates, muffled voices through barred windows, and the ever-present tension that hung in the air.

As I passed the gate near maximum security where I'd once encountered "Popeye," I noticed three unfamiliar faces. They were seated near the gate, their expressions calm but distinctly out of place among the usual hardened inmates. Two of them appeared to be around my age—one with a beard, the other clean-shaven—and the third was noticeably older, with grey hair and a weathered demeanour.

"Hello there," one of them greeted in English, the accent unmistakably Irish. Intrigued, I walked over and struck up a conversation.

They introduced themselves without fanfare, their demeanour casual. When I asked why they were there, they answered with nonchalance: "Fake passports."

"Fake passports?" I repeated, my curiosity piqued. It didn't make sense. They were Irish, so why would they need British passports? Irish passports were just as good, with similar access to countries requiring visas. Something about their story didn't add up.

"Why are you in maximum security for a trivial charge?" I pressed.

"For our own protection," one of them replied with a shrug, as if that explanation should suffice. The answer only deepened my suspicion. Other European and North American inmates weren't separated for their safety, so why these three?

The exchange gnawed at me as I made my way to the education department. Later, at the administrative office, I casually inquired about the three Irishmen. The reaction was immediate and telling. The guards exchanged wary glances before one of them leaned in closer and lowered his voice.

"You don't know who they are?" he asked.

"No, should I?" I replied.

"They're IRA."

The words hit like a hammer. Irish Republican Army.

"What are they doing here?" I asked, my voice steady but my mind racing.

"They were caught training the guerrillas. Teaching them how to use explosives, including how to turn household plumbing pipes into missile launchers for shooting down aircraft."

My stomach churned. This wasn't just another odd encounter in the labyrinth of La Modelo. These men, members of the IRA, were here to support the very guerrilla forces responsible for killing our colleagues and attempting to destroy everything we were working toward. I couldn't help but wonder if they'd played a role in the attack that brought down our Air Tractor in Catatumbo. The possibility was sickening.

From that moment on, my perspective shifted. I avoided any further contact with them, steering clear of the gate where they often loitered. If our paths crossed, I made no acknowledgment, offering them nothing but silence. They, of course, had no idea who I was or my role in the operations they were so determined to undermine.

But I knew who they were. I knew what they stood for. And I despised them for it. It wasn't just professional—it was personal. The thought of them assisting the guerrillas to kill pilots, mechanics, and ground crew I considered family left a bitter taste that lingered long after I left the prison each day.

Back at my quarters that evening, the weight of the revelation settled heavily on me. The enemy wasn't just out in the jungles or hiding behind the guise of coca farmers. They were here, within these very walls, plotting and scheming in ways I hadn't fully imagined. It reinforced what I'd always known but sometimes tried to forget: this was a war, and we were all its combatants, whether we chose to be or not.

I'd faced many challenges since taking on this mission, but something about these men— their quiet arrogance, their calculated detachment—unnerved me in a way few others had. They were a stark reminder that the danger wasn't just theoretical or distant. It was real, immediate, and often much closer than I cared to admit.

I continued my routine visits into the patios, stepping into the strange and often surreal world of La Modelo. On one such visit, I sought out the South African man I had met during one of my earlier excursions into Patio 3—the one who had mistakenly thought I was the British ambassador. His demeanour was always friendly, and his cell was a quiet respite from the chaos that usually surrounded me in the prison.

When I arrived, he greeted me warmly and invited me into his cell. It was cramped, like all the others, but neat and surprisingly homey. A small stack of books sat neatly in one corner, and a tiny portable typewriter perched on a makeshift desk made from repurposed materials.

"Do you like pancakes?" he asked with a grin.

Caught off guard but intrigued, I nodded. "Yeah, sure."

With an air of practiced efficiency, he pulled a small hotplate out from under his bed. It looked ancient and well-used, with bare wires that he plugged directly into the socket. The hotplate glowed a fierce red as he placed a tiny frying pan on it and poured in a pre-made batter mix from a reused plastic bottle. Within moments, the rich, comforting smell of pancakes filled the cell. He served them hot, with a dollop of jam, and we sat on the edge of his bunk eating together. The juxtaposition of eating pancakes with jam in the middle of a Colombian prison wasn't lost on me—it was one of those moments that felt absurdly normal despite the circumstances.

As we ate, he opened up about his situation. He told me he was serving time for drug smuggling and admitted, without much bitterness, that he still had a long stretch ahead of him. His calm acceptance of his fate was disarming. My eyes wandered to the typewriter on the desk, and I asked if he was a writer.

"Of sorts," he replied, wiping his hands on a scrap of cloth. "I help the other inmates. Legal petitions, formal requests—anything official. They pay me enough to cover my 'rent' here in Patio 3."

"That's resourceful," I said, impressed. "Do you get much work?"

"Not anymore," he said, his tone growing somber. "The typewriter's broken. There's a tiny sprocket inside that's cracked, and I can't find a replacement."

I asked him for the model, and he grabbed a small scrap of paper to write it down. It was an Olivetti, a brand I vaguely recognized. "I'll see what I can do," I told him, though I wasn't sure how much luck I'd have.

A couple of days later, while walking through Bogotá's bustling city center, I came across a tiny shop with a faded sign that read: *Olivetti Official Distributor.* The place was packed wall-to-wall with shelves of typewriter parts and other mechanical odds and ends. The air smelled of grease and aging metal. I approached the shopkeeper and asked about the sprocket, showing him the piece of paper with the model's name scribbled on it. Without hesitation, he pulled out an exploded diagram of the typewriter on a dusty old computer screen. I recognized the part immediately, and within minutes, he returned from the backroom with a small bag containing three sprockets.

"How much?" I asked, half-expecting a steep price.

"Six thousand pesos," he said.

I handed over the equivalent of two dollars, amazed at how easy it had been. Clutching the bag, I couldn't wait to deliver the news.

As I was walking back to the car park where I had parked up, a booming voice called out, "Professor! Is that you?"

The accent was unmistakable—Nigerian. I turned and spotted him immediately: one of the Africans I'd taught in La Modelo, the ones who had spent 21 months inside simply for being poor and staying in a dodgy hotel. He was beaming, his wide smile cutting through the chaos of the street as he strode toward me.

Before I could say anything, he threw his arms around me in a bear hug, nearly knocking the wind out of me. "It's so good to see you!" he said, still grinning.

"It's good to see you too," I replied, genuinely pleased. There was something heartwarming about seeing someone walk free after all they'd been through.

"How are you, Professor?" he asked quickly. "Are you well?"

"I'm doing fine," I said. "What about you?"

He waved off the question with an exaggerated shrug, his eyes already drifting toward my wallet as I reached for some spare cash. "Professor, can you give me 2,000 pesos for a coffee?" he asked.

It wasn't much—about a dollar—and I was more than happy to oblige. I opened my wallet and began pulling out the small bill when I noticed his expression change. His eyes lit up, locking onto a 50,000-peso note tucked just inside.

"Actually," he said, his tone suddenly urgent, "can I have that one instead?" He pointed a finger at the larger bill.

I raised an eyebrow. "So you don't want the 2,000 pesos anymore?"

"No, no," he said eagerly, his grin widening. "I want the other one."

I couldn't help but laugh. "Nice try," I said, handing him the smaller note. "Don't get greedy."

He took it with a sheepish grin and clapped me on the shoulder. "Thank you, Professor. You are a good man!"

I walked away, still chuckling to myself. Even on the outside, these guys never missed a chance to try their luck. Some things, it seemed, would never change.

The following Monday, after finishing my morning classes, I made my way back into Patio 3. When I handed the South African man the sprockets, his reaction floored me. He held the small bag like it was a treasure, his face lighting up with sheer gratitude. For a moment, I thought he might cry.

"You have no idea what this means to me," he said, his voice cracking slightly. "Let me pay you back."

"Don't worry about it," I said, waving him off.

"No, I insist," he replied. "At least let me make you some pancakes."

And so, I found myself once again sitting on the edge of his bunk, eating pancakes and talking about life. The simplicity of the moment was humbling.

The following day, as I stood at the front of the classroom, watching the inmates trickle in one by one, I couldn't help but notice that something was off. Normally, the men ambled into class with an air of indifference—gruff and tired, but resigned to the routine. Today was different. The atmosphere was thick with suppressed laughter and smirking faces, tempered only by an undercurrent of palpable irritation.

In particular, one young inmate seemed to be the epicenter of it all. He was a chubby guy, no older than 25, with a round face and a perpetually slumped posture. He plodded to his seat, his eyes cast downward, and slumped into the chair with a sigh that seemed to come from the soles of his shoes. As he did, the others began filing past him, each taking a moment to deliver their own form of punishment.

One smacked him lightly on the back of the head.
Another banged his shoulder as he walked past.
A third just looked at him with disgust and spat out the word, *"Veintiuno!"*—"Twenty-one!"—his tone dripping with derision.

The word spread like a chant among the others as they all muttered it under their breath, each delivering their own sneer or smirk as they settled into their seats.

I watched the whole scene unfold with growing curiosity. What the hell was going on? "Twenty-one?" What was that supposed to mean? I didn't say anything during class; I had enough trouble keeping these guys on task as it was. But during the break, my curiosity got the better of me. I walked up to the young man, who was now sitting alone at his desk, poking dejectedly at a crumb of bread from his snack.

"Hey," I said gently, pulling up a chair beside him. "What's this all about? Why is everyone calling you 'twenty-one'?"

He looked up at me, his face a mix of embarrassment and frustration. For a moment, he didn't answer. He just shifted uncomfortably, as though deciding whether or not to tell me. Finally, with a heavy sigh, he relented.

"There was an escape yesterday," he mumbled, his voice low enough that I had to lean in to hear.

That piqued my interest. "An escape? What happened?"

He glanced around, making sure no one was close enough to listen, then began his story. It turned out he was from the north wing—*the* north wing, the one run by the guerrillas. Those patios operated under their own law, a sort of shadow government, and everyone knew it. Every so often, they'd orchestrate a tunnel escape. The process, I learned, was almost ritualistic in its structure.

"First," he explained, "the tunnel gets dug—quick, narrow, and dirty—but just enough to do the job. Before anyone escapes, they use it to bring in weapons and drugs to keep control and make money."

The tone in his voice suggested he wasn't proud of this knowledge, but in prison, it wasn't like you had a choice.

"Then, the guerrilla leaders get to leave first," he continued. "Their guys. After that, it's the turn of the regular inmates—but only the ones who *paid* for it. You gotta pay to get out."

"Paid?" I asked, genuinely intrigued. "How much?"

He scratched the back of his head awkwardly. "Anywhere from five thousand to twenty thousand dollars."

I nearly whistled at the price. "That's not cheap."

"Yeah," he muttered. "It's a business."

"So what does 'twenty-one' have to do with this?" I pressed.

He sighed again, this time deeper, heavier. "I was number twenty-one on the list."

I frowned, trying to understand. "And?"

He looked up at me, his eyes narrowing with a mixture of frustration and humiliation. "And I got stuck."

"Stuck?"

"In the tunnel," he clarified, his face going red. "It was narrow, and, well..." He gestured helplessly to his ample frame. "I couldn't fit."

The image flashed through my mind—him wedged in a narrow, dark tunnel, his legs flailing, the alarmed shouts of the others behind him. I fought the urge to laugh, but he kept going.

"They tried to pull me out. Tied a rope around my legs and yanked as hard as they could. By the time they dragged me free, the tunnel collapsed behind me."

"Collapsed?" I asked, stunned.

"Yeah," he said bitterly. "They tried to reopen it, but that's when the alarm went off. The guards heard something and started closing everything down. Everyone after me—everyone from twenty-two on—had to crawl back to their cells."

I sat back in my chair, processing the absurdity of it all. No wonder the other inmates were pissed at him. He hadn't just failed to escape; he'd ruined the escape for everyone else.

"And now they're mad at you," I said, stating the obvious.

He nodded miserably. "They keep saying, '*Veintiuno,* you ruined it.'"

"And what happens now?"

He shrugged. "Nothing. The guards found the collapsed tunnel this morning, and they'll seal it up. The guys after me are just going to have to wait for the next one."

I shook my head, trying to imagine how someone could both afford to pay thousands of dollars for an escape and yet somehow end up stuck halfway through. It was almost laughable.

"Why are you here today?" I asked, genuinely curious. "Why not hide out in your cell until they calm down?"

"Because I still need the discount," he said flatly, referring to the reduced sentences they earned by attending class.

Of course. For all the humiliation, for all the anger from his fellow inmates, he wasn't about to give up his chance at shaving time off his sentence. It was, I had to admit, a kind of resilience in its own right.

"Well," I said, standing up and clapping a hand on his shoulder. "Maybe next time, don't volunteer for tunnelling duty."

He shot me a look that suggested the joke didn't land, but I couldn't help myself. I walked back to the front of the room, chuckling under my breath as I thought about the sheer absurdity of it all.

As I left La Modelo that day, the world outside this cramped place returned with a starkness that hit me like a cold wind. The brief normalcy of pancakes and quiet conversation was gone, replaced by the weight of what this place truly was. This prison—this chaotic microcosm of humanity—was a tangle of contradictions.

The South African with his typewriter and pancakes reminded me that for all the monsters and villains confined here, there were still ordinary men—decent in their own way—who had been ground down by bad decisions, cruel luck, or simply the wrong company. It was hard to reconcile that quiet breakfast with other moments: the hollow arrogance of the so-called naval "Captain," or the idiotic bravado of a fake helicopter pilot who didn't know the controls of his own aircraft. And then there were the IRA men, weaving their web of destruction, or Popeye—the embodiment of casual violence, his chilling laughter a reminder of the lives he'd taken.

Even in the same day, La Modelo could lurch from the absurd to the horrifying. I couldn't help but think of the chubby inmate, humiliated and mocked for collapsing an escape tunnel, his girth costing countless others their shot at freedom. Or the Nigerian I'd once known, now free but still begging on the streets of Bogotá, his joyful shout for a coffee turning into a plea for my larger bills the moment he glimpsed them. These lives were trapped in cycles that seemed impossible to break.

La Modelo wasn't just a prison—it was a battleground, a stage for the bizarre, the tragic, and the grotesque. There were tunnels dug with desperation, weapons hidden under floors, and tunnels collapsing under human weight, like some twisted metaphor for the futility of escape. There were typewriters that brought purpose and pancakes that brought comfort. And yet, for every small flicker of normalcy, there was the sharp edge of reality waiting to cut through it.

Walking back through the security gate and past the barbed-wire topped walls—some curious, some hollow, some murderous—I realized how profoundly unsettling this place was. It was impossible to reconcile these moments of humanity with the darkness that surrounded them. La Modelo was a world unto itself: cruel, absurd, and yet still capable of producing fleeting glimpses of something pure, even beautiful.

But those moments were fragile. Like sunlight trickling through cracks in stone, they were easily swallowed by the shadows.

In August 2001, we welcomed the arrival of the first two Ayres S2 Turbo Thrush aircraft to our fleet. It marked a pivotal moment, as these planes were specifically modified for the gruelling and dangerous missions we undertook. Over the next six months, through to February 2002, the remaining four aircraft arrived, completing our batch of six. These were no ordinary crop dusters; they were warhorses, purpose-built for the harsh realities of our operations. Known for their Narcotics Eradication Delivery Systems (NEDS), these planes were armoured and equipped to endure hostile fire while delivering precision spraying to coca fields deep in guerrilla-controlled territory.

The Turbo Thrush had a reputation for agility and toughness. Developed by Ayres specifically for the United States Department of State, this version featured a reinforced, armoured cockpit and engine designed to withstand small-arms fire—an ever-present threat in the fields of Colombia. Though not as large or powerful as the Air Tractor AT-802, it was a precise tool for eradication missions, perfect for navigating the treacherous and dense terrain where coca cultivation thrived.

The day the first shipment arrived was a spectacle. A massive C-5 Galaxy transport aircraft, one of the largest in the western world, landed on the tarmac, dwarfing everything around it. Watching the cargo bay doors slowly open to reveal two gleaming Turbo Thrush planes, carefully packed side by side, was like seeing reinforcements arrive on a battlefield. The sense of anticipation among the ground crew was palpable. These planes were more than just machinery; they were symbols of our evolving strategy, tools that could change the course of our fight.

The Ayres Turbo Thrush was smaller than the Air Tractor AT-802, but what it lacked in size, it made up for in finesse. It could carry around 500 gallons of herbicide, significantly less than the AT-802's 800 gallons, but its manoeuvrability and speed were unmatched. The cockpit felt snug, almost intimate, and every control felt within reach, giving the pilot a profound sense of connection to the aircraft. Its Pratt & Whitney PT6A turboprop engine delivered power that belied its size, enabling sharp climbs and quick responses—essential in regions where speed and precision could mean the difference between life and death.

In contrast, the Air Tractor AT-802 was a behemoth. Its sheer size and capability made it a different kind of weapon in our arsenal. The aircraft felt like a fortress in the sky, with its 1,295-horsepower engine effortlessly lifting heavy payloads and delivering them across vast fields. Its long wings and sturdy frame made it a stable and reliable platform, capable of covering enormous areas in a single run. But what the AT-802 had in power, it lacked in finesse. Navigating tight turns or avoiding sudden threats in the dense jungles of Colombia required a more agile machine—this was where the Turbo Thrush truly excelled.

As we incorporated the Turbo Thrush into our operations, it quickly became clear that it was a pilot's aircraft. Flying it felt personal, as if the plane were an extension of your will. It lacked the imposing stature of the AT-802, but its responsiveness and compact design made it ideal for the unique challenges we faced. For those flying into hostile territory, the Turbo Thrush's armoured cockpit provided an added layer of confidence, a protective cocoon against ground fire that was often as much psychological as it was physical.

Yet the Air Tractor AT-802 remained indispensable for larger operations. When sheer volume and coverage were required, the AT-802 was the undisputed king. Flying it felt like commanding a tank in the sky—unwavering, powerful, and capable of handling anything thrown its way. Its ability to endure heavy payloads while maintaining steady handling made it invaluable for missions covering extensive fields.

Still, as I watched the first Turbo Thrush lift off, its engine roaring and the spray system primed, I couldn't help but feel a deep sense of satisfaction. This was the aircraft we needed for our most dangerous missions. Its agility, combined with its armoured cockpit, made it the best choice for navigating the labyrinthine fields of Catatumbo or the steep mountains of Cauca. For the pilots, it meant a fighting chance—a faster exit, a better shield, and the reassurance that their machine was built to bring them home.

These new arrivals weren't just planes; they were a commitment to doing the job better and safer. They reminded us that in this relentless fight, our tools mattered as much as our determination. Every time a Turbo Thrush soared into the sky, it carried with it not just herbicide but also the weight of our hopes—that with precision and perseverance, we might one day see an end to the coca fields that fuelled so much pain and conflict.

At the beginning of 2001, our operational demands were at an all-time high. With three bases now fully active, stretching almost the length of Colombia, the logistical challenges alone were immense. I found myself constantly moving between these bases—Larandia in Caquetá, Tumaco on the Pacific Coast, and Santa Rosa del Sur in Bolívar—coordinating personnel shifts, overseeing operations, and delivering briefings on new protocols. These flights became my routine, and the Cessna 208 Caravan was my trusty steed.

The Caravan, with its long range, reliable performance, and autopilot capabilities, was perfect for these missions. I needed an aircraft that could carry both cargo and passengers while sparing me the constant manual handling that smaller planes required. Hands-on flying was exciting but draining, especially with the distances I was covering. The Caravan was a workhorse, and I relied on it heavily.

The first time I climbed into the Caravan's cockpit, I was struck by its unassuming but sturdy design. The high-wing configuration, robust landing gear, and spacious cabin hinted at its utilitarian nature. It wasn't flashy or fast, but it was dependable, built to handle everything from paved runways to remote dirt strips.

The cockpit layout was straightforward, clearly designed with practicality in mind. For someone like me, used to the complexity of airliners and the nimbleness of smaller helicopters, the Caravan presented a unique balance of simplicity and capability. Its controls were heavier than I expected, requiring a firm hand, but they responded with reassuring precision.

The Caravan's Pratt & Whitney PT6A turboprop engine delivered smooth, reliable power, even when fully loaded. Takeoff was steady rather than thrilling—this wasn't a machine designed for quick climbs but for endurance. As the wheels lifted off the runway, the aircraft transitioned effortlessly into flight, and I was reminded why this plane was such a staple in rugged aviation environments worldwide.

Cruising at around 160 knots, the Caravan wasn't fast by any stretch, but it was stable. Long flights gave me time to reflect, plan, and even enjoy the breathtaking Colombian landscapes. From the dense jungles of Caquetá to the rolling hills near Bolívar, the vistas were stunning, even as they hid the dangerous realities of our mission.

The autopilot feature was a blessing, especially during these lengthy transfers. While the Caravan required more hands-on attention than an airliner, its modern avionics suite made navigation straightforward. I often found myself appreciating the balance this plane offered—simple enough to feel connected to the aircraft but advanced enough to ease the burden of solo operations.

Each base posed unique challenges for landings. Tumaco's coastal strip was often plagued by unpredictable winds, while Santa Rosa's runway required careful handling due to its uneven surface. Larandia, with its military-grade infrastructure, was the most straightforward. The Caravan handled all these conditions with ease, its rugged landing gear absorbing rough touchdowns like a champ. It wasn't graceful, but it got the job done.

The Caravan's versatility became more evident with each flight. Whether I was ferrying personnel, hauling spare parts, or even carrying sensitive equipment, it adapted seamlessly. Its spacious cabin could be reconfigured as needed, making it invaluable for our operations. In many ways, it felt like a Swiss Army knife in the sky—reliable, efficient, and ready for anything.

Flying the Caravan often felt like a return to the roots of aviation. After years in high-tech cockpits and sleek helicopters, this plane offered a raw, practical experience that I found oddly fulfilling. There was a sense of accomplishment in mastering its quirks and adapting to its steady pace. It was a reminder that flying wasn't just about speed or agility—it was about resilience and purpose.

The flights weren't just logistical necessities; they were a lifeline connecting our operations. As I landed at each base, I carried with me updates, supplies, and a sense of continuity for the teams working tirelessly on the ground. These flights allowed me to witness the dedication of our crews firsthand and gave me the opportunity to address their concerns directly.

Each takeoff, each landing, was a small victory in a larger, ongoing battle. The Caravan became more than just a tool—it was a symbol of our collective effort, bridging the vast distances and challenges that defined our mission. And as I climbed into its cockpit for yet another journey, I couldn't help but feel a deep sense of gratitude for the role it played in keeping us moving forward, one flight at a time.

At the start of my visit to Santa Rosa del Sur, the memory of the downed plane lingered heavily in the air. This base had been home to the team we lost, and their absence was palpable. While there, a new operation was unfolding—one that promised to be a major blow against the cocaine trade. Intelligence had pinpointed a massive cocaine production site deep in the jungle. This wasn't just about fumigating coca fields; this time, the mission aimed to capture the workers, seize the cocaine, and dismantle the manufacturing operation before they could scatter.

The mission started in spectacular fashion. The helicopters—Blackhawks, a few Hueys, and even a Little Bird—roared to life on the runway. Armed troops boarded, weapons glinting in the harsh sunlight, their expressions a mix of focus and determination. It felt like a scene straight out of *Apocalypse Now*, with the rotors kicking up dust and the jungle echoing with the unmistakable thrum of engines. As they lifted off, the sky filled with their presence, the air vibrating with purpose.

The plan was straightforward: the helicopters would secure the site, engage any resistance, and hold the area until we could assist with extraction. They were airborne for over two hours, leaving those of us on the ground to wait, restless and tense. Then the call came through—success. The site had been secured, several workers detained, and an enormous stash of cocaine discovered. They needed us to help transport prisoners and contraband.

I climbed into the cockpit of the Cessna Caravan, its engine humming with familiar reliability. The airstrip they directed us to was barely more than a dirt track carved out of the jungle. From the air, it looked like a narrow scar in the greenery, its rough edges blending into the dense foliage. The Caravan handled it well, touching down with a bump and rolling to a stop just short of where the Blackhawks were parked. Soldiers waved us forward, guiding us toward the extraction zone.

As I stepped out of the Caravan, the scene was surreal. The jungle was alive with noise—birds squawking, insects buzzing, and the occasional crackle of a soldier's radio. At the edge of the clearing, the land dipped into a small path leading into the trees. Nestled there, partially hidden by the dense canopy, was the cocaine "kitchen." It was a crude structure of bamboo, covered with a black tarpaulin riddled with holes from helicopter gunfire. The smell of chemicals lingered in the humid air, acrid and overpowering.

The site was a disturbing yet fascinating display of brutal efficiency, a grim testament to the ingenuity of those entrenched in the drug trade. Beneath the sprawling tarpaulin riddled with bullet holes, the heart of the cocaine kitchen revealed itself—a chaotic arrangement of tools, chemicals, and machinery. Large plastic vats sat at the center, their stained surfaces bearing the telltale marks of countless batches of coca leaves soaked in toxic solvents. Nearby, press machines—some manual, others crudely modified with hydraulic components—stood ready to squeeze every last drop of alkaloid-rich liquid from the leaves.

Makeshift drying tables, constructed from planks of wood and rusted metal frames, lined one side of the structure. They were used to evaporate the liquid extracted from the coca leaves, leaving behind the sticky residue that would eventually be transformed into coca paste. This was no polished industrial operation; the tools were crude, often cobbled together from whatever materials could be scavenged or smuggled into the jungle. Yet, it was devastatingly effective.

Scattered haphazardly across the site were containers of chemicals essential to the process. Kerosene, gasoline, sulfuric acid, and ammonia—many in reused plastic jugs with faded or missing labels—spoke to the dangerous and highly toxic nature of the work being carried out here. The smell was overwhelming, a sharp and acrid mixture that clung to the humid air and burned the throat with every breath. These chemicals were key to breaking down the coca leaves and extracting the alkaloids, but their careless storage and use made the site a powder keg of potential disaster.

Despite the primitive tools and chaotic layout, the operation ran like a well-oiled machine. Workers would soak the leaves in vats filled with kerosene, stomping on them to ensure the solvents penetrated every fibre. The soaked leaves would then be pressed, the resulting liquid filtered to remove impurities. This liquid would be treated with sulfuric acid and sodium carbonate, causing the coca alkaloids to precipitate out as a paste. The paste was then dried on the tables, its texture and colour closely monitored by the chemists overseeing the operation.

Further down the line, the coca paste would be refined using even more chemicals—acetone, ether, and hydrochloric acid—until it became the pure white powder known as cocaine hydrochloride. This final product, neatly packaged into one-kilogram bricks, lay in a massive pile under the tarpaulin, each brick a testament to the relentless efficiency of the operation.

Nearby, a group of young men sat on the ground under heavy guard. They were the workers—barefoot, shirtless, and gaunt, dressed in little more than tattered jeans. Their expressions were a mix of resignation and fear. They had been caught red-handed, but it was clear they were merely cogs in a much larger machine. Behind them, under the jungle's canopy, lay the real prize: a mountain of cocaine bricks, meticulously packed and stacked, each brick weighing a kilo. The soldiers reported the haul at an astonishing three tonnes.

It was astonishing to think that such a rudimentary setup, hidden deep in the jungle and operated with minimal resources, could produce tonnes of cocaine capable of flooding international markets. Here, in this isolated and makeshift laboratory, the foundation of a global trade was laid—one that reached far beyond Colombia's borders to devastate communities, enrich cartels, and spark endless cycles of violence and exploitation.

The decision was made to destroy most of the cocaine on-site. Two tonnes were stacked at the edge of the runway, where soldiers rigged it with high explosives. The remaining tonne was to be transported back to Bogotá for evidence and publicity purposes—a stark visual of the fight against the drug trade.

When the explosives detonated, the fireball was immense, a violent burst of heat and light that seemed to swallow the jungle. The shockwave rippled through the clearing, and the air filled with a dense white cloud. It was an eerie sight, watching the remnants of that destructive trade hang in the air like ghostly mist. Then the realization hit—some of that mist was cocaine.

The soldiers assured us the fire had consumed the bulk of it, but the fine powder coated everything, including us. I remember coughing, wiping at my face, and realizing with some alarm that I might have inhaled more than I wanted. I have never done cocaine before, HONEST!, except if you count at a party about 20 years earlier with a girl I was trying to impress, I sneezed it all out and blew away most of the supply, much to the annoyance of everyone ate the party, especially the girl, but I experienced no effects. Thanks to this cloud, for the next three days, I battled a headache and a strange, jittery energy that I couldn't quite shake.

Once the smoke cleared, we began the extraction. The captured workers were loaded into the Caravan under heavy guard. Despite my rank and position, the soldiers decided the cocaine bricks would be transported in the Blackhawks—they didn't trust me, or perhaps the small plane, with such a valuable and volatile cargo. I couldn't blame them.

As we taxied down the makeshift runway for takeoff, I glanced back at the prisoners. They sat quietly, their hands bound, their faces blank. What would become of them? Were they just pawns, easily replaced in this brutal game? The answers didn't matter in the moment. What mattered was getting them—and myself—out of there safely.

As the Caravan lifted off, leaving the jungle and its haunting scenes behind, I couldn't help but reflect on the enormity of it all. The scale of the operation, the resources involved, and the sheer human cost weighed heavily. For every tonne of cocaine destroyed, how many more were being produced elsewhere? For every worker captured, how many more would take their place?

This mission had been a victory, a tangible blow against the cartels. But it was also a reminder of the complexities of this war—how intertwined it was with poverty, corruption, and desperation. The jungle below faded into the distance, but its shadows lingered in my thoughts. We had won a battle, but the war was far from over.

That evening, after the dust had settled and the adrenaline of the mission began to wane, a few of us contractors decided to celebrate. The success of the day deserved at least one night of relaxation—one chance to laugh off the tension and drink away the lingering shadows of our work. We made our way to a local bar, the kind you only find in these forgotten corners of Colombia. From the outside, it looked like a ramshackle hut, the walls patched together with corrugated metal and splintered wood, the roof sloping unevenly as if it might cave in at any moment. A single yellow bulb hung over the entrance, casting just enough light to make the place look inviting—or at least intriguing.

Inside, the atmosphere was warm and familiar. Wooden tables, mismatched chairs, and a bar made of rough-hewn planks stood against the far wall. The smell of fried food and cheap rum mixed with the faint scent of cigarettes, and a crackly old radio played salsa music in the background. At this early hour, there were only a few patrons—locals who glanced up at us briefly before returning to their drinks. We took a table at the far end of the bar, close enough to see the action but far enough away to mind our own business.

We were halfway through our second round of beers when the entertainment began. Two locals, both wiry and sun-weathered, started play-fighting in the middle of the bar. At first, it was all good fun—a farce, really. They'd each grabbed a pen, holding them downward in what I could only assume was their best impression of a Hollywood knife fight. They lunged and swung their arms theatrically, though they stayed a good two feet apart. It was ridiculous—like a scene from a B-movie no one wanted to watch.

But the playful laughter faded quickly. Something in their jabs—maybe a misstep or an offhand insult—turned the mood sour. The pens were suddenly gone, replaced by real knives that seemed to appear out of nowhere. Both blades were short—maybe six inches—but their presence was enough to make the bar hush. The two men began circling each other cautiously, their bravado visibly faltering. What had started as a performance was now a standoff, but it was comical in its own way. They kept stepping backward, not toward each other, the distance growing until it was impossible they could do any real harm.

I couldn't help myself. I turned around on my seat, watching them with a mix of disbelief and amusement. "You'll have to get closer to each other if you actually want to stab him," I said dryly, my voice dripping with sarcasm. Our group burst into laughter, loud enough to draw the attention of everyone in the bar. The two men froze, turned to glare at me, muttered something under their breath that I didn't bother deciphering, and promptly stomped off in opposite directions. The spectacle was over.

"This is so Colombia," I said, shaking my head. "They skip the fists and go straight for the knives. Not that they plan to use them." It was a strange dynamic I'd noticed in these small towns—flashes of aggression that rarely ended in real violence. It was all about saving face, showing strength without crossing that final line. A show, really. Bravado, nothing more.

As the night wore on, the bar began to fill. The radio grew louder, the tables more crowded, and the air grew thick with laughter and chatter. Then the girls arrived. A group of them—no more than seventeen or eighteen, but already carrying themselves with a confidence that belied their age—drifted toward our table. They were stunning, as many Colombian girls are: dark eyes, radiant smiles, and an effortless charm that could disarm even the most stoic man.

One of them sat next to me. She had an innocent face but wore a T-shirt with a puppy dog on it and the words *"I'm Cute"* written in bold letters across the front. She leaned in close, tilting her head up and smiling, her very ample chest almost in my face. "¿Qué significa esto?" she asked in perfect innocence, gesturing to her shirt.

The temptation was there—the kind of moment that could so easily turn into something I'd regret. She was close, her chest pushed forward just enough to make sure I noticed. I cleared my throat, managing a smile, and translated the words for her in my best Spanish.

"It means 'I'm cute,'" I said simply, avoiding the unspoken invitation in her eyes.

The other guys weren't nearly as restrained. They had started in with the corny lines—the kind of pick-up attempts you'd hear in an old war movie. "You know," one of them said, leaning in toward another girl with a dramatic sigh, "we could be dead tomorrow. Our job... it's dangerous. So..." He let the thought hang in the air like it was some kind of golden ticket. I rolled my eyes, finding the whole thing both cheesy and sad.

To my surprise, the girl shied away from him and slid closer to me, grabbing onto my arm and leaning against me as if seeking protection. She looked up with that same expectant smile, and for a brief second, it almost worked. Almost.

I stood up, gently peeling her hand off my arm. "Lo siento," I said softly. "Tengo que irme." I turned to the guys, shaking my head. "I'm heading back to the base."

They groaned and teased me as I grabbed my jacket, but I didn't care. As I stepped out into the cool night air, I felt proud of myself. It wasn't about resisting temptation, really— it was about being true to the person I'd promised to be. Martha deserved that much, and so did I.

As I walked back to the base, the distant sounds of music and laughter faded behind me. The mission had been a success, and we'd all needed the release, but I knew what really mattered. Tomorrow, the fight would continue, and I needed to be clear-headed for the days ahead. This war demanded everything—discipline, strength, and integrity. Tonight had been a small test, and I'd passed it. For that, I felt a quiet sense of victory.

In early September, the base buzzed with an unusual intensity as news broke of an impending VIP visit. U.S. Secretary of State Colin Powell, one of the most prominent figures in American politics, was coming to Colombia. This visit was to underscore the U.S. commitment to Plan Colombia, solidify relations with President Andrés Pastrana, and assess firsthand the progress in the fight against drug trafficking and insurgent groups. Powell's presence was a big deal, a diplomatic statement that the world was watching and supporting Colombia's struggle for stability.

The announcement sent the base into overdrive. The transformation was immediate and relentless. Days before his arrival, every corner of the installation was meticulously cleaned, scrubbed, and polished. Trash was non-existent, weeds vanished, and lawns were trimmed to near-military precision. The smell of fresh paint lingered everywhere as walls, curbs, and even some vehicles received a touch-up. No detail was too small for inspection.

The base commander, a man whose stern demeanour could make seasoned soldiers snap to attention, patrolled the grounds like a general preparing for inspection by royalty. Flanked by a small entourage, he checked every detail, barking orders to correct anything that didn't meet his exacting standards. When he turned his focus to our team—the civilian contractors—his orders were clear and direct: stay out of sight.

"If you must appear," he commanded, "you're to wear your airline uniform. And don't be carrying your pistol. No exceptions."

The implication was crystal clear. Our role in this high-profile visit was to be invisible. If Powell ventured into our territory, I was to stay in my office, quietly managing operations without so much as a handshake. It wasn't exactly a morale booster, but we understood the optics. This was politics, after all.

On the day of Powell's arrival, the atmosphere was electric. The base stood at full attention, soldiers in their sharpest uniforms forming neat lines, their faces a picture of discipline. As the whine of jet engines approached, heads tilted skyward. The U.S. Secretary of State's aircraft descended onto the runway—a gleaming Gulfstream V, its white body accented with a blue belly, and "United States of America" emblazoned in bold lettering across its side. The plane seemed to radiate authority and purpose.

Ahead of it, another aircraft—one of "my" Cessna Caravans—had touched down, carrying members of the press. Cameras clicked furiously as Powell disembarked, flanked by his security detail. He moved with the practiced ease of a seasoned statesman, offering waves and handshakes to the Colombian and U.S. military officials awaiting him.

For the next several hours, Powell toured the base in a meticulously choreographed sequence. Groups of soldiers and police officers, each carefully positioned for photographs, greeted him with respect and deference. He inspected facilities, nodded in approval at presentations, and exchanged words with key figures. His itinerary included viewing some of the anti-narcotics equipment funded by U.S. aid and meeting personnel involved in operations, "my" equipment, where I figured I should be. Who better than me should explain our work to him, after all my English was probably the best on the whole base.

From my vantage point, I could hear the hum of activity but saw little of the man himself. He didn't get invited into our offices, where everything was planned, as I had been instructed to keep to my office. Still, I couldn't help but glance out occasionally, catching glimpses of the entourage as they moved from one location to another.

But the visit was cut short. Powell's original plan included traveling to Santa Rosa to observe operations closer to the frontlines. Those plans were abruptly cancelled. The date was September 11, 2001.

It was a little before 9 a.m., and we were in the same time zone as New York. I had just settled into my office at Larandia, a mug of lukewarm coffee in hand, when I heard a commotion echoing through the corridor. Raised voices, hurried footsteps—the unmistakable hum of something out of the ordinary. I stepped into the hallway and stopped a young soldier who was rushing past.

"What the hell is going on?" I asked.

He paused just long enough to catch his breath. "A plane hit the World Trade Center in New York."

My immediate thought was that some hapless pilot of a light aircraft had gotten too close, misjudged his route, and clipped the building. It was tragic, but accidents like that could happen. "A light plane?" I asked.

"No, sir. An airliner."

I froze. An airliner? That was no accident. My mind raced as I made my way toward the officers' *casino*—what the Colombians called their mess hall—where I knew there was a large TV perched high on a stand. As I entered, the place was already packed. Soldiers and officers alike sat or stood, their faces turned upward, illuminated by the glow of the television.

The news was chaos. Confusion reigned on-screen as reports came in—erratic, fragmented. They were saying a Boeing 767 had struck the North Tower of the World Trade Center. My heart sank. A Boeing 767—the same aircraft I had flown for years. I knew its size, its power, and now, its potential for destruction. The image on the screen was surreal, smoke billowing out of the skyscraper, flames licking the air like some grotesque spectre.

And then it happened. The second plane struck.

The South Tower erupted in an explosion of fire and debris as the second Boeing screamed into it. A collective gasp filled the room, followed by stunned silence. It was now unmistakable: this was no accident. Someone had done this deliberately. But who? And why?

The shock deepened when, one by one, the towers fell. Those buildings, the very ones that had made me dizzy when I looked up at them during my visit last year, crumbled into dust. It was inconceivable. For hours we sat there, glued to the TV, watching the horror unfold. Four planes—four acts of calculated terror. The images of the Pentagon in flames and the field in Pennsylvania where United Flight 93 had crashed haunted us. The sense of helplessness, the sheer magnitude of the loss—it was impossible to process.

Very little work got done that day. Everyone was trying to grasp the enormity of what had just happened. I gathered with our team, a somber huddle of Americans, Colombians, and a handful of other nationalities. Most of the Americans were visibly shaken, their thoughts turning to home. Some were desperate to leave immediately, to get back to their families, to their country that had just been so viciously attacked. I understood; hell, I would have felt the same. They were granted leave without question.

As the United States declared its war on terror in the days that followed, we began to wonder what it would mean for us here in Colombia. Would this shift in focus jeopardize our war on drugs? Would our funding dry up? Would we suddenly find ourselves abandoned? We had no answers, but the uncertainty was palpable.

A couple of days later, in the midst of all the chaos, I made my usual phone call to Philip. He was still in the hospital back in the UK, recovering—or so I thought. When the call connected, instead of hearing his gruff and cheerful voice, I was transferred to an administrator.

Her voice was soft, but her words struck like a blow. "I'm sorry to inform you that Mr. Philip Harrison passed away."

The room spun. "What?" I croaked, barely able to form the word.

She explained that he had succumbed to respiratory complications, brought on by over 50 years of smoking. "He passed peacefully," she added gently, "on the morning of September 11th at 9 a.m."

The time caught in my throat. Nine a.m.—the same hour the first plane had hit the North Tower. While the world reeled from the attacks, Philip had quietly slipped away. In the UK, it had been the afternoon, six hours ahead of New York, but still, the irony gnawed at me. September 11th would always be remembered as a day of global tragedy, but for me, it would also carry a deeply personal weight.

"He left a letter," the administrator said after a pause. "Would you like me to read it to you?"

I nodded, though I knew she couldn't see me. I was too stunned to speak.

Her voice trembled slightly as she read his final words. "I've had a good life these last two years, thanks to you, son. I'm so happy you found Martha. She's the best thing that ever happened to you, and I know you'll be fine with her by your side. You brought me back to life, and I'll never forget it. I love you."

Tears blurred my vision, and I felt my throat close up as if someone were squeezing the breath out of me. My mind flooded with memories—our breakfasts at the house, his teasing of Martha, his adventures with Jacky, his smile as he embraced his newfound family. Two years wasn't enough. It would never be enough.

I wanted to say so much in return—to tell him that *he* had brought *me* back to life too, that I loved him, that he had been more of a father to me than I could have hoped for. But the line was silent, and the words choked inside me.

I hung up the phone, tears streaming down my face as I sat there alone. Philip was gone, and this time, it was final. The house would feel emptier without his presence, his laughter, his stubborn resilience. And as much as I tried to hold onto the memory of those two wonderful years, the pain of his loss settled heavily in my chest.

That morning—September 11th, 2001—would be etched into history as a day of unfathomable grief and terror. For the world, it was the day everything changed. For me, it was the day I lost my father.

Chapter 12: Blackhawk Down!

In February 2003, we found ourselves once again back at the Santa Rosa base, a familiar place now etched into our routines, where the humid air carried the constant whir of helicopters and the smell of grease and sweat. The mission had been planned several days earlier, and intelligence suggested this would be a straightforward operation. A small *kitchen*—a clandestine cocaine lab—had been identified, and it was supposedly lightly guarded, a handful of workers and a few farmers in an area not protected by any guerrilla forces. It sounded almost routine, a quiet swoop-and-seize mission that would disrupt the flow of narcotics from this pocket of the César Province.

I was part of the air support team for the operation, flying one of the UH-1H Hueys alongside a Blackhawk and another Huey. The Blackhawk was the centerpiece of the mission, loaded with six crew and seventeen heavily armed soldiers—men trained to move fast and hit hard. The plan was simple: I would scout ahead to identify a clear landing zone, and then the Blackhawk would sweep in, unload the soldiers near the jungle clearing, and secure the site. With any luck, we'd capture the workers, seize the drugs, and be back at base before sundown.

We took off early in the morning, the engines roaring as the aircraft lifted into the pale dawn sky. The familiar hum of the Huey settled into a rhythmic vibration that was oddly comforting, despite the nerves that always lingered at the start of a mission. The Blackhawk thundered ahead of us, its dark silhouette powerful and imposing, while the second Huey hung back slightly. The target was only about 150 kilometers north of Santa Rosa, near the small towns of *Curumaní* in César Province. The terrain here was unforgiving—dense jungle stretching endlessly under a low, iron-gray sky.

The flight was uneventful for the first hour. I hovered at about 200 feet, scanning the tree line for a suitable landing spot for the Blackhawk. The weather was turning sour, heavy clouds rolling in like an advancing army. The rain started light but quickly became a torrent, slashing against the windshield and obscuring visibility. It was one of those situations where you had to fly more by instinct and instruments than by sight.

Then it happened.

Out of nowhere, the first gunshots cracked through the rain, startlingly loud even over the roar of the rotor blades. The dull *thud* of rounds striking metal followed immediately after, and I knew we were under fire. I swung the Huey hard, pulling up and banking away in a sharp climb to get out of range. My heart pounded as I pushed the aircraft as fast as it would go, scanning the jungle below for the source of the attack.

"Taking fire!" I barked into the radio, my voice clipped with adrenaline.

To my surprise, the Blackhawk didn't retreat. Instead, it swooped low like a bird of prey, its machine gunners opening up with a deafening burst of fire. The door gunners unleashed a relentless stream of bullets, joined by the soldiers firing from the open bay doors. Muzzle flashes flickered in the dim light as tracer rounds ripped into the jungle below. For a brief moment, the air was chaos—gunfire, rain, and the mechanical scream of the helicopters cutting through it all.

I lost sight of the other Huey in the confusion, and my focus narrowed to staying airborne and alive. As I climbed out of the immediate area, a sudden, calm voice came over the radio.

"We're going down."

It was the Blackhawk pilot. The words were delivered with a shocking level of composure, as though he were announcing an engine test rather than imminent disaster. I swung my head around just in time to see the Blackhawk, thick black smoke trailing from its engine, diving straight for the treetops. A moment later, the jungle swallowed it whole, the treetops shuddering as the aircraft disappeared.

A massive plume of black smoke erupted upward, a dark, ugly column rising from the greenery below. My stomach dropped, and for a second, I just stared, frozen in disbelief. *Holy shit*. The Blackhawk had been shot down.

Shaking off the shock, I circled back to confirm the crash site. The rain was still coming down in sheets, and my mind raced as I fought to keep my hands steady on the controls. There it was—an open wound in the jungle where the Blackhawk had gone down. I couldn't linger. I had no way of knowing if the attackers were still out there, waiting for another easy target. With a sick feeling in my gut, I radioed back to base, my voice strained but steady.

"Blackhawk down. Repeat, Blackhawk down. Coordinates incoming."

Back at Santa Rosa, the response was immediate but chaotic. The shock of losing an aircraft hit everyone hard. The commanding officers scrambled to put together a rescue operation, but word quickly came from Bogotá—a veto. They wouldn't authorize an immediate recovery mission. The area was deemed too dangerous, too volatile, and the risk of another ambush was too high.

It took days for a recovery team to be sent out. By then, I had already returned to Larandia, but I couldn't shake the image of that plume of smoke rising from the jungle. I learned later from hushed conversations around the base that the recovery mission had been grim. They found the wreckage, but there were no survivors.

The news spread like wildfire, but details were sparse. The media picked up fragments of the story—"helicopter shot down in César Province"—but they didn't know the half of it. That evening, when I made my regular call to Martha, I heard the worry in her voice before she even asked the question.

"I saw on the news… was that you? Were you on that mission?"

For a moment, I hesitated. I could picture her sitting on the couch in the living room, clutching the phone, her face tight with concern. She didn't need to know the details, not really.

"No," I said finally, softening my voice to reassure her. "I was on the other side of the country, nowhere near it."

The words hung in the air like a lie, though technically it was true. I wasn't the one in that Blackhawk. I wasn't the one who never made it back. But I had been there. I had seen it. And as I sat in the quiet of my office that night, staring at maps spread across my desk, I couldn't escape the weight of it.

We had all known the risks. Every time we flew out, every time we hovered over coca fields or skimmed low over the jungle, we knew what could happen.

Flying missions in Colombia during this period was not for the faint of heart. While the threat of being shot down by hostile fire loomed large, accidents were an equally relentless adversary. The unforgiving conditions of this country's geography and climate turned every flight into a high-stakes gamble. Between treacherous weather systems, mechanical stress, and the demands of low-altitude flying, our aircraft were constantly tested to their limits—and sometimes beyond them.

Colombia was a land of extremes. The dense jungles, vast plains, and winding rivers stretched endlessly below, broken only by the jagged peaks of the Andes. The terrain was breathtaking but deadly for a pilot. Navigating narrow valleys, threading through steep cliffs, and skimming over jungle canopies at barely 100 feet demanded a focus that bordered on obsession. There was no room for error. Even a brief lapse in concentration could mean slamming into the side of a mountain or clipping a tree, and that was before you factored in the ever-present risk of ground fire.

The weather was no kinder. In the lowlands, sudden thunderstorms would roll in without warning, sending walls of rain so thick you couldn't see the rotor blades in front of you. In the mountains, fog could appear like a phantom, swallowing entire peaks in a matter of minutes. Flying in these conditions was akin to dancing blindfolded on the edge of a cliff.

You trusted your instruments, you trusted your instincts, and sometimes you just hoped the odds were in your favour.

The aircraft themselves were pushed to the brink. The planes and helicopters we flew were workhorses, rugged and dependable, but we were asking them to perform in the harshest conditions imaginable. The fumigation aircraft—Air Tractors and Turbo Thrushes—were designed to fly slow and low, ideal for precision spraying but dangerously exposed. At these altitudes and speeds, there was no margin for mechanical failure. A fuel line rupture, a hydraulic leak, or a simple engine hiccup could be catastrophic.

And yet, we flew. We flew because that was the mission, and there were always more fields to spray, more labs to shut down, and more operations to execute.

But sometimes, the jungle won.

I remember one crash vividly. It wasn't even due to hostile fire, though we initially thought it might be. A Turbo Thrush went down in the Caquetá region. The pilot, a Colombian contractor who was a few months into the job, had been spraying a patch of coca fields nestled deep in the rainforest. It was supposed to be a routine run—clear weather, a straightforward flight path. But halfway through the spray pattern, something went wrong. Maybe it was a mechanical failure, maybe it was pilot error; we never did get the full story. The plane clipped the top of a tree, losing part of its wing. At that altitude, there was no chance of recovery.

The wreckage was found a day later, hidden under the jungle canopy. A recovery team had to machete their way through miles of thick vegetation just to reach it. The aircraft was twisted and mangled, half-buried in the mud. There wasn't much left to salvage. The pilot hadn't stood a chance.

The loss hit all of us hard. Whether it was one of our own contractors or a local pilot, the pain was the same. We were a family of sorts, bonded by the shared risks we faced every time we went up. Whenever someone didn't come back, it reminded us all of how fragile that bond was, how quickly the jungle could snatch someone away. That pilot had flown beside me only a week earlier, laughing over coffee in the mess hall about the absurdity of it all—how we were fighting this impossible war against coca plants and cartels in machines that were constantly on the edge of breaking down.

These crashes were not isolated incidents. There were others—some we could blame on the weather, others on mechanical failures, and a few where the cause remained an open question. I once heard of an Air Tractor that went down in the mountains near Tumaco, where the ridges are steep and unrelenting. The pilot had been flying a standard mission when a downdraft grabbed the aircraft and dragged it straight into the slope. The impact left a crater. Another time, one of the Hueys lost tail rotor control in mid-flight. The helicopter spun like a top before crashing into a clearing, miraculously leaving the crew alive but shaken and bloodied.

When accidents like these happened, there was always a scramble to piece together the story—what had gone wrong, how it could have been prevented. But even with investigations and safety reviews, we all knew the truth: we were flying in conditions that no amount of training or preparation could completely account for. The risks were baked into the job.

And then there were the international repercussions. Many of the crew members on these missions were foreign contractors—Americans, Canadians, even a few Europeans—working alongside Colombian nationals. Whenever one of the American contractors went down, the fallout reached all the way to Washington. Questions would be raised. Was it worth it? Was enough being done to protect the crews? The newspapers would jump on it, painting stories of doomed missions and reckless operations, which only added fuel to the controversy surrounding Plan Colombia.

It was frustrating at times because we were just trying to do the job. None of us took the risks lightly. We all knew what we signed up for, but we also believed, in our own way, that what we were doing mattered. Every field we sprayed, every operation we supported, felt like a small victory—a chip taken out of a monolithic problem.

But the losses stayed with us. Every time I stepped into the cockpit, I thought of the pilots who hadn't made it back. I could see their faces, hear their voices, and I carried their memory with me. I told myself I'd fly smarter, safer. I double-checked every system, studied every map, and never let my guard down. Because in the jungle, there were no second chances.

We were living on the edge, threading the needle between success and disaster, one flight at a time. The machines we flew were sturdy, the crews were skilled, but the risks—those never changed. Every mission was a roll of the dice, and the only certainty was that the jungle always kept the score.

Martha became increasingly concerned as news of these crashes and incidents reached her. Every time she saw the look on my face after a particularly close call or heard about another aircraft that hadn't come back, her anxiety grew. She didn't mince words when we spoke about it. "You're the boss," she said firmly, more than once. "Your job is to manage operations, not to fly around the country risking your life. What's the point of all this if something happens to you?" I understood her worry; she had every right to feel that way. But it wasn't so simple for me. I had always believed that a leader should never ask someone to do something they weren't willing to do themselves. I couldn't justify sitting safely at the base while others flew into danger. It felt like a cop-out, like I'd be betraying the very people who put their trust in me.

I told Martha as much, trying to explain the pride I felt when I strapped into the cockpit, joining the men on the front lines. "If I don't fly," I argued, "how can I expect them to? How could I look them in the eye and ask them to take these risks if I won't?" But she wasn't convinced. "They respect you because you lead, not because you're flying into harm's way," she said quietly. "But I need you here too." Her words stayed with me longer than I cared to admit. She was right—there was a lot at stake, and not just for me. I was torn, caught between my duty to the mission and my duty to the people I loved. I could see the strain it put on Martha, how every time I walked out the door, she held her breath until I came back. I started to wonder if my insistence on flying was less about leadership and more about proving something to myself—proving that I was still as capable and fearless as I'd always been.

In the end, I promised her I'd be smarter about it. I couldn't stop flying completely—it was too much a part of who I was, and the missions still called to me—but I would fly less, leaving the bulk of the operations to the pilots who were there to do just that. It wasn't an easy decision, and I worried about how the men might see it. But I realized that real leadership wasn't just about being present on the battlefield—it was also about being present for the people who needed me most, both on the ground and back at home. Martha, as always, was my anchor, pulling me back from the edge just when I needed it most.

By mid-2003, the dangers of our work seemed to intensify with every mission. Each day in the skies over Colombia was a gamble, with stakes higher than most people could imagine. The bullet holes in our aircraft had long become routine, but what was happening now felt different—more organized, more aggressive. The FARC and other armed groups were clearly adapting, becoming bolder and deadlier.

It was late August when the first incident rattled us all. On August 26, 2003, a spray plane—a small fumigation aircraft—came under fire in the northern part of the country. The pilot, a seasoned American contractor, was mid-operation, flying low over the coca fields when rifle fire erupted from the tree line. At that altitude, there was little room for error.

The reports that came in were jumbled at first. The plane had been hit—no one knew how badly—but the pilot managed to keep it steady enough to execute an emergency landing on a rough patch of ground. He was alive, miraculously unhurt, but stranded in hostile territory. Helicopters from the army were scrambled immediately. I remember pacing the floor of my office at Larandia as the operation unfolded, my hands clenching and unclenching as I waited for news.

An hour later, the army choppers reached him. I breathed a sigh of relief when I heard he'd been pulled out safely. But when I saw the spray plane later, flown back in pieces, it was clear how close he had come to dying. Rifle rounds had punctured the fuselage, the engine cowling was shredded, and one wing looked like it had barely held on. How he'd managed to land that thing was beyond belief. It was the kind of skill only desperation and experience could produce.

But even as we were processing this near miss, worse news was waiting just around the corner.

The southern jungles of Colombia were always the most perilous, their remote regions controlled by the FARC and other insurgents who saw us as a direct threat to their livelihoods. **Late August 2003** brought another incident—one that hit us like a punch to the gut.

A U.S.-contracted spray plane had gone down during a mission deep in FARC territory. This time, there were no miraculous landings, no heroic rescue. The aircraft, reportedly fired upon, crashed into the dense jungle. For hours, there was silence as search-and-rescue teams scrambled to locate the wreckage, hoping against hope that someone might have survived.

But the news that filtered back was grim. There were fatalities among the crew members—contractors who had become friends, colleagues, and, in some ways, family. These were men who had sat at the same mess tables, swapped stories over late-night beers, and flown the same dangerous skies that I had. Their loss hit the entire operation hard.

The jungle claimed its secrets fiercely. Recovery efforts were painstakingly slow, and rumors swirled that the crash site had been tampered with before our teams arrived. Bodies were recovered, the wreckage cataloged, and questions left unanswered. The FARC had sent another message, loud and clear: we were not welcome in their skies.

That year, incidents involving spray aircraft became alarmingly frequent. Reports came through almost weekly—planes hit by ground fire, emergency landings on makeshift strips, pilots narrowly escaping death.

By the time September rolled in, we had logged 225 incidents of ground fire against our spray planes during operations in 2003 alone. The numbers were staggering, but for those of us in the thick of it, it was far more personal. Each round fired wasn't just a statistic—it was aimed at someone's father, brother, husband, or friend.

We had five U.S. contractors die in air-related incidents in the span of just seven months. Not all of these were caused by hostile fire, but in the unforgiving terrain of Colombia, the line between mechanical failure and enemy action was often blurred.

In February, one of "my" Cessna 208 Caravans, the one I'd flown into the jungle kitchen and flown out the captured farmers, carrying both U.S. and Colombian personnel, went down in a region controlled by the FARC. The crash itself was bad enough, but what followed was unthinkable. An American and a Colombian were executed shortly after the crash, their deaths a cold and deliberate act. Thomas Janis, a U.S. pilot. A Colombian Army intelligence officer, Sgt. Luis Alcides Cruz, was executed alongside him. Three others— contractors— Thomas Howes, Keith Stansell and Mark Gonsalves were captured and held hostage for over five years before being rescued on July 2, 2008, during Operation Jaque. Operation Jaque was a Colombian military operation that resulted in the successful rescue of 15 hostages, including former Colombian presidential candidate Íngrid Betancourt.

Just a month later, in March, another Cessna 208 went down during a rescue operation, sent to recover the crew of the first crash. This time, three Americans lost their lives. The weight of those deaths hung heavy on all of us, as we asked ourselves what more could be done to keep our people safe.

Then, in April, tragedy struck again. During a routine spraying operation, one of the Air Tractors crashed. The pilot, an American contractor from Texas, didn't make it, he was 31. Mechanical failure, weather, or enemy fire—it didn't matter. The result was the same: another name added to the growing list of lives lost in this relentless war.

Back in Bogota at the Colombian Antinarcotics Directorate offices at the airport I was given the numbers.

Between 2000 and 2003, the aerial eradication program had achieved staggering numbers—over 380,000 hectares of coca sprayed, a figure that represented more than 8% of Colombia's cultivatable land. That kind of scale was almost impossible to comprehend. From the cockpits of our aircraft, those sprawling coca fields stretched endlessly across the jungle—green upon green, cultivated patches breaking the natural wild of Colombia's landscape. And yet, this was where the war on drugs was being fought, acre by acre, sortie by sortie.

The Colombian Antinarcotics Directorate, or DIRAN, remained at the heart of this effort, coordinating the operations with a mix of precision and urgency. They were the ones overseeing the aerial spraying missions, ensuring each sortie was meticulously planned and logged. But by 2003, the program had grown beyond anything we had initially imagined. The addition of armed helicopters—escorts that flew with us to provide security—had become essential. The threat from the ground was too real to ignore anymore. FARC, along with other armed groups, had made it clear that every fumigation flight over their territory would be contested, often with bullets. Their fire wasn't random; they knew we were threatening their lifeline, and they were willing to kill to protect it.

We were now operating a fleet of twenty-four aircraft, each one devoted to eradication. Air Tractors, Turbo Thrushes, and Cessna Caravans all carried their weight, while the helicopter gunships—Hueys and Blackhawks—hovered nearby, ready to engage any threat on the ground. It was organized chaos: planes spraying, escorts watching the tree line like hawks, and pilots constantly scanning for flashes of light from rifles aimed at the sky.

Numbers were always contentious, though. The State Department and DIRAN figures often painted slightly different pictures of success, owing to variations in their monitoring mechanisms. The United Nations-funded SIMCI (Sistema Integrado de Monitoreo de Cultivos Ilícitos) relied on a more localized "integrated monitoring system" to measure eradication outcomes, and their numbers were more optimistic. While the U.S. State Department estimated a 15% reduction in coca cultivation from 2001 to 2002—down from 169,800 hectares to 144,450 hectares—DIRAN's figures told an even more dramatic story: a 29.5% reduction, with coca cultivation plummeting from 145,000 hectares to 102,000 hectares.

These figures gave us something to hold onto—a sense that our efforts were not in vain. The Andean Counterdrug Initiative (ACI) had pumped hundreds of millions of dollars into the program: $380 million in FY2002 and $439 million in FY2003. The financial backing was there, and with it came more equipment, more fuel, more sorties. But even those impressive numbers didn't tell the full story.

In the early stages, back in 2000 and 2001, despite nearly doubling the number of acres sprayed—from 116,090 acres to 232,180 acres—coca cultivation had reportedly increased by 25%. It was a sobering realization, a reminder of just how resilient and resourceful our adversaries were. The cartels adapted quickly, relocating fields deeper into the jungle, building hidden pathways for smuggling, and paying local farmers to replant almost as soon as we'd sprayed an area.

But 2002 brought the first glimmer of hope. The State Department reported that our intensified spraying efforts—303,057 acres of coca and 7,516 acres of opium—had finally yielded a tangible result: a 15% reduction in coca cultivation and an even more dramatic 25% reduction in poppy fields. It was the first documented decrease in years.

The reports were encouraging, but I knew firsthand what those percentages meant in reality. Each hectare sprayed represented hours of work—pilots flying low and fast, weaving through hostile airspace while ground fire snapped at their wings. For every victory celebrated in the boardrooms of Bogotá or Washington, there were men and women risking their lives in the skies and on the ground. The numbers didn't tell the stories of bullets slamming into fuselages, emergency landings on dirt strips, or pilots who didn't make it home.

One memory stood out to me as I reflected on all this. I was at Santa Rosa when one of the DIRAN officers came into our operations center with the latest figures from the State Department. He slapped a folder down on the table and smiled broadly.

"Fifteen percent!" he exclaimed. "The first decrease in years! This is working!"

I looked at the papers and nodded, trying to match his enthusiasm. I wanted to celebrate those numbers, but all I could think about were the five Americans we had lost that year alone. Their names were etched in my mind, their stories a constant weight on my conscience. Was it worth it? Did the numbers justify the sacrifices we had made?

I looked up at him and forced a smile. "It's progress," I said simply.

Because, in truth, it was. For every setback, every loss, there were gains—however incremental. We were putting pressure on the cartels, forcing them to adapt, relocate, and invest more resources to sustain their operations. Every hectare sprayed was one less that could fuel violence, corruption, and addiction.

Back at the base that evening, I stood by the runway, watching the fading light cast long shadows over the aircraft parked in neat rows. The hum of an engine somewhere in the distance was a familiar comfort, a sound that spoke of work still to be done.

I thought about how far we'd come. Just a few years earlier, our operations had been sporadic, underfunded, and chaotic. Now, with the backing of Plan Colombia, we had fleets of aircraft, armed escorts, and real momentum. The scale of the effort was unlike anything I'd ever seen.

But I also knew this war was far from over. The coca fields we eradicated today would likely reappear somewhere else tomorrow. The cartels were nothing if not resourceful, and the jungle was vast. The reports we sent back to Bogotá and Washington looked good on paper, but on the ground, we still saw too many farmers planting coca, too many fields hidden in the green expanse below.

As I walked back to my office, I thought about the men and women—pilots, soldiers, contractors—who made those numbers possible. Each flight they took was a silent act of courage, a mission that pushed back, however slightly, against the shadow that loomed over Colombia.

We were making a difference. I had to believe that.

Chapter 13: Under Attack

On February 13, 2003, the day began like any other at the Larandia military base in Caquetá, Colombia—a place tucked deep in the jungle and heavily fortified against the omnipresent threats posed by the Revolutionary Armed Forces of Colombia (FARC). The morning was humid, the air already heavy with the smell of the earth and aviation fuel from the parked fumigation aircraft that sat silently on the edge of the runway.

I had just finished a hectic week of flying operations and, as was routine, was now standing before about 30 young soldiers, barely out of their teens, conducting an english class on modal verbs. A blackboard had been set up on the hard standing near the runway, improvised benches and plastic chairs spread haphazardly across the area. Behind me, the wire fence marked the perimeter, a frail divider between us and the dense, unforgiving jungle that stretched for miles.

The lesson felt surreal in that setting. I found myself explaining words like *"can," "could,"* and *"should"*—simple concepts that seemed laughably out of place for a group of soldiers at a base under perpetual siege. And then it came.

A sound—a deep, resonant "whump"—cut through my words like a blade. For a moment, I dismissed it, a trick of the mind perhaps. But the sound came again—"whump"—pause—"whump"—followed by the unmistakable concussive roar of explosions. The earth shook, and dust rose into the air. My brain clicked: mortars.

I scanned the sky instinctively, hoping my eyes would betray me and I'd find nothing, but no—this was real. The jungle on the far side of the perimeter fence spat fire and destruction as FARC guerrillas lobbed mortar rounds toward us. Their targets were unmistakable: our fumigation aircraft and hangars, the symbolic and practical tools of Colombia's anti-drug campaign and income for the guerillas.

The first explosion hit, smaller than I expected—a small mortar round, likely fired hastily and in volumes. The reaction was instantaneous. The young soldiers—children, really—threw themselves to the ground in sheer terror. Some ran for cover, their panic raw and primal. I heard shrieks, the voices of boys caught in a moment for which their training had not prepared them. A small defensive position nearby had been manned by one soldier, barely older than his comrades. His 7.62 Galil assault rifle—an Israeli-made weapon—quivered in his hands as he crouched behind the sandbags, head down. He started firing blindly into the air.

"Get down, Señor!" he shouted over his shoulder, his voice cracking, sweat pouring down his face. I glanced at him, incredulous. The bullets were going up—straight up—sure to rain back down on us.

"Soldier, stop shooting!" I shouted, pointing toward the jungle, where the mortar fire was originating. "They're over there, in the jungle! Not in the clouds! That's where WE operate"

I admit, for one reckless moment, I was tempted to grab his rifle myself—to at least give us a chance at hitting something real. The Galil was very similar to the rifle I had used in the navy so I knew I could handle it, certainly better than this……. child in a uniform. But instead, I sprinted toward the makeshift office buildings at the far end of the tarmac, my body screaming with adrenaline as explosions continued to thunder behind me. The ground quaked, and debris struck the pavement like angry fists. I knew, in those eternal seconds, that the guerrillas weren't aiming for us; they wanted the planes. Disable the fumigation aircraft, and they could cripple the eradication efforts—the very heart of the government's war on coca production and their funds.

And then, just as suddenly as it began, the shelling stopped. The silence that followed was deafening, surreal. Dust hung in the air, and the only sound was the ragged breathing of the soldiers who dared to lift their heads from cover. The FARC, like ghosts, had vanished back into the jungle, leaving no trace of their presence except the chaos they had wrought.

The damage was significant but not catastrophic. The mortars had missed their primary targets—the aircraft themselves—but the shrapnel had torn through maintenance facilities and sent jagged holes through wings and fuselages. Each aircraft stood damaged, like wounded soldiers, but none beyond repair. Within a week, the engineers had them all airworthy again—a testament to their grit and determination.

The attack on February 13, 2003, was not an isolated event. It was part of a broader guerrilla strategy to halt the aerial eradication campaign. For the FARC, coca was more than a crop; it was a financial lifeline, funding their war against the state. The fumigation planes represented an existential threat, and targeting them was a calculated move in a conflict where every hectare of coca lost was a blow to the insurgency.

The incident was a stark reminder of the stakes involved. The soldiers I taught that morning—boys forced to become men—saw firsthand what it meant to be in a war where the enemy hid in the trees, struck without warning, and disappeared before you could blink. For them—and for me—it was a lesson far more profound than anything I could have taught on a blackboard. It was a lesson in survival.

And so the war continued, relentless and unforgiving. The jungle remained the guerrillas' ally, the aircraft our shield, and the soldiers, the scared boys who fired blindly into the air, our fragile line of defence.

Chapter 14: Game Over

The fumigation efforts in Colombia—particularly the aerial spraying campaigns aimed at eradicating the coca crops—were a complex, unrelenting war of their own. Between 1994 and 2006, these operations were repeatedly suspended, disrupted by a shifting combination of political pressures, environmental concerns, and fierce social resistance. Each year brought a new set of challenges, and by 2005, the program faced its most serious scrutiny yet.

That year, mounting criticism from civil society and international organizations grew louder, condemning the use of glyphosate for its alleged health risks and ecological damage. Ecuador, Colombia's neighbour to the southwest, claimed that the fumigation had crossed into its border regions, affecting their environment and communities. Of course, to me, this was utter nonsense, a convenient diplomatic talking point rather than a reflection of reality. Still, the political noise was deafening, and the suspensions became harder to avoid.

By then, my own contract—originally meant to last five years—was coming to an end. The uncertainty hanging over the program meant my renewal was limited to just one more year. A clear sign, if there ever was one, that the end of this chapter was drawing near. By 2006, when the fumigation operations were suspended yet again, I knew it was over. The job was done. I was done.

I remember that conversation with Martha, my rock and my voice of reason in all this chaos. She looked at me, eyes full of worry, and said, "You have to find a new job—one where they aren't trying to kill you every day."

She was right, of course. But I couldn't help myself. A wry smile tugged at my lips, and I said, "But where's the fun in that?"

The truth was, for all the danger, the noise, the mortar fire, and the near-death brushes in the jungle skies, this life had given me something most people never find—a purpose. For six years, I had been part of a mission bigger than myself, flying through jungles, dodging bullets, and watching young soldiers turn into men far too soon. I had been on the frontlines of a war against a crop that had ravaged nations and lives. And now, it was over.

As I packed up my things, I looked back at the hangars one last time. The aircraft, worn but resilient, sat quietly in the humid air, no longer carrying the scars of shrapnel or jungle debris. For all their imperfections, they were symbols of what we had done—what we had tried to do.

The jungle, as always, loomed beyond the fences, untouched and eternal. It swallowed up everything eventually: bullets, dreams, enemies, and friends. And perhaps it was better that way.

For me, though, it was time to move on—to seek out whatever came next. Even now, as I write this, I sometimes catch myself staring at the sky, looking for the faint silhouette of a Bell

LongRanger or Huey helicopter or a Cessna Caravan, flying low over a canopy of endless green. And for a fleeting moment, I'm there again—dodging mortar fire, hearing the rush of wind, and chasing something most people will never understand.

But that's the thing about a life lived on the edge—it's hard to leave behind.

But what now? That was the question I kept coming back to as I sat around the house in Bogotá, the silence pressing in like a weight. After years of living on the edge, navigating warzones, flying through hostile skies, and dodging bullets both literal and metaphorical, the stillness felt unnatural—almost suffocating. I could hear the hum of the city outside, the occasional honk of a horn or murmur of voices, but inside, it was just me and my thoughts.

The first idea, of course, was to return to the airlines. Flying had always been my core, my skill, my purpose. But the airline industry had changed since I'd last been in a cockpit with passengers. The once-stable profession had been disrupted by a flood of low-cost carriers—cheap fares, tight margins, and crappier working conditions. These outfits hired low-hour pilots fresh out of flight school who were desperate to build experience or older captains who had nowhere else to turn. The stories I'd heard about life in those cockpits were less than glamorous—flying long hours for a fraction of the pay, being nickel-and-dimed for onboard food and drinks, and getting treated like a glorified taxi driver rather than a professional aviator. That wasn't a future I could see for myself.

There were better opportunities in China—a booming aviation market where pilots were in constant demand. The pay was good, and the contracts were tempting. But when I mentioned it to Martha, her reaction was immediate. "China? Absolutely not." I couldn't blame her. After everything we'd been through, she wanted stability and familiarity, not the alien experience of living in a faraway land where even the food and language would be a daily struggle.

The UK was a natural option for me, but Martha's visa situation threw a wrench into that plan. Getting her permission to live in Britain was a bureaucratic nightmare we didn't have the energy—or resources—to tackle. Spain, however, was another story. The UK was still in the EU back then, which made relocating to Spain an easy option for me, and for Martha, it was nearly guaranteed. The idea of Barcelona intrigued us both: a cosmopolitan city with sunshine, beaches, and an easier transition for Martha, given her native Spanish. It was somewhere we could start fresh, together.

Once the seed of Spain had been planted, I began brainstorming ways to make a living. NetJets, the leader in private aviation, operated in Spain, catering to wealthy clients who didn't have the time or inclination to fly commercial. I knew of NetJets' reputation—they were the gold standard in private flying—and the thought of flying sleek, modern jets for discerning clients had a certain appeal. It wasn't the airlines, but it wasn't low-cost carriers either. It was professional, prestigious work. Maybe this could be the next step.

But then there was the business itch. During my time in the UK, while juggling flying and other responsibilities, I had worked for a while in financial services, and I liked the industry. I liked the idea of making money work, of growing it, and helping others grow theirs. But trying to build a financial services business while based in Colombia wasn't realistic. As much as I loved the country, the stigma remained—mention Colombia to prospective European clients, and all they'd think of were cartels and cocaine.

Still, I explored other ideas. Gold and emeralds were abundant in Colombia—treasures pulled from the earth—but while the markets existed, the logistics were complex, and I wasn't convinced it would be worth the effort. Besides, it didn't set my pulse racing.

Then there was a moment of absurdity that made me laugh out loud: a man I had met in La Modelo, a former ambassador, suggested I help with a military coup in Africa. He said I was the perfect candidate—a skilled pilot with leadership experience, connections, and a certain level of fearlessness. It was ridiculous, of course, and I had no intention of being dragged into someone else's revolution. But it was telling of the life I had led so far that such an offer didn't entirely shock me.

Still, the idea of Africa lingered. Not for a coup, but for a more practical opportunity: diamonds. Diamonds were mined legally in places like Zaire (now the Democratic Republic of Congo) and Ghana under the oversight of the Kimberley Process, ensuring they weren't "blood diamonds" tied to conflict. There was potential there, I thought. I could combine what I had learned about gold and precious stones with this market, acting as a middleman for European buyers. But it was uncharted territory, and I would need to do a lot more research.

In the back of my mind, I always knew I could fall back on something smaller—something tangible. I thought of my model airplanes, the tiny aircraft that had kept me sane in Colombia, carving balsa wood into miniature versions of the machines I loved. In Europe, I might get more money for them. Perhaps I could build models on the side, enough to cover the bills while I figured out what came next.

Then another idea crept in—one that felt truer to where I had been and where I was headed. Teaching. It was something I had done throughout my life: training cadets in the Navy, standing at the head of a classroom in La Modelo, even guiding younger pilots as a captain. I half-jokingly considered myself an "extreme teacher" by this point, having taught English and aviation to men who were anything but typical students. The trouble was, if I wanted to teach at a higher level—university, for example—I needed credentials. I didn't have a PhD or even a master's degree. I would have to start with an MBA, something I could do in Spain while building a new life for us.

And so, I stood on the precipice of another leap into the unknown. Leaving Colombia wouldn't be easy. I had come to love the country—its landscapes, its people, its raw, unfiltered energy. It had given me danger and adventure, but it had also given me love and family.

Spain was calling, though. I imagined myself in Barcelona, walking along Las Ramblas, looking out at the Mediterranean, and wondering what new opportunities awaited me there. I didn't have a job lined up, or a clear plan, but that wasn't new to me. I'd done this before, leapt into the void and trusted myself to figure it out.

This time, though, I wouldn't be going alone. Martha would join me, eventually. I would set things up first, find work, and carve out a place for us in that sun-drenched city by the sea.

After everything I had seen and done—the jungle, the planes, the prison classrooms, the men with guns—what was one more leap? At least now, the unknown didn't scare me. It excited me.

And yet, as I began preparing for this next chapter, I couldn't help but reflect on what I was leaving behind. My time in Colombia had been unlike anything else in my life, a tapestry of danger, camaraderie, and purpose. It had been more than just a job—it was an adventure that had reignited a part of me I thought I'd left behind when I left the Royal Navy.

In Colombia, I had felt, in many ways, like I was back in the military—living with discipline, taking on important responsibilities, and experiencing the deep bonds that come from shared challenges. The camaraderie of my team, the respect we had for one another, and the friendships we forged under fire were things I would carry with me forever. These weren't just colleagues—they were my brothers and sisters in arms, and I knew I would stay in touch with many of them for years to come.

The people of Colombia, too, had left an indelible mark on me. There was a warmth and resilience to them that I had never encountered anywhere else. Whether it was the earnest kindness of a prison inmate who offered me pancakes in his cell or the way Martha's fierce determination mirrored the spirit of her homeland, the people I met during my years there were unforgettable. I couldn't count the times strangers welcomed me into their lives with open arms, their smiles as bright as the Colombian sun.

And, of course, there was no forgetting the beauty of the women I had known—intelligent, graceful, and unapologetically vibrant. They embodied the energy and allure of Colombia itself, a country as unpredictable as it was breathtaking.

Colombia had become a part of me in ways I never anticipated. It wasn't just the language I had learned or the streets of Bogotá I had memorized. It was something deeper—a connection that felt woven into my very identity. From then on, whenever a South American heard my Spanish and asked where I was from, I would smile and say, "Soy un Anglo-Rolo," borrowing the affectionate nickname for people from Bogotá. It felt right. It felt true.

No place could ever compare to the experiences I had in Colombia, and I knew I would miss it dearly. The jungle skies, the camaraderie, the people, the chaos—it was all part of me now. And though I was leaving, I also knew that I would return. Colombia wasn't just a chapter of my life; it was a part of my soul.

For now, though, it was time to start again. Martha and I would find our future, whatever it was, together. Adventure would always call to me, and when it did, I would answer. But as I looked ahead to Spain, I carried with me the spirit of Colombia, knowing it would never truly let me go.

If, after reading all of this book and you're not sure if it really happened, go to a small town in Yorkshire, England called Batley, go to a working men's club and ask those that remember a short son of a baker, a real "Posh, southern bastard, and they will tell you, "It's all bollocks!, he was full of shit!"

GALLERY

None of the following images were generated by A.I or have subject to alteration with photoshop.

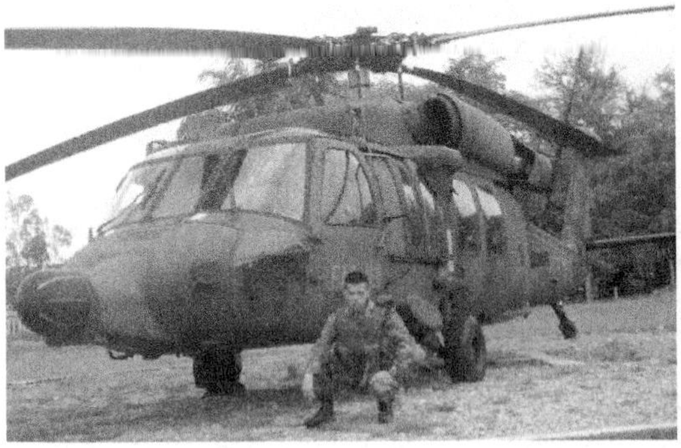
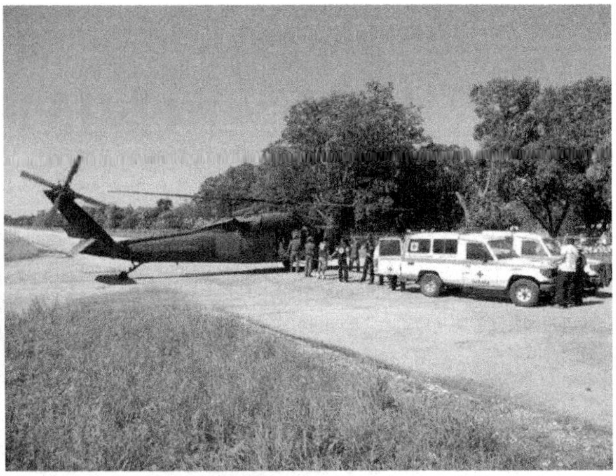
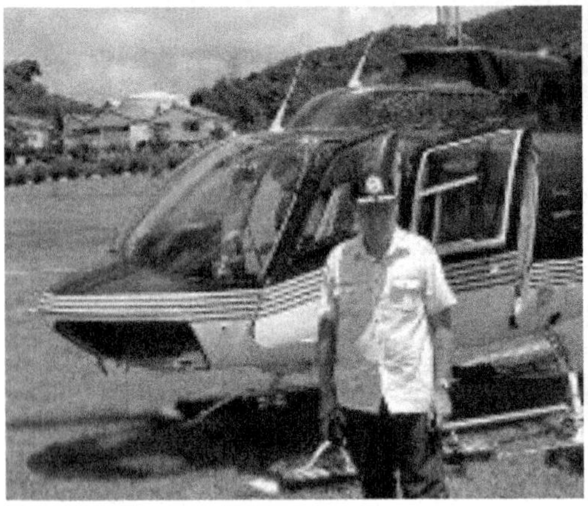
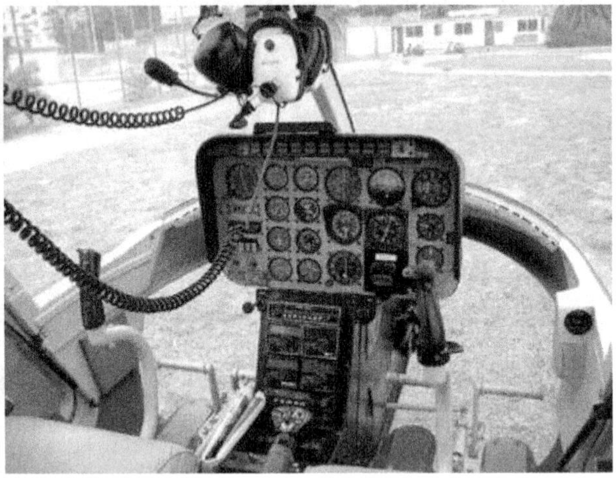
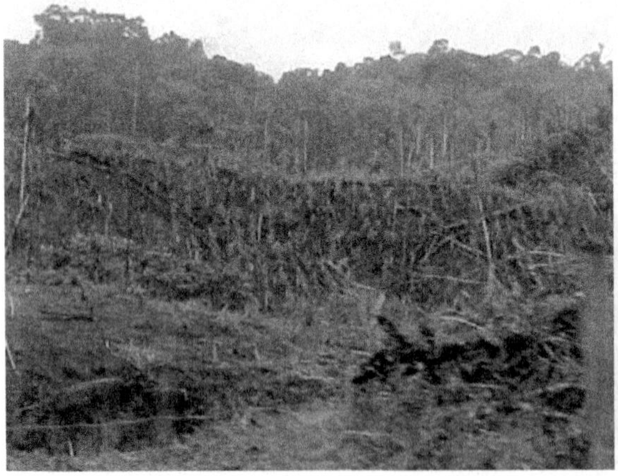
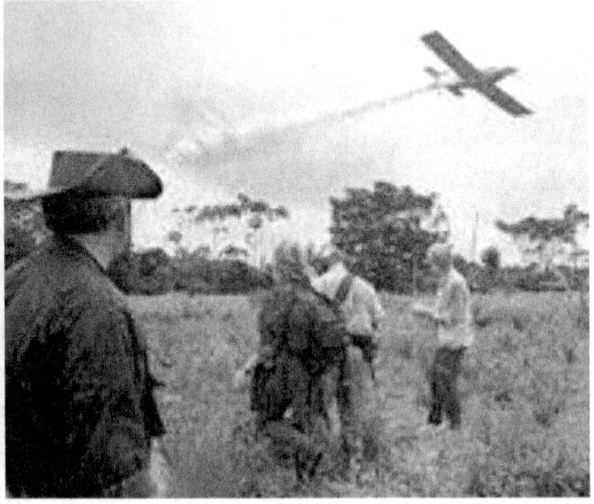

181

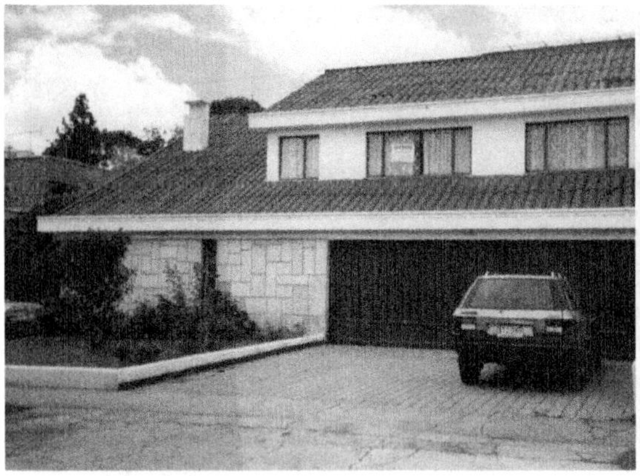

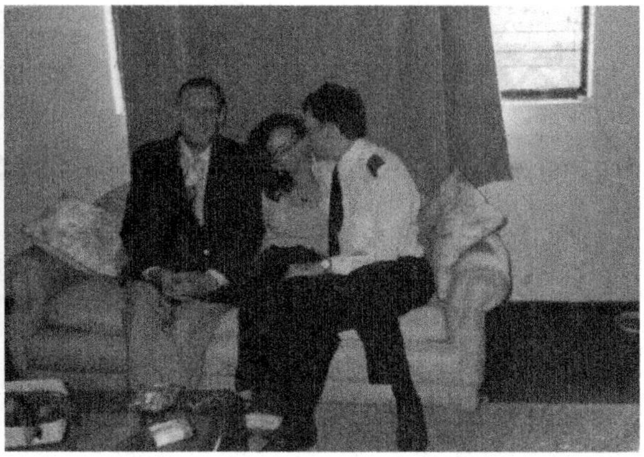

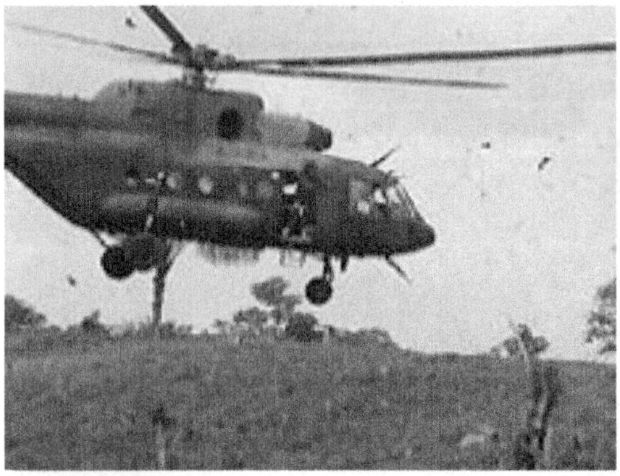

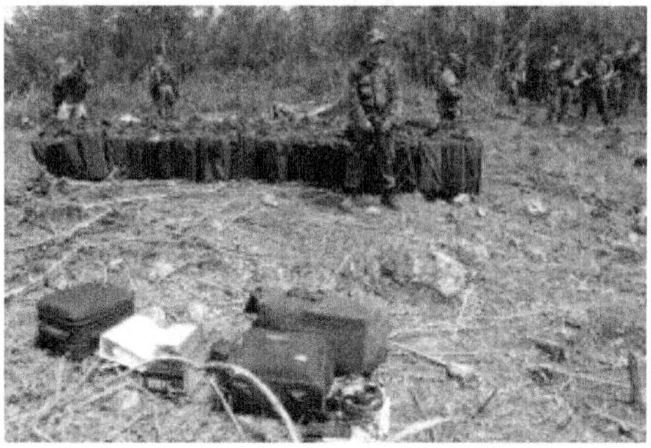

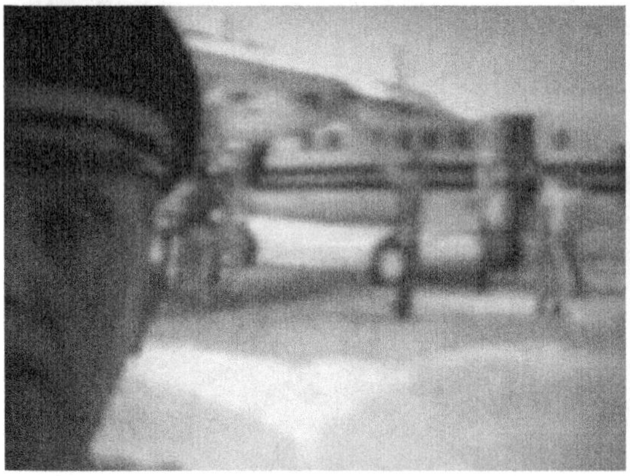

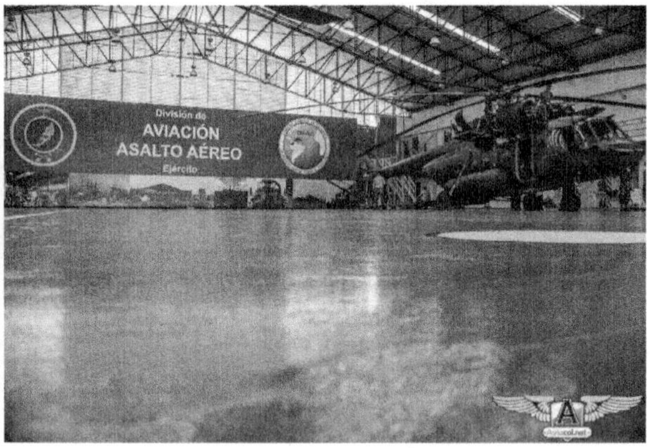
División de
AVIACIÓN
ASALTO AÉREO
Ejército

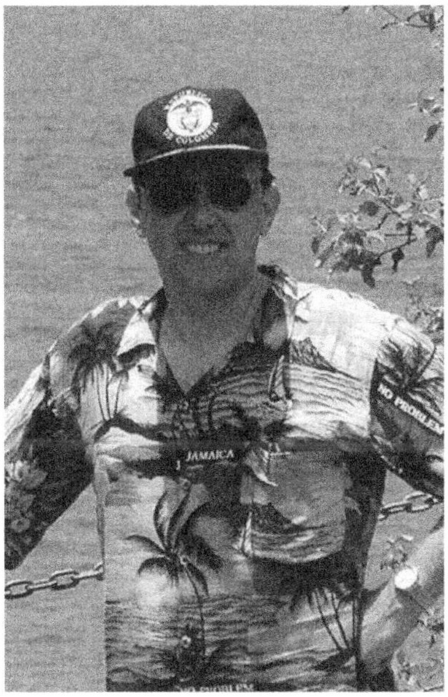
JAMAICA
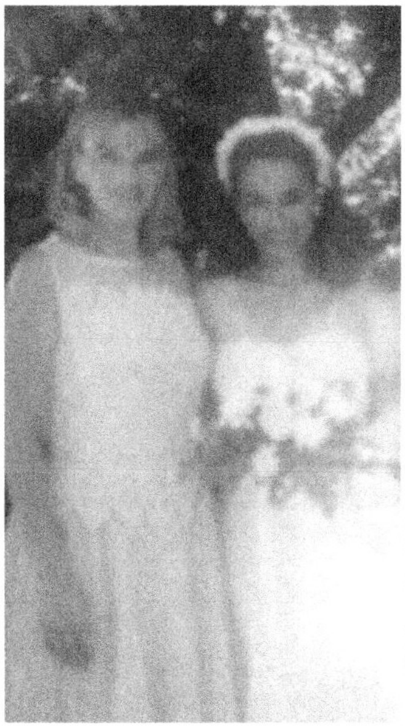
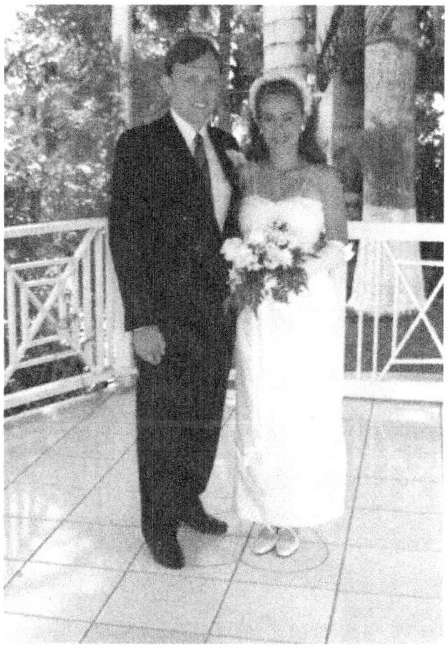
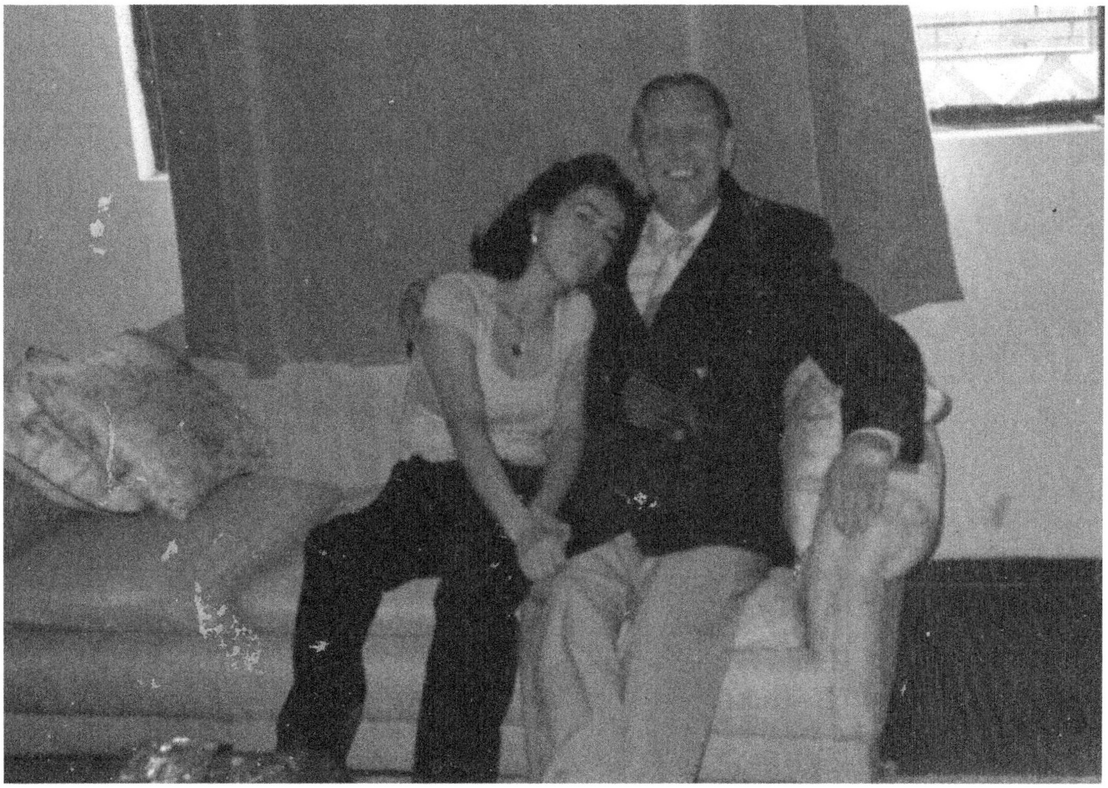

Printed in Great Britain
by Amazon